GILGAMESH

GILGAMESH

Translated from the Sîn-leqi-unninnī version

JOHN GARDNER
JOHN MAIER

with the assistance of
Richard A. Henshaw

VINTAGE BOOKS
A DIVISION OF RANDOM HOUSE
NEW YORK

For Fathers and Mothers

a-a-ᵈen-ki zà-ṁi

kù-ᵈinanna-ke₄ zà-ṁi-zu-dùg-ga-àm

First Vintage Books Edition, October 1985
Copyright © 1984 by Estate of John Gardner
and by John Maier
Map copyright © 1984 by David Lindroth, Inc.

Library of Congress Cataloging in Publication Data
Gilgamesh. English.
Gilgamesh: translated from the Sîn-leqi-unninnī version.
Translation of: Gilgamesh.
Bibliography: p.
I. Gardner, John, 1933–1982.
II. Maier, John R.
III. Henshaw, Richard A. (Richard Aurel), 1921–
IV. Title.
[PJ3771.G5E5 1985]   892'.1   85-40132
ISBN 0-394-74089-0 (pbk.)

9B8

CONTENTS

PREFACE

"There is," George Steiner has written, "a special *miseria* of translation, a melancholy after Babel." This *Gilgamesh* takes what Stephen Mac-Kenna called a "chaste freedom" in presenting a very ancient literary work. The translation assumes a number of things about *Gilgamesh* that, like most things ancient and remote, are subject to question. *Gilgamesh* is the "late" or "standard" version of a collection that reaches back to a Sumerian hero of the early Third Millennium B.C. The late version is written in the Akkadian language and was composed in the Middle Babylonian Period (1600–1000 B.C.), no later than the thirteenth century, by an exorcist-priest, Sîn-leqi-unninnī. There is a long history of the Gilgamesh stories, and the late version offers only one moment of it —a moment, though, that we consider so compelling that, like many others working in French, German, Danish, Finnish, Georgian, Hebrew, Italian, Russian, Swedish, Czech, and, of course, English, we too are tempting that melancholy after Babel to translate it again.

Gilgamesh is a work, we feel, that is best approached as seventy-two more or less complete poems. The story line can be sketched briefly, but as is the case with many traditional stories, whose original audience knew fairly well the overall design of the story, the pleasure lies not so much in the plot but in smaller segments that make up the whole. Most translations of the Gilgamesh stories follow the traditional twelve-tablet format that seems to have been universal once the different Gilgamesh stories were brought together into an "epic" unity. Not all of them, though, pay close attention to the subdivisions of the text into columns. The late version is written in cuneiform or "wedge-shaped" characters on twelve clay tablets, a number suggesting the twelve books or cantos of Western epic poems. Each tablet is inscribed front and back, in six columns read left to right and top to bottom. Often an episode will begin in one column and end in another. We hope to show, however, that the column is an important unit of composition—and a convenient way to move through the work poem by poem. Sîn-leqi-unninnī attempted to give his Second Millennium poem the look of his Third Millennium Sumerian forerunners—stately, dignified, unhurried, often repetitive— and the division into six columns served his purpose well.

This translation follows the standard text of *Gilgamesh*: R. Campbell

Thompson's *The Epic of Gilgamesh: Text, Transliteration, and Notes* (Oxford: Clarendon Press, 1930). His work has since been augmented and in some cases corrected by new discoveries of Gilgamesh texts in the Middle East, and we have attempted to keep the new materials in mind; but Campbell Thompson's is still the basis of any new translation. Many translations and critical studies have been consulted. Because this is not a new edition of the text and because it is designed to be read by people like us, non-specialists, the notes are not exhaustive. The hundreds of philological and textual problems that are of great importance to the specialist are usually ignored here; they are beyond our modest competence, and the reader who needs to know about them can probably already find his way through the vast material written about *Gilgamesh* in the hundred years since it was discovered by George Smith. The notes make reference only to the most readily accessible works in English, like James B. Pritchard's edition of *Ancient Near Eastern Texts Relating to the Old Testament*, 3rd ed. (Princeton: University Press, 1969), in which E. A. Speiser and A. K. Grayson have presented much Gilgamesh material. Others are general works like Samuel Noah Kramer's *History Begins at Sumer* (Philadelphia: University of Pennsylvania Press, 1981), Thorkild Jacobsen's *The Treasures of Darkness* (New Haven: Yale University Press, 1976), and A. Leo Oppenheim's *Ancient Mesopotamia* (Chicago: University of Chicago Press, 1964).

One work, though, has been especially important and is referred to often. Jeffrey H. Tigay's *The Evolution of the Gilgamesh Epic* (Philadelphia: University of Pennsylvania Press, 1982) became available as we were completing our work. It summarizes so much earlier work on the *Gilgamesh* that Tigay has, we feel, relieved us of the burden of reproducing earlier scholarship; indeed, it would be pretentious to reproduce it when a reference to Tigay will take the reader to a discussion and bibliography of the original scholarship. But Tigay's book is much more than a compendium of earlier work. He shows that the "late" version of *Gilgamesh* is a work in its own right with its own stylistic peculiarities and innovations. He maps out the "evolution" of the *Gilgamesh* from its early Sumerian forms through the first great effort at unification in the Old Babylonian Period, through Middle Babylonian, Hittite, and Late Assyrian versions until it finds a stable form. That we are deeply indebted to this work of impeccable scholarship will appear on nearly every page.

Many friends and colleagues have provided ideas and support for this work, and we thank them for their help, especially Marilyn Gaddis Rose, Susan Thornton, Liz Rosenberg, Walter P. Bowman, Grace Alvarez-Altman, Paul Ferguson, Robert Gilliam, Norma Lawrence, Cynthia La-Pier, Paul F. Hoye, and John B. Alphonso-Karkala. Our sometimes unorthodox views have been voiced at meetings of the American Oriental Society, the International Association for Philosophy and Literature, the Conference on Literary Onomastics, the Society of Biblical Literature, the Translation Research and Instruction Program at SUNY Binghamton, and the New York State Asian Studies Conference. With all of that support we might have been expected to get it right; where we have failed, the mistakes are ours alone.

We would also like to acknowledge, as the source for the text and monument sites indicated on the map, "L'Épopée de Gilgameš—a-t-elle été fixée dans l'art?", by G. Offner, in *Gilgameš et sa légende*, edited by Paul Garelli (Paris: C. Klincksieck, 1960); and we are happy to acknowledge our gratitude to the British Museum and Oxford University Press for permission to reproduce material in the Appendix.

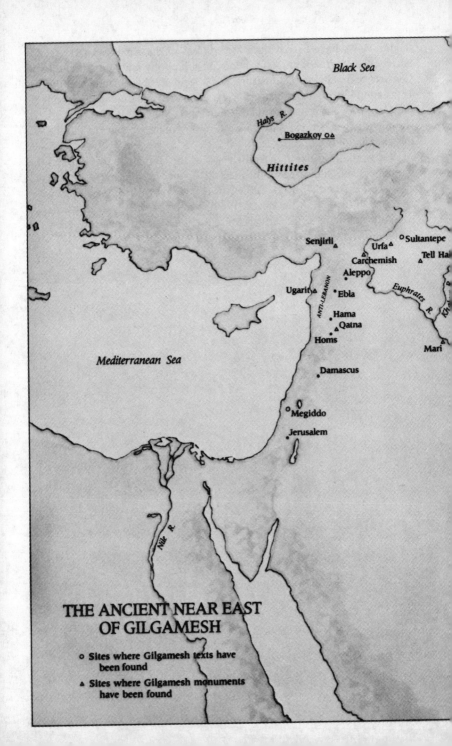

THE ANCIENT NEAR EAST
OF GILGAMESH

○ Sites where Gilgamesh texts have
been found

△ Sites where Gilgamesh monuments
have been found

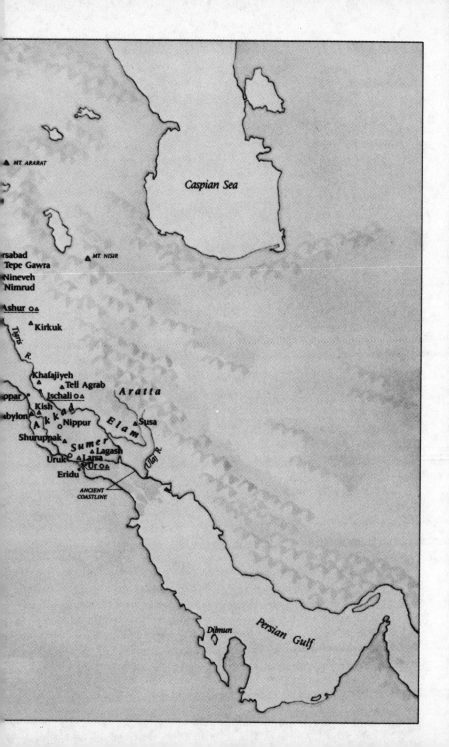

Introduction

THE ONE WHO
SAW THE ABYSS

John Gardner died in a motorcycle accident on September 14, 1982, leaving a typescript of *Gilgamesh,* the last work he completed before his death. There is a certain irony in that, for the version of the Gilgamesh stories he had worked over the years to translate develops a simple, terrible truth: death is inevitable, but the works a person achieves can gain a kind of immortality, as it has for the Sumerian hero of the stories. John Gardner worked in many artistic modes. He was, above all, a novelist and writer of short fiction; but he was also a literary critic, teacher, composer, librettist, playwright, painter, woodworker, and author of children's books. He was trained as a medievalist and was at home in the great traditions of Western literature. Little wonder, then, that he pursued scholarly studies and translation, writing books about Chaucer and transposing ancient works like *Jason and Medeia* (1973). The Gilgamesh stories are older than anything else he worked with—the earliest stories date back to nearly 2600 B.C.—and they come from an Ancient Near Eastern culture that is very remote indeed from the modern, Western world; but they represent simply another direction Gardner was taking in his work. He had worked night and day in late August and September to complete the typescript. Such strenuous work was habit with Gardner. What prompted him to finish the manuscript was a very practical concern: he planned to use the typescript for his course in the Epic at the State University of New York at Binghamton, and the document had to be ready for his students to use at the beginning of the Fall Term.

What Gardner completed just days before he died was his part in a project that has taken nearly ten years to complete. Together with Richard Henshaw, the only Assyriologist of the three of us who worked on the *Gilgamesh,* I had been poring over Sumerian and Akkadian literary works since 1972, and had spent some eighteen months between 1974 and 1976 examining the cuneiform ("wedge-shaped") texts, transliterations of the cuneiform characters into roman letters, and translations of what has come to be known as *The Epic of Gilgamesh* since its discovery in the ruins of ancient Mesopotamia (modern Iraq) just over a century ago. With Henshaw's help, I had prepared a rough translation of the text and generated large files of notes on every line of Akkadian, the language of the text, the language of the ancient Babylonians and Assyrians. Most of the material had come from the Library of Ashurbanipal in ancient

Nineveh, a library assembled during the reign (668–627 B.C.) of that Assyrian king. The *Gilgamesh* tells of a king of the important Sumerian city-state of Uruk (modern Warka) during the Second Early Dynastic Period (2700–2500 B.C.). It was thought that the material from the Library of Ashurbanipal reflected much earlier work, and scholars have found that to be the case. Fragments of older versions have been found and studied, some reaching back to the centuries just after the reign of Gilgamesh himself, back to the time of the earliest writings in any language yet deciphered—and not much later than the invention of true writing itself (about 3000 B.C.).

Gardner and I began work on what was intended to be a translation for the non-specialist in 1976, after one of Gardner's visits to the Brockport Writers Forum. *Gilgamesh* is the most significant literary work to come out of ancient Mesopotamia. It was worked and reworked for two thousand years, kept alive by a tradition of scribal schools set up in Sumerian times (and lasting into the early Christian era). Judging from the different versions, the spread of fragments across the Ancient Near East, and the different languages in which the Gilgamesh stories appear (Sumerian, Akkadian, and Hittite), *Gilgamesh* was the most popular of works composed in the Sumero-Akkadian literary tradition. Recently, Jeffrey H. Tigay (*The Evolution of the Gilgamesh Epic,* 1982) has synthesized the hundred years of modern scholarship on the text of *Gilgamesh* and has been able to isolate many of the features of the "late" version attributed to the poet Sîn-leqi-unninnī, the version followed here. Seven earlier compositions in the Sumerian language have survived, and several fragments in Akkadian earlier than our version. Gardner was much taken by the fragments of an Old Babylonian (2000–1600 B.C.) Gilgamesh epic, and much of the studying done by Maier and Gardner was devoted to the similarities and differences among the versions, especially the Old Babylonian fragments. We were happy to discover that many of our intuitions were borne out in Tigay's painstaking work. The importance of *Gilgamesh* is such that every specialist in cuneiform literature and the languages of the Ancient Near East has studied at least part of the work, and the specialist has the text in the original and by now hundreds of scholarly articles to help him through *Gilgamesh*. For the most part, these texts and articles are virtually inaccessible to the outsider. The great value of Tigay's *Evolution* for our work has been to reduce the space needed to argue a point he has already demonstrated. We have not hesitated to question some of the interpretations offered by specialists. From the start, our aim was, in the parlance of programmers, a "top-down" translation that emphasized large sections of literary discourse (schemata, speeches, verse paragraphs, columns, tablets, large narrative movements), rather than a "bottom-up" translation that begins with cuneiform signs (and fragments of signs) and gradually builds up words and lines. At first, we were open to almost any type of translation. We considered a prose translation of the Akkadian poetic lines; and we thought about the technique that has been successful in some biblical translations: paraphrase. Although there are a few instances of paraphrase and a number of places where we have eliminated the scholar's brackets (for reconstructions in the text) and parentheses (doubtful constructions or translations), we have settled for a "chaste" translation of *Gilgamesh*, one that, in particular, preserves the integrity of the poetic line. Tigay's work has simplified the task of annotation, and we draw upon his work and the work of others very frequently. Our disagreements come mainly in larger questions of interpretation, where we have tried to exonerate the scholars by separating them from our own wild surmises.

John Gardner's part in the project was, finally, to decide upon the reading of the lines. The typescript he completed in his last days took care of that. Except for the usual problems of an unedited first draft, the typescript is complete, and it forms the basis of this edition. From the start it was intended that I would put the manuscript together, with introduction, notes, and an appendix on translating the *Gilgamesh* for those who know little about the writing system, languages, and tools available to the translator today. One would like to have had Gardner's counsel through all stages of the preparation of the manuscript. It is enough, though, that his last work is one powerful enough to express the force of his personality.

Gardner's life was filled with projects, and he had to work on *Gilgamesh* in the odd hours when he could pull himself away from his parents' home in Batavia, New York, or from the schools where he taught—in his last years, SUNY Binghamton. His interest in *Gilgamesh*, though, stretched back before the time we first met at Brockport. *The Sunlight Dialogues* (1972) is a novel pervaded by Mesopotamian thought. It contains the most explicit statements about *Gilgamesh* Gardner wrote—even though the remarks are made by his *persona* in the fictional work. The novel is set in the Batavia of 1966, but is laced with the Mesopotamiana of four thousand years ago. The dialogues of the title are exchanges between the hero, Taggert Hodge ("the Sunlight Man"), and Batavia Police Chief Fred Clumly. All four dialogues focus on the values of an ancient civilization that stands in sharp contrast with Western civilization. The Sunlight Man is convinced that Western civilization is collapsing, that only by going beyond the Judeo-Christian and Greco-Roman traditions to the values of ancient Babylon can any sense be made of what is happening in our society today. The last of the dialogues, "The Dialogue of the Dead," discusses Gilgamesh. At the time Gardner wrote *The Sunlight Dialogues*, he knew *The Epic of Gilgamesh* only in translation, and the translation he knew had lopped off the last of the twelve tablets of the original and had substituted in its place a Gilgamesh story with a very different point to make and in a very different language, Sumerian. The Sunlight Man thought *The Epic of Gilgamesh* "obscure" and "undramatic," even "lifeless." He thought that the poetry of that Akkadian epic was "intricate" and suited more to elaborate description and oration and hymnic address than to the action-stories we think of as "epic." He could see the beauty of technique in the ancient work, with its careful segmentation, echoing devices, repetition and counterpointing that played one scene against another, one speech against another. Mainly, though, the Sunlight Man is less concerned about the artistic technique—of great interest to a writer of fiction, of course—than he is with the truth *The Epic of Gilgamesh* has to offer us. He uses the ancient work to tell us about the freedom to act.

Gilgamesh, according to this early Gardner account, tries every sort of scheme for achieving immortality—and fails. He tries to find personal immortality, eternal youth, lasting fame, the glory in achievement (building a great city), establishment of a lineage—only to fail in every attempt. The answer to this desperate human dilemma is simply, the Sunlight Man claims, the power to act. Taggert Hodge, the Sunlight Man, tells the Police Chief, "And so, in answer to your question, one acts to maintain the freedom to act, but the ultimate act, the act which comes when the gods command it, is utterly impersonal, a movement of the universe, a stroke by, for, and of sole interest to—the gods."[1] When all of the illusions of personal immortality are stripped away, there is only the act to maintain the freedom to act. Why, then, act at all? For Gardner's Sunlight Man, if not for Gardner himself, the answer to this age-old human question is the main thrust of *The Epic of Gilgamesh:* "because action is life."

The action of *Gilgamesh* is difficult to interpret after many thousands of years, but relatively easy to follow. It is a double quest. Gilgamesh sets out to make a name for himself and succeeds, with his friend Enkidu, by defeating a demonic figure, Humbaba, and then the terrifying Bull of Heaven. By the midpoint of the story, Gilgamesh and Enkidu have indeed established their names and boast about their achievements in riddles. Just at the moment of greatest success, though, the gods announce an unexpected and arbitrary decision: one of the men must die. Enkidu is chosen. In what is surely the most moving death scene in ancient literature, Gilgamesh eulogizes his friend and in deep grief strikes out upon the long road, insisting there must be some ultimate meaning in his friend's death.

In his grief Gilgamesh breaks through territory no human had ever visited. Time and again he is told his search is in vain. Better to enjoy the pleasures of life than to puzzle out the meaning of life. He forces himself even across the Waters of Death to demand an answer.

Mesopotamian thought divided human history by the Flood. What first fired the enthusiasm of the West when George Smith discovered the first of the *Gilgamesh* tablets a century ago[2] was the stunning discovery of a Flood story, older and more detailed than the biblical account, told by a Noah-like character, Utnapishtim. It is to Utnapishtim, the only human to have escaped the general fate of mankind, that Gilgamesh forces his way. Like Herakles, Utnapishtim had been raised to a life "like that of the gods." It was his cunning, however, rather than his heroic deeds (Herakles) or his piety (Noah), that marked him as special. Gilgamesh comes to him demanding an answer.

The answer comes close to crushing Gilgamesh: there is no permanence. Enkidu will not return. Gilgamesh himself will not escape death. Even the Flood story, which tells of the saving of mankind, contains a hidden sting: henceforth mankind must live in a hostile environment, threatened by the lion and the wolf, by famine and plague. Still, Gilgamesh rallies. By the end of his quest, Gilgamesh has cast away the hideous rags of skin he had been wearing on his journey. He is cleansed. He returns to the civilized world with, if not a cheerful mien, at least a sense of obligation to the living. He returns to his goddess, Ishtar, and to his city, once again as king.

THE STORIES IN GILGAMESH

Many find in *The Epic of Gilgamesh* only flat despair, but John Gardner was not one of them. The work has a strong story line, but a summary of the action is likely to miss the richness of the poetry—and to emphasize the negative. Still, it is useful to keep an outline of *Gilgamesh* in mind, for a mark of *The Epic of Gilgamesh* is the intricate way in which a number of Gilgamesh tales and other, non-Gilgamesh traditions have been stitched together into a well-designed unity.[3] The work is divided into twelve six-columned clay tablets, for a total of seventy-two columns of text. Although parts of *The Epic of Gilgamesh* are still missing today, the overall design is clear.

TABLET I

Column i. An introduction to the work as a whole, it emphasizes two accomplishments of the hero, Gilgamesh, one of which is to be narrated, the other already complete when the story begins. Gilgamesh is the seer, the one who discovered things secret, who found out about the time before the Flood divided history, and who cut his discoveries into a *narû*, or stone monument. His other work is the city walls of Uruk (modern Warka), which modern excavators have discovered made a circuit of some six miles around. At the center of the city is the temple complex called Eanna ("House of Heaven"), sacred dwelling of the chief deity of the city, the goddess Ishtar.

Column ii. A description of Gilgamesh is followed by the distress of the citizens, who cry out that their king is oppressing them. The gods hear the lament and create a double for Gilgamesh in the wild, Enkidu the fighter. Enkidu, who knows only the life of the animals in the wild, is spotted by the Stalker, who is worried that this Enkidu is disturbing the hunt.

Column iii. The Stalker reports to his father, who tells the Stalker of the powerful Gilgamesh living in the city and suggests a plan to trap Enkidu: ask Gilgamesh for one of the temple women, a love-priestess who can turn Enkidu from the animals he lives with. The Stalker takes the woman into the wilderness, where she waits for Enkidu.

Column iv. The seduction of Enkidu. In the most sexually explicit scene in Akkadian literature, the priestess traps Enkidu, sleeps with him for "six days and seven nights," and fills his mind with civilized matters. She tells him of Gilgamesh, and he speaks for the first time, boasting of his prowess, anxious to confront the hero in the city.

Column v. Enkidu's boast continues. The priestess urges him on with an extended description of the city and Gilgamesh. Gilgamesh, as the scene shifts to the city, reports to his mother, the divine Ninsun, about a dream he has had in the night. She "unties" the dream by repeating it.

Column vi. Ninsun completes the "untying" of Gilgamesh's dream by interpreting it. Gilgamesh reports a second dream, like the first about

Enkidu, and she interprets that one as well. Gilgamesh is anxious to meet this dream-figure, to acquire a friend. The scene shifts once again to Enkidu and the priestess sitting together.

TABLET II

Column i. Badly broken. From an Old Babylonian parallel text, it would appear that Enkidu is introduced to the arts of civilized life by the temple priestess.

Column ii. Badly broken. Apparently, the education of Enkidu continues. By the end of the column, Enkidu has entered the city of Uruk. The two heroes meet as Gilgamesh prepares to enter the "bride house," apparently to insist upon the right to deflower the brides of the city. Enkidu blocks his way, and the two men fight.

Column iii. Badly broken. It appears (from the Old Babylonian parallel text) that the column narrates the great fight. The two wrestle—and suddenly become fast friends.

Column iv. Broken. Gilgamesh praises the strength of Enkidu, and the two men embrace like brothers.

Column v. Fragmentary. The column contains a description of the terrifying guardian-demon, Humbaba, whom the god Enlil has made guardian of the "cedar forest." Gilgamesh will set about to make a name for himself by challenging the guardian Humbaba.

Column vi. Badly broken. Fragments of a dialogue between Gilgamesh and Enkidu.

TABLET III

Column i. The elders of the city advise Gilgamesh on the campaign against Humbaba. Gilgamesh takes Enkidu into the temple, Egalmah, where he seeks Ninsun's help.

Column ii. Ninsun performs a ritual to the god Shamash for the protection of the two heroes in their campaign against Humbaba.

Column iii. Almost completely lost. Preparations for the fight with Humbaba continue.

Column iv. Badly broken. Ninsun, goddess and mother of Gilgamesh, adopts Enkidu.

Column v. Too broken for translation. Preparations for Humbaba continue.

Column vi. Badly broken. The elders of the city entrust Gilgamesh to Enkidu's care. Preparations for Humbaba completed.

TABLET IV

Columns i–iv. Almost completely missing. A small fragment of the first column shows that Gilgamesh and Enkidu have begun their journey to the land of the cedar forest.

Column v. Broken. In one passage, Enkidu encourages Gilgamesh in preparation for the fight with Humbaba.

Column vi. Broken. Now Enkidu expresses fear, and Gilgamesh must urge his friend on as they approach the gate of the cedar forest. They enter the forest.

TABLET V

Column i. Gilgamesh and Enkidu wonder at the entrance of the cedar forest. They begin the journey into the forest when the text breaks off. A parallel text, though, tells of dreams Gilgamesh received in the night and the beginning of Enkidu's interpretation of the dreams.

Column ii. Badly broken. A reference to a "three-stranded towrope" indicates a wisdom saying about two men overcoming obstacles.

Column iii. Quite broken at the beginning, the column tells of a second dream Gilgamesh receives in the cedar forest and of Enkidu's interpretation of the dream. The men plunge farther into the forest, and pour out an offering to Shamash, asking for a dream.

Column iv. A third, terrifying dream comes to Gilgamesh.

Columns v–vi. Only a few signs remain from these columns in which Gilgamesh and Enkidu confront the demon Humbaba and kill him. Parallels in Old Babylonian and Hittite texts suggest something of the intensity of the battle—and of a moral problem that emerges once Humbaba is defeated. In both parallels, it is Enkidu who counsels Gilgamesh to kill Humbaba. Gilgamesh strikes him, but Enkidu delivers the final blow. In the Hittite version, Humbaba pleads for his life, offering to become Gilgamesh's servant, but Enkidu argues against it, and they cut Humbaba down. In any case, by the end of Tablet V the long narrative of establishing a name by defeating Humbaba, already suggested by the end of Tablet II and covering Tablets III, IV, and V, ends in success for Gilgamesh and Enkidu.

TABLET VI

Column i. The narrative takes a decisive turn in this well-preserved text. The goddess Ishtar is attracted to the heroic Gilgamesh and offers to make him her lover. Gilgamesh responds to the proposal with a list of insults and the question "Which of your lovers have you loved forever?"

Column ii. Gilgamesh continues the insults to the goddess Ishtar in a catalogue of Ishtar's lovers. In a fury, Ishtar turns to her father, the high god Anu, for help.

Column iii. Ishtar asks Anu to send the Bull of Heaven to punish Gilgamesh, and Anu agrees, provided that the city of Uruk has grain stored to survive seven years of stress. Ishtar assures Anu she has provided for her people, and the Bull of Heaven descends.

Column iv. The account of the battle with the Bull of Heaven is broken, but it is clear that both Gilgamesh and Enkidu engage in the fight.

Column v. Gilgamesh and Enkidu defeat the Bull of Heaven, and Enkidu further insults Ishtar. The heroes celebrate their victory and boast of their prowess.

Column vi. Very brief. Gilgamesh holds a joyous celebration. The heroes rest—only for a moment. A dream comes to Enkidu that will turn joy to woe.

TABLET VII

Columns i–ii. Quite broken. Enkidu weakens, apparently because the gods in council have decreed that Enkidu must die for having destroyed Humbaba and the Bull of Heaven. Gilgamesh is distraught. Enkidu addresses the door of the cedar forest, as if it were human, in a speech full of regret.

Column iii. Enkidu curses first the Stalker and then the temple priestess who had transformed him into a civilized human. Shamash, the sun god, hears the curse and upbraids Enkidu, reminding him of the honors he has received in his friendship with Gilgamesh.

Column iv. Enkidu then blesses the temple priestess. He tells Gilgamesh of a terrifying dream he has had of the netherworld, the house of darkness.

Column v. Lost.

Column vi. Only part of the column remains. The progress of the strange illness that has seized Enkidu is marked, and Enkidu reflects upon the anger of a god that has robbed him of a hero's death in battle.

TABLET VIII

Column i. Gilgamesh delivers a beautiful eulogy.

Column ii. Gilgamesh continues his eulogy, and his grief intensifies.

Column iii. The mourning of Enkidu continues. The text breaks off after a few lines.

Column iv. Very little remains of the column. The few lines suggest that the column describes a statue raised in Enkidu's memory.

Column v. Very little remains. What survives suggests a ritual Gilgamesh performs for Enkidu.

Column vi. Lost.

TABLET IX

Column i. Still grieving, Gilgamesh cries out in fear of death. He begins the long journey that will take him to Utnapishtim, the only human to escape the death decreed for all humans.

Column ii. Gilgamesh approaches the mountains of Mashu, guarded by scorpion-demons, male and female. The scorpion-demons speak to each other about Gilgamesh.

Column iii. Gilgamesh tells the Scorpion-man that he intends to journey to Utnapishtim. The Scorpion-man responds that no human has made such a journey.

Column iv. The Scorpion-man opens the gate for Gilgamesh to enter. The journey into the darkness begins.

Column v. The journey into the great darkness continues. Finally, light breaks out, and Gilgamesh finds himself in the Garden of the Gods.

Column vi. Very little of the column survives. Apparently, it is devoted to the Garden of the Gods.

TABLET X

Column i. Gilgamesh's journey continues. He reaches the dwelling of Siduri the Barmaid, a manifestation of the goddess Ishtar. She inquires about his terrible journey, and he recounts the adventures of the two friends.

Column ii. Gilgamesh tells Siduri of his deep grief. She, too, insists that his journey is dangerous and futile—but she advises him on the way to make the journey across the waters of death. He finds a way to confront the Boatman who can make the crossing.

Column iii. Gilgamesh once again recounts his adventures and his grief to the Boatman, Urshanabi. Gilgamesh cuts poles for the voyage, and the two begin the journey across the waters.

Column iv. The journey across the waters of death is accomplished. Utnapishtim watches the boat in the distance.

Column v. Gilgamesh finds his destination and speaks to the sage Utnapishtim. Utnapishtim tells of the parentage of Gilgamesh.

Column vi. Much is missing of the column, but the final lines survive. They give Utnapishtim's answer to Gilgamesh's desperate quest for the meaning of life: there is no permanence.

TABLET XI

Column i. Utnapishtim begins his account of a secret of the gods: the Flood. He recalls the trick by which the god Ea allows mankind to know of the Flood and to prepare for its coming.

Column ii. Utnapishtim describes the boat and its launching.

Column iii. The Flood comes with its terrifying fury and finally recedes.

Column iv. Utnapishtim lets birds fly out of the boat. When the crow does not return, Utnapishtim leaves the boat and offers sacrifice to the gods. The gods argue about the Flood. Utnapishtim challenges Gilgamesh to a test: remain awake for six days and seven nights.

Column v. Gilgamesh fails the test. Gilgamesh is cleansed and is prepared to return to Uruk when the wife of Utnapishtim chides her husband's inhospitality.

Column vi. Utnapishtim offers Gilgamesh a final secret, a plant called "The-Old-Man-Will-Be-Made-Young." Gilgamesh secures the plant but loses it when a serpent carries it away. Gilgamesh and the Boatman return to the city of Uruk.

TABLET XII

Column i. The story has no clear chronological relationship to the narratives in the previous tablets, for Enkidu is alive. He offers to enter the underworld to bring out a drum and beater that have fallen into the world of the dead. Gilgamesh gives Enkidu detailed advice that will enable him to enter the underworld and return.

Column ii. Enkidu does everything he was not to do, and he is seized by the earth. Gilgamesh begins a search for a god who can bring Enkidu back to the living.

Column iii. Rebuffed by the gods Enlil and Sîn, Gilgamesh finds the temple of Ea. With Ea's help, the ghost of Enkidu escapes the underworld, and the friends try to embrace.

Column iv. In a dialogue, Enkidu tells Gilgamesh of the fates of humans in the underworld.

Column v. Much of the column is lost. Enkidu continues to describe the fates of humans in the netherworld.

Column vi. A brief column. Enkidu describes more of the fates, ending with the spirit who has no one left alive to love him: the spirit must make his way in the underworld with only the scraps tossed into the gutter—eating what no dog would touch.

THE CHARACTERS OF GILGAMESH

The narrative is long and complex, and many lines of *The Epic of Gilgamesh* have not yet been recovered. Still, the main lines are clear, and enough is known of each tablet to see the overall design clearly. The main figure is, of course, the hero Gilgamesh.[4] Except in the early parts of the work, when the focus is on Enkidu, and in the story-within-a-story account of the Flood, Gilgamesh is the center of attention. He is a mature human at the opening of the work, in the sense that his position as king of the city of Uruk is already secure, and one of the works for which he was remembered, building the walls of the city, is already in the past. In another sense, his physical maturity and his status are only the background for his "education," which takes place in two distinct stages. In the first, which takes up exactly the first half of the story, Gilgamesh must establish a name for himself, a process of individuation that demands preparations (physical, emotional, and spiritual) for an initiating encounter with the demonic Humbaba. In the second, Gilgamesh, having lost his friend and brother, must pass through stages of melancholia and dissolution of the self, a dark night of the soul, from which he emerges intact but profoundly different from the boisterous and arrogant champion who made up riddles about his name after he defeated the Bull of Heaven.

Gilgamesh is also the story of the double. If Gilgamesh is two-thirds god and only one-third human, his double, Enkidu, seems to reverse the ratio. If Gilgamesh is outwardly the same at the beginning and the end of the work, the story of Enkidu everywhere emphasizes change. For Enkidu, it is a story of birth, development in the wild, a step-by-step initiation into the life of a civilized man, courageous acts, and death. It is the story of Everyman. (It is also the story of the emergence of mankind from the wild, a parable of culture, the best worked-out Mesopotamian speculation about *lullû-amēlu*, the First Man.)[5] Once the men fight, they become friends immediately. The relationship is tested and confirmed time and again, and expressed in one of the most moving elegies to have come down to us from the ancient world. The love of Gilgamesh and Enkidu is likened to that of husband and wife and to the bond between brothers. Indeed, Enkidu is brought into the family of Gilgamesh, adopted by the goddess-mother of Gilgamesh, Ninsun.[6] Enkidu is, perhaps, the more physical of the two—though Gilgamesh wins the fight between them—and those things over which humans are so anxious— sexual desire, revenge, and the like—are expressed in the actions of Enkidu with an immediacy and vigor that contrast with the lordly Gilgamesh. Consider the two insults the heroes give to the goddess Ishtar in Tablet VI. Gilgamesh insults her with a lengthy, detailed, and clever speech, while Enkidu is brusque, and he throws a part of the slain Bull of Heaven into her face.[7]

The large contours of *Gilgamesh* follow, then, the two equal but different heroes through a few major adventures. The number of columns and poetic lines given to the different episodes may strike the modern reader as strange or disproportionate. The story of the heroes' fight against Humbaba, for example, is introduced as early as the second tablet, and covers fully three tablets. The fight itself (V.vi), though, is quite brief. Indeed, for a society that is supposedly so competitive and warlike,[8] there is almost an ellipsis of battle in *Gilgamesh*. The three fighting scenes —Gilgamesh vs. Enkidu, the heroes vs. Humbaba, and the heroes vs. the Bull of Heaven—are certainly important to the action, but in contrast to, say, *The Iliad*,[9] the fighting is brief, stylized, and though direct, remarkably free of detail.

On the other hand, although they are some of the worst preserved sections of *Gilgamesh*, the preparation for the fight with Humbaba is developed at great length. Gilgamesh was, according to the *Sumerian King List*, a Sumerian king during what modern historians consider the Second Early Dynastic Period of Sumer (ca. 2700–2500 B.C.),[10] and the defeat of the guardian of the cedar forest may cast in mythic form an historical event, the capturing of valuable woodlands or the establishing of trade involving wood—a precious commodity almost totally lacking in the plain that constitutes Sumer (southern Iraq). The story in *Gilgamesh* focuses on none of this. Rather, it concentrates on the decision to make a name for the heroes, a debate involving the elders of the city about the merits of the expedition, rituals to assure the gods' blessings, the difficult journey, and dreams. Since Humbaba was established as guardian of the cedar forest by no less an authority than the most powerful of the gods, Enlil, the decision to challenge that authority involves grave dangers and a moral dilemma. The sun god Shamash is the protector of the heroes in this endeavor, and in the version of the story that is followed in our translation, Shamash is the instigator of Gilgamesh's plan to battle Humbaba.[11] Ninsun, the mother of Gilgamesh, offers a libation to Shamash and asks the god what had become the central question:

> "Why have you raised up my son Gilgamesh and laid on him a
>   restless heart that will not sleep?
> Now you push him to go
> on a long journey to the place of Humbaba,
> to face a battle he cannot know about
> and travel a road he cannot know
> until the day he goes and returns,
> until he comes to the forest, the cedars,
> until he kills Humbaba the ferocious one
> and has removed from the land any evil you hate." (III.ii)

By this late version, the question of moral responsibility has entered the story, and the battle against Humbaba has taken on a mythic dimension it had not had before: Gilgamesh as the instrument of the sun god in his battle against the forces of evil.

The high gods in the Sumerian and Akkadian pantheon are as much the invention of the poets as of any of the forces that act on the development of religious institutions.[12] Shamash, whose character as sun god was very ancient, was from Sumerian times an important god, but never one of the Four (Anu, Enlil, Ea, and the Great Goddess) thought to have greater power than the hundreds of other gods.[13] The sun god had nothing like the importance of the sun in, say, Egyptian mythology. The sun's battle[14] with evil appears to be a late addition to the Gilgamesh stories, and it is not clear if *Gilgamesh* presents anything like a consistent theological picture. In the late version, Shamash certainly dominates the first half of the story—and then virtually disappears. The second half is dominated, if at all, by a god with a very different "character," Ea. And the whole late version is overladen with the divine being whose presence enters in a subtle way indeed—the Great Goddess, Ishtar.

Shamash is Justice, and he prompts the battle with Humbaba as a confrontation with the Shadow. This complex of light, the good, and the development of the heroic ego (through battle the hero establishes a "name") is well known in myths throughout the world.[15] Less well known is the second phase and the elusive god who dominates the second journey, in *Gilgamesh* the god Ea.

The second phase begins with the illness that seizes Enkidu as Tablet VII opens. Before he dies, Enkidu curses the Stalker and the temple woman who had brought him to civilization. Shamash calls down to Enkidu, reminding him of the advantages that life in the city has given him: food of the gods, drink of kings, a "great garment," the companionship of Gilgamesh, power, honor—and fame. Enkidu's anger is assuaged, and he turns from curses to blessings. It is not enough, though, to remove the fear of death. A full tablet is given over to the rites of mourning, especially Gilgamesh's elegy and a statue fashioned in Enkidu's honor. As his grief intensifies, Gilgamesh strips himself of his office and his identity. His "equal" gone, Gilgamesh turns himself into his double, into a savage form for a very different journey. Everywhere he travels his quest is subject to mockery. The Scorpion-man, the gods (presumably) in the Garden, the Barmaid, Siduri, even the Boatman, Urshanabi, insist his quest is futile. He attempts to go where no human has gone—and succeeds, only to find that the wisdom he seeks will not remove death or bring back Enkidu. The agonizing journey of Tablets IX and X is full of wearying repetition. Everywhere Gilgamesh rehearses the life spent with Enkidu; everywhere he is asked why he wastes himself in such deep grief.

He sets out to find Utnapishtim, the sage who like Noah saved mankind from the Flood. Utnapishtim is the unique case of a human defeating death. For his help in the Flood he is rewarded with something like the life of the gods. To find him, Gilgamesh must risk the waters of death itself, where a touch of the water will kill him. Looking for the secret of life and death, Gilgamesh instead is given a story. Adding a second narrator, Utnapishtim, and a story-within-a-story—a first-person narrative at that—further removes Gilgamesh from the simple directness of the sun god, Shamash.

Through Utnapishtim Gilgamesh finds the god of the watery abyss, Ea. The story of the Flood, with its many resemblances to the biblical version (though considerably older than Genesis), was what first excited the excavators who found the *Gilgamesh* tablets in the ancient city of Nineveh.[16] The Flood is only part of one tablet, Tablet XI, but the columns are quite long and the story is presented in fine detail. Much of it is like the biblical Flood, but the narrative difficulties that arise in Genesis 6–10, where all the divine roles have to be carried by one figure, Yahweh, are resolved in the polytheism of *Gilgamesh*. The Flood is the result of the deeply irrational fiat of the powerful Enlil. No reason is given to justify the Flood.[17] Indeed, Enlil is chided for commanding the Flood "without talking it through," that is, in the Assembly of the Gods. The gods themselves are frightened by the ferocity of the destruction, and the Great Goddess, identified with Ishtar, loudly laments the destruction of mankind.

Mankind is saved by a trick. Enlil has forbidden the gods to tell humans of the plan to destroy them. So Ea, whose very "character" is cunning,[18] finds a way to reveal the plan—by speaking to a wall, behind which, it happens, is the sage Utnapishtim. But Utnapishtim is faced with a dilemma, one that requires yet another trick. He must somehow persuade the people of his city to build a great boat without knowing the true nature of the mission. He succeeds in this because Ea provides him with a cunning speech, a beautifully designed, richly metaphoric speech that supports two entirely different interpretations. The people are delighted, and celebrate after the building of the boat as if they were celebrating the New Year's Festival.

The cunning of Ea allows one man to survive, and with him the seed of animals to repopulate the earth. But Utnapishtim finds another clever twist to the story. Ea tells Enlil, first, to punish only the evildoers—not mankind as a whole; and he offers a kind of trade: instead of a Flood, let humans live in a hostile world—the world of lions and wolves, famine and plague. Gilgamesh is asked to ponder Ea's words. Although one man, Utnapishtim, has been spared death, Gilgamesh must give up the dream of achieving a like fate.

Gilgamesh finally accepts the wisdom, but not without resistance. When he returns to Uruk, he returns as king, to life. Tablet XI ends with a clear echoing of the opening of Tablet I. Ea will be heard once more in *Gilgamesh*, though, in the difficult Tablet XII. Although there is no question that this tablet belongs to *Gilgamesh* and completes it,[19] it is the most difficult of the parts to account for. Jeffrey H. Tigay has shown in great detail how the Gilgamesh stories "evolved" from a group of Sumerian tales that arose not long after the historical Gilgamesh lived, through different versions to the one that provides the basis of this translation, the Neo-Assyrian version from Nineveh.[20] Changes in the versions are important enough that, after Tigay's analysis, the kind of composite Gilgamesh that has prevailed in translations will be deeply suspect from now on.[21] Our translation, then, attempts to render the version attributed to the poet Sîn-leqi-unninnī[22] as faithfully as possible, as his version is reflected in the so-called standard texts. Tigay's work throws into even stronger relief the strange character of the twelfth tablet, a very close Akkadian translation of a Sumerian original.[23] Whatever reasons prompted the inclusion of this tablet, the god who helps Gilgamesh in the story is Ea.

Tablet XII is unusual in that it breaks the narrative line of Tablets I through XI. When it begins, Enkidu is still alive, and the tablet presents a different version of Enkidu's death. He offers to enter the underworld to retrieve two objects, the nature of which is still disputed, but seem to be drum and beater. Gilgamesh gives Enkidu detailed advice on entering and returning from the underworld, but Enkidu does just the opposite and is trapped forever. Gilgamesh goes weeping to the gods Enlil and Sin, but they do nothing to help. Only Ea listens to Gilgamesh's petition. Ea instructs the god of the dead, Nergal, to open a hole in the earth so that the ghost of Enkidu can escape from the underworld.[24] Significantly, it is the ghost of Enkidu, not the complete man, who escapes, and his tale of the underworld is anything but pleasant, especially because it ends on the bleakest of notes—the fate of one who dies with no one on earth to care for his memory; his fate in the underworld is by far the least appealing of all fates.[25]

Gilgamesh, Enkidu, and Utnapishtim are the major human characters in the story. In spite of some extraordinary powers and adventures, they are recognizably human figures. The gods may speak and sometimes act like humans, but they are recognizably immortals, of a different nature. Shamash and Ea are the most important of the deities in the story, although the old sky-father, Anu, makes an appearance in Tablet VI, and the most powerful of the gods, Enlil, is depicted in both halves of the story, a god all the more to be feared because of his arbitrary exercise of power. All of these are traditional Mesopotamian characters, well-defined and relatively "flat" characters from literary sources that stretch back into the Third Millennium. Perhaps the most important of the gods in *Gilgamesh*, though, is less well defined, though just as traditional: the Great Goddess, Ishtar.[26]

In his close analysis of the different versions of Gilgamesh stories, Jeffrey H. Tigay observes a number of small but pervasive changes in wording related to Ishtar.[27] The most interesting of these are formulas describing the city of Uruk; where in Old Babylonian texts Uruk is consistently "Uruk of the broad places," the later version has instead "Uruk *supūri*," "Uruk of the Sheepfold." Whatever historical, economic, and social reasons may have caused the growth of the city as an institution in ancient Mesopotamia, Mesopotamian thought consistently regarded the city as the dwelling-place of a god. Characterizing the city as "of the Sheepfold" draws attention to the temple complex at the center of the city and recalls the Sacred Marriage performed there between the goddess and the king as high priest.[28] Mythologically, the Sacred Marriage was depicted in the love story of Ishtar and Tammuz, mentioned prominently in Tablet VI. Tammuz, a human taken as the lover of Ishtar, was considered a king before Gilgamesh; but he is most often the shepherd, and the love-making of Ishtar and Tammuz takes place in pasture or sheepfold or storehouse.[29] The shift from "Uruk of the broad places" to Uruk *supūri* suggests a renewed interest in the cultic center—and Ishtar's importance for the very being of the city.

The shift is confirmed by a second one noted by Tigay. Where Uruk is called "the abode of Anu" in the Old Babylonian texts, the city becomes regularly "the abode of Anu and Ishtar" in the later version.[30] The reference is specifically to the temple complex, Eanna, the scene, historically, of a most intriguing religious transformation. Eanna was originally a temple devoted to the cult of Anu, head of the pantheon, and his divine consort, Antum. Already in Sumerian times, though, Ishtar (Sumerian Inanna) had supplanted the divine consort and installed herself in Eanna, virtually eclipsing Anu himself. Anu, like other celestial gods, withdraws and becomes remote, inactive—what Mircea Eliade calles the *dei otiosi*.[31] Ishtar, Anu's "daughter," is by far the more active partner in *Gilgamesh*. Anu is appropriately remote, entering into *Gilgamesh* only to do Ishtar's bidding (Tablet VI) and recalled by her in an obscure reference in the Flood story (Tablet XI).[32]

These small details indicate the degree to which Gilgamesh's city has become in the late version of *Gilgamesh* increasingly identified with Ishtar. These shifts counter the prevailing notion that Ishtar is depicted only in a negative way in *Gilgamesh*, that the poet is somehow deeply antagonistic to the goddess.[33] Certainly the episode carefully placed in the center of *Gilgamesh* (Tablet VI) shows a dangerous and treacherous Ishtar. When she offers to make Gilgamesh her lover and presents him wondrous gifts,[34] Gilgamesh rebuffs her in a particularly biting exchange, insulting her and offering as proof the many lovers she has had—beginning with Tammuz—and whose fates were cast by their involvement with her. Ishtar, who is goddess of both love and war, does not take the insults lightly. She implores Anu to send the Bull of Heaven to punish Gilgamesh and Enkidu; Anu, at first resisting, gives in when she threatens to let loose the dead to overtake the living. To Gilgamesh's insults are added two more: the Bull of Heaven is defeated by the heroes, and Enkidu flings a part of the Bull into her face.

The episode is indeed central to *Gilgamesh*, and it needs to be read in a number of ways. Certainly the arrogance of the heroes is both admirable and deeply mistaken: a violation of the very boundary between mortals and immortals that the poem treats again and again. The gods, in Mesopotamian thought, do not exist for mankind. Indeed, the reverse is true. One constant feature in stories about the First Man, for example, is that man is formed by the gods to relieve the gods of work. Gilgamesh and Enkidu, like most heroes of myth, are breakers of barriers, pushing their way beyond normal limits. And the irrationality of the gods, represented in the poem by Enlil, may sanction the risk-taking of the heroes.

It is easy to focus so intently on the Ishtar of Tablet VI that her presence is missed elsewhere. A notable addition to the Flood story, for example, is the explicit identification of Ishtar with the mother goddess. It is Ishtar who is given the compassionate address to the gods, when she is sickened by the slaughter of her "children." Even more significant, for Gilgamesh, is that his return to Uruk after his agonizing journey across the waters of death is a return to his role as king and a return to the "house of Ishtar." His kingly role, we suggest, has as its heart the Sacred Marriage Gilgamesh so bitterly scorned at the center of the work.

More subtle yet are the complex manifestations of Ishtar. The Great Goddess, rather unlike the great male gods, is multidimensional. *Gilgamesh* depicts that polymorphous and sometimes contradictory nature in a great variety of ways. The goddess is mother—even where, in Tablet XII, she is Ereshkigal, goddess of the underworld. There, Enkidu has entered the netherworld and is seized by a most unusual death. He had been warned by Gilgamesh that the "lament of the netherworld" (*tazimtu erşeti*, XII.i.28) would seize him if Enkidu failed to take precautions. The lament itself, which sounds much like a lullaby in the Akkadian and which is paralleled in ritual texts and myths elsewhere, indeed does take him:

> The lamentation of the netherworld seized him:
> *She who sleeps, she who sleeps, the Mother of Birth and Death,*
> *who sleeps,*
> *Her clean shoulders no garment covers,*
> *Her breast like a stone bowl does not give suck.* (XII.ii.46–49)[35]

The mother who dominates this lullaby is, like "Mother Earth," goddess of both birth and death. Elsewhere, the goddess appears in one form as a goddess in the cedar forest (ᵈIrnini, V.i.6) and as the Barmaid, Siduri (X.i.1), another manifestation of Ishtar. The temple prostitute who seduces and then instructs Enkidu (I.iv) is in Ishtar's service, an identification that is strengthened in Tablet VI, when Ishtar calls her women together after Enkidu has insulted her (VI.v.16–17). Since the names of the goddesses tend to separate the functions of the Great Goddess enough to confuse the modern reader, better to consider the variety of mother, whore, maiden, death-crone, priestess, wife, and the like manifestations of a single underlying feminine archetype.[36] She may be Aruru in the story of the birth of Enkidu (I.ii), but she is most often named by the most widespread of her names, Ishtar.

The image of the Great Goddess in *Gilgamesh* is of particular importance today, thousands of years after the text was composed, because the Mesopotamian goddess in some way confirms but in other ways disturbs a pattern that becomes all too common in the long history of Western civilization: the dethroning of the Great Goddess. Another group of texts, not nearly as old as the *Gilgamesh* but important because of their close relationship to the Bible, the Nag Hammadi Library,[37] has shown the remarkable persistence of the Great Goddess even into early Christian times and emphasizes all the more the orthodox rejection of the Feminine in Judeo-Christian tradition. Time and again, the Nag Hammadi texts portray a feminine divinity equal to the Father. The texts know a divine trinity of Father, Mother, and Son instead of what comes to be the orthodox Blessed Trinity of Father, Son, and Holy Spirit.[38] In the texts she is known by many names: Mother, Barbelo, Sophia, Zoe, and the like. Her role in the Creation of the universe and the Creation of mankind is quite complex, but generally she is exalted. The Nag Hammadi texts often challenge the orthodox interpretation of the story of Eve, and Eve is exalted because of her connection with the Great Goddess. The most shocking of the texts, "The Thunder, Perfect Mind," proclaims the paradoxical nature of the goddess:

> For I am the first and the last.
> I am the honored one and the scorned one.
> I am the whore and the holy one.
> I am the wife and the virgin.
> I am [the mother] and the daughter.
> I am the members of my mother.
> I am the barren one
>   and many are her sons.
> I am she whose wedding is great,
>   and I have not taken a husband.
> I am the midwife and she who does not bear.
> I am the solace of my labor pains.
> I am the bride and the bridegroom,
>   and it is my husband who begot me.
> I am the mother of my father
>   and the sister of my husband,
>   and he is my offspring.[39]

The shocking presence of the goddess in the theological and mythological speculation of the Judeo-Christian tradition only serves to underscore the degree to which the goddess was rejected and degraded by the orthodox tradition.

Although there is evidence that Yahweh was thought to have a consort at different times in Israelite history,[40] the Hebrew Bible has only scorn for the Queen of Heaven worshipped by those who would corrupt the purity of the worship of Yahweh. Jeremiah, for example, warns the women among the Jews who persist in following the Queen of Heaven. The women claim

> "We have no intention of listening to this word you have spoken to us in Yahweh's name, but intend to go on doing all we vowed to do: offering incense to the Queen of Heaven and pouring libations in her honor, as we used to do, we and our fathers, our kings and our leaders, in the towns of Judah and in the streets of Jerusalem: we had food in plenty then, we lived well, we suffered no disasters. But since we gave up offering incense to the Queen of Heaven and pouring libations in her honor, we have been destitute and have perished either by sword or by famine." The women added, "When we offer incense to the Queen of Heaven and pour libations in her honor, do you think we make cakes for her with her features on them, and pour libations to her, without our husbands' knowledge?" (Jeremiah 44:16–19) [41]

Jeremiah responds by showing them the consequences of their worship: ruin. Even more vividly, the much later text, Revelation, returns to the Great Goddess as the symbol of all that opposes true religion. One of the seven angels takes John

> in spirit to a desert, and there I saw a woman riding a scarlet beast which had seven heads and ten horns and had blasphemous titles written all over it. The woman was dressed in purple and scarlet, and glittered with gold and jewels and pearls, and she was holding a gold wine cup filled with the disgusting filth of her fornication; on her forehead was written a name, a cryptic name: "Babylon the Great, the mother of all the prostitutes and all the filthy practices on the earth." (Revelation 17:3–6)

The other great source of Western tradition, Greek mythological thought, is often considered more open to the feminine. After all, goddesses were important in Greek religion and were celebrated in Greek literature: Hera, Athena, Aphrodite, Artemis, and Demeter, to name but a few. Close investigation has shown, however, the way the Greeks almost systematically reduced the powers of the goddesses.[42] Probably the most striking case is the capture by Apollo of the most sacred ground in Greece: the sanctuary at Delphi.[43] The god Apollo, Averter of Evil, god of purification, god of prophecy (and later identified with the sun), is often thought to embody the most conspicuously Greek characteristics of rationality and order.[44] Among the inscriptions at his shrine at Delphi are the Apollonian maxims "Curb thy spirit," "Observe the limit," "Hate hybris," "Bow before the divine"—and "Keep woman under rule." [45] The Greeks sought advice from Apollo through the priestesses at Delphi, who uttered prophecy while in a state of ecstatic possession. The presence of women in the cult of Apollo, though, is an indication of a profound change that took place in the sanctuary. The Greeks knew this most rational of the gods had his origins outside Greece. He was a foreigner, like Dionysus, possibly from Asia Minor. Greek myth explains Apollo's capture of Delphi as an heroic act, displacing the original divine being, Mother Earth.[46] By killing the great serpent, Python, at the very place where Earth had her sacred center, Apollo established himself as the god in command of all the powers that had been invested in the Great Goddess.

If orthodox Judaism and Christianity, on the one hand, and Greek thought, on the other, display the degradation of the Great Goddess, the two main sources of Western civilization make it difficult to recover the positive character of the Mesopotamian Great Goddess. In particular, the deep connection with the powers of sexuality has been disturbed. One of the most important minor characters in *Gilgamesh* is an unnamed prostitute, a priestess in the service of Ishtar. The woman, identified only by her cultic role (*šamḫātu* and *ḫarīmtu*), is the instrument who brings Enkidu from the wild to the civilized state. Through her he gains consciousness, language, identity. Through her he learns what it is to be human. This is, perhaps, not surprising in a culture in which sexual allure is a divine attribute, where the god Enki is portrayed as praising his own phallus and Ishtar's explicit sexual powers reveal her command over all life. How shocking it would be, today, to portray Yahweh in such a way. The Virgin Mother of Christian orthodoxy (who is, of course, not divine) is taken as the very opposite of the Virgin Mother of Mesopotamian culture. Consider only the shock in recent years when the early Christian document "The Gospel of Philip" portrayed the relationship between the feminine Wisdom and Christ in sexual terms.

As for the Wisdom who is called "the barren," she is the mother of the angels. And the companion of the Savior is Mary Magdalene. But Christ loved her more than all the disciples and used to kiss her often on her mouth. The rest of the disciples were offended by it and expressed disapproval. They said to him, "Why do you love her more than all of us?" The Savior answered and said to them, "Why do I not love you like her?" When a blind man and one who sees are both together in darkness, they are no different from one another. When the light comes, then he who sees will see the light, and he who is blind will remain in darkness.[47]

Nothing is more difficult for the modern reader, then, than the connection in *Gilgamesh* between the Great Goddess and the prostitute in her service. So important is it in the version of Sîn-leqi-unninnī, however, a version that is centuries older than the earliest biblical or Greek text, that it has led us to characterize the two major narrative movements in *Gilgamesh* as "Apollonian" and "Dionysian." The Apollonian phase ends with explicit comments on the prostitute.

THE APOLLONIAN PHASE (*Gilgamesh* I.i–VII.iv)

The Great Goddess is evident throughout *Gilgamesh*, as Aruru, Irninni, Siduri, Ereshkigal, and Ishtar. The complexity of the goddess must be seen against the relatively simple story lines dominated by Gilgamesh and Enkidu. The two phases might properly be called the phases of Shamash and Ea. "Apollonian" and "Dionysian" should not be taken as implying Greek influence on *Gilgamesh*, which even in its late version is considerably older than Greek texts. We rather consider the distinction in light of Friedrich Nietzsche's "The Birth of Tragedy from the Spirit of Music" (1871). The Apollonian/Dionysian duality, originally proposed to explain the co-existence of opposing principles in Greek tragedy, has been proposed as a useful typology of alternative world views, structures of consciousness, and even right brain/left brain specialization.[48] Where Apollo dominates a world of cause and effect, Dionysus reveals a cosmic unity. If man is on the one hand *Homo faber*, with his tools of reason and logic, he is on the other hand *Homo ludens*, the player, dominated by imagination, fantasy, and intuition. If Apollo rules the left hemisphere of the brain, Dionysus holds sway in the right. Freud is on one side, Jung the other. The Apollonian world is a "male-dominated, hierarchically organized, class-structured society. It emphasizes virtues that have been traditionally considered masculine (control and rationality) and hence it thrives best in situations where: the head controls the body; capital governs the corporation; reason controls emotions; the male is the ruler of the family."[49] The Dionysian vision, on the contrary, embraces the matriarchal societies and planting cultures, "where the cycle of the seasons and the dependency on Mother Nature is a primal fact of existence. It places high value on the 'feminine' virtues of surrender, trust and nurturance."[50]

Nietzsche saw the individual at the heart of Apollonian consciousness. "This apotheosis of individuation knows but one law—the individual, i.e., the delimiting of the boundaries of the individual, *measure* in the Hellenic sense. Apollo, as ethical deity, exacts measure of his disciples, and, that to this end, he requires self-knowledge." [51] Sharing the same shrine, as if to confirm their mutual dependence, the "barbaric" Dionysus reveals to us that "despite all its beauty and moderation, . . . existence rested on a hidden substratum of suffering." [52] At the center of Greek tragedy is the suffering of the hero. But even in suffering the two gods pull in different ways. The plastic art of Apollo "dispels the suffering of the individual by the radiant glorification of the *eternity of the phenomenon:* here beauty triumphs over the suffering inherent in life." [53] Dionysian art, which Nietzsche saw primarily in the music of Greek tragedy, is something else. It "too, wishes to convince us of the eternal joy of existence: only we are to seek this joy not in phenomena, but behind them. We are to recognize that all that comes into being must be ready for a sorrowful end; we are forced to look into the terrors of the individual existence—yet we are not to become rigid with fear: a metaphysical comfort tears us momentarily from the bustle of the transforming figures." [54]

Sîn-leqi-unninnî took traditional stories and wove them into a unity that we are only now coming to recognize. The *action* that dominates the first half of *Gilgamesh* is the heroic exploit of Gilgamesh and Enkidu in battle against Humbaba. Of the various elements brought together to form a coherent narrative (preparation; debate; cultic acts; the journey; dreams; battle; conclusion), an innovation transforms the tradition in a profound way: the role of the sun god, Shamash. [55] The earliest Gilgamesh tales knew what prompted the hero: he must make a name for himself. Gilgamesh is rather confident that establishing a name is the first necessity of the great one. The fear of death must be brushed away in the endeavor. But Sîn-leqi-unninnî deepens the motivation. Now it is Shamash who has "laid on" Gilgamesh "a restless heart that will not sleep." And the urgency is explained by the way the stakes have changed. Humbaba is not just a symbol of the enemy or of the precious commodity of lumber for a treeless Mesopotamia. Humbaba stands for "any evil" Shamash "hates." At once, the heroic task has taken on the dimensions of the battle against the Shadow, Apollo against Python or Mithras slaughtering the Bull.

Depth psychology sees in this hero myth the ego's conflict with the Shadow, which contains the hidden, repressed, and unfavorable aspects of the personality. [56]

The battle between the hero and the dragon is the more active form of this myth, and it shows more clearly the archetypal theme of the ego's triumph over regressive trends. For most people the dark or negative side of the personality remains unconscious. The hero, on the contrary, must realize that the shadow exists and that he can draw strength from it. He must come to terms with its destructive powers if he is to become sufficiently terrible to overcome the dragon. I.e., before the ego can triumph, it must master and assimilate the shadow.[57]

If the battle with Humbaba (and, perhaps, also the battle with the Bull of Heaven in Tablet VI) is charged with this conflict, at once cosmic and personal, this does not exhaust the interest in Shamash, Averter of Evil. Shamash is also, like Apollo, the god of the dream—at least in this work. Gilgamesh's mother, Ninsun, herself a minor deity, is active in his cult. Her major role is interpreting dreams and dispensing advice in *Gilgamesh*. Shamash, unlike Ishtar in Tablet VI, does not reveal himself bodily to speak to the heroes. He reveals his truths through dreams, which must be interpreted.

The hero myth acts in concert with another story, though, and it is in the other story that the role of Shamash is indeed striking and surprising. The story is the education of Enkidu. Enkidu is seduced by the prostitute and alienated from the wild beasts with whom he has lived. Early in *Gilgamesh* Enkidu is prepared for his entry into the city by the help of the prostitute. The story retreats until, in what must be one of the earliest deathbed scenes in literature, it suddenly returns in a most extraordinary way (VII.iii).

As Enkidu weakens, he curses the Stalker and the prostitute—decreeing their fates. His anger is understandably great. But his anger is turned not by, as one might guess, Ishatar, but by Shamash. The third column is badly broken, but we are fortunate to have Shamash's speech preserved in its entirety.[58] The *form* of the speech should be noticed first. Shamash speaks "from afar," and his speech is appropriate to the Apollonian rational mind. It is an argument, carefully balanced, directed to the intellect, calm, connected, and clear:

> "Why, Enkidu, do you curse the love-priestess, the woman
> who would feed you with the food of the gods,
> and would have you drink wine that is the drink of kings,
> and would clothe you in a great garment,
> and would give you beautiful Gilgamesh as a companion?
> Listen: hasn't Gilgamesh, your beloved friend,
> made you lie down in a great bed?

Hasn't he made you lie down in a bed of honor,
and placed you on the peaceful seat at his left hand?
The world's kings have kissed your feet.
He will make the people of Uruk weep for you, cause them to
   grieve you,
[will make the women], the whole city, fill up with sorrow for
   your sake.
And afterward he will carry the signs of grief on his own body,
putting on the skin of dogs and ranging the wilderness."

The column ends with Enkidu's response: his angry heart "grew still." It does not mean the end of terror for Enkidu. As his sickness deepens, he is given a vision of the underworld, where the inhabitants eat dust and fly about in darkness on "a garment of wings." If death is no less painful for Enkidu and Gilgamesh (VII.vi), Enkidu has discovered that life—civilized life, given him by the prostitute—has indeed been rich. Enkidu responds by blessing the prostitute (VII.iv). Decreeing the fate again does not change the curse, but it adds blessings, balancing the good and evil in the life of Ishtar's servants.

The *content* of Shamash's speech, then, may strike the modern reader as unusual and unexpected. But it reinforces a truth underscored often in *Gilgamesh:* death is inevitable and terrifying; but life ("food of the gods," "the drink of kings," a "great garment," a beloved friend, honor, and memory), seen as civilized life, is precious. Together, form and content reveal the triumph of the rational mind, with its logical skill and its harmony of memory (past delight) and imagination (what the future holds). It is the final learning, much like achieving the stage of formal operations in the psychology of Jean Piaget,[59] in the education of Enkidu. And it reveals much about the organizational skill of the poet-narrator.

THE DIONYSIAN PHASE (*Gilgamesh* VII.v–XII.vi)

No matter how much one may lay up the positive, life-enhancing messages that appear in *Gilgamesh*, the overwhelming truth it conveys is the bitter message of death and loss. It is, as generations have characterized it, a protest against death. Some even see in *Gilgamesh* a direct challenge to traditional values, traditional religion—perhaps all religion. Readers have long noticed that the great confidence Gilgamesh shows in his preparations to meet Humbaba, where life is easily worth risking for the sake of a name, turns to flat despair once Gilgamesh's beloved is taken from him. From the triumphal journey outside the city that marks the first half of *Gilgamesh* the narrative turns to terror, the dark night of the soul.

The entire Tablet VIII appears to be devoted to the formal grieving of Gilgamesh and the city. Gilgamesh delivers a lengthy and beautiful eulogy and, acting as both priest and king, raises a statue in Enkidu's memory. The last two columns of the tablet are fragmentary, but they suggest ritual activity, activity that may have had special relevance for the priestly author, Sîn-leqi-unninnī. From a Nietzschean standpoint, the eulogy would mark the last trace of the Apollonian, where eloquence gives expression to deep feeling within the confines of Gilgamesh's will. The mask begins to crack, but Gilgamesh manages to hold together both privately and publicly, maintaining his dignity and his kingly (and priestly) role. Shamash had, though, told Enkidu that after Gilgamesh had caused the city to weep he could "carry the signs of grief on his own body,/ putting on the skin of dogs and ranging the wilderness." The collapse is narrated in Tablet IX.

Greek tragedy, Nietzsche maintains, "in its earliest form had for its sole theme the sufferings of Dionysus."[60] The dismemberment of Dionysus by the Titans provides a metaphor for the profound transformation of Gilgamesh at this moment in the story. As he casts off his garments and departs the city of Uruk, he loses all that has moored him to society and to civilization itself. The turn recalls the way Enkidu had been described *before* his transformation by the prostitute. Gilgamesh enters the wild and becomes one with it. In his grief he becomes indistinguishable from his double, Enkidu; he becomes Enkidu. At every stage on the agonizing journey, the question of his identity is raised anew. Everyone he meets—the scorpion-demons, the gods in the Garden, Siduri, the Boatman, Urshanabi, Utnapishtim—remind him that the desperate, futile journey is wasting him away. The device used by the poet is relentless repetition: Gilgamesh's strength is wasted, his face sunken; evil fortune has entered his heart, undermined his looks. The story of Enkidu is retold at each stage, and the litany of his grief only renews the suffering again and again.

Two small devices set off the terror of Gilgamesh's quest. One is a simile that in its very incongruity deepens the wound. After all he has undergone, Gilgamesh is told that his "face is like that of a man who has been on a long journey!" Indeed the journey is long. Whether it takes him through the real world or the celestial world, as has been suggested,[61] or through an imaginary landscape, is in one sense irrelevant. It is an inner journey. All of it is significantly "out there," beyond the walls of Uruk—beyond a public role, beyond civilization, uncharted. Gilgamesh presses on through territories to find an answer to the problem of death, territories that had been barred to humans. And part of the irony of Gilgamesh's quest is that he closes the way for other humans just as he is opening up the territory. The second device underscores this. In IX.iv–v Gilgamesh travels through a world of darkness. Hour after hour he travels; thick the darkness; there is no light; he can see neither behind him nor ahead of him.[62] The simple, exact repetition—a vestige of Sumerian poetic style even older than the Akkadian in which this work is cast—is a stunning image of the agony of Gilgamesh's dismemberment.

If the heroic battle with the monster suggests one necessary stage in the developing consciousness of the individual, the "symbolic means by which the emerging ego overcomes the inertia of the unconscious mind,"[63] the ordeal of Gilgamesh suggests the second stage, the archetype of initiation. Anthropologists have long studied the rituals of passage, of which the festivals of Dionysus are an ancient example.[64] In these death and rebirth rites, the ego is lost; "identity is temporarily dismembered or dissolved in the collective unconscious."[65] Orpheus, Dionysus, Christ—all have been taken by their followers to have experienced the ordeal of death and rebirth. The lonely pilgrimage is a widespread symbol of this in literature, and we think it the main reason for the extraordinary impact of the second half of *Gilgamesh*.

Joseph L. Henderson has pointed to the contrast in what we are calling the two phases of *Gilgamesh*.

> There is one striking difference between the hero myth and the initiation rite. The typical hero figures exhaust their efforts in achieving the goal of their ambitions; in short, they become successful even if immediately afterward they are punished or killed for their *hybris*. In contrast to this, the novice for initiation is called upon to give up willful ambition and all desire and to submit to the ordeal. He must be willing to experience this trial without hope of success. In fact, he must be prepared to die; and though the token of his ordeal may be mild (a period of fasting, the knocking out of a tooth, or tattooing) or agonizing (the infliction of the wounds of circumcision, subincision, or other mutilations), the purpose remains always the same: to create the symbolic mood of death from which may spring the symbolic mood of rebirth.[66]

There is, of course, no possibility of avoiding death in *Gilgamesh*. The agonizing journey does not give Gilgamesh hope of personal immortality; nor does it bring Enkidu back to life. Yet, Gilgamesh *is* cleansed. He puts on the great garment after he casts away the filthy skins he had been wearing. He does return to Uruk, to his kingship, and to Ishtar. (It is important to notice that the magical plant, "The-Old-Man-Will-Be-Made-Young," given him by Utnapishtim [XI.vi], is not devoured by Gilgamesh. He intends to offer it, rather like the eucharist, to the citizens of Uruk. We take this as a symbol of the full renewal of Gilgamesh's public, i.e., priestly and kingly, role; and the altruism marks the transcendence of mere egoistic values.) The return is narrated in a brief, solemn manner. In one sense, of course, nothing has changed: mankind has not been spared death. But there is a kind of learning that has taken place, a second kind of thinking that we can consider Dionysian. In contrast to Shamash's wisdom in Tablet VII we are given the cunning of Ea in Tablets XI and XII.[67]

The lonely journey of Gilgamesh is a movement away from the center (Uruk, with all its demands on king and priest); but it is also a journey into the archaic. *Gilgamesh* announces from its first line that it celebrates the hero who has seen the *nagbu* (I.i.1), which we have translated "the abyss" for the many resonances that term retains. The term *nagbu* had a range of meanings, from "spring" and "fountain" and "underground water"—all of particularly great importance in arid Mesopotamia, where water is life—to a meaning found in poetic texts, "totality," the all.[68] Even as the source of water, it is often used as an epithet of the gods, especially the god whose "place" is the *abzu* (Akkadian *apsû*, with much the same semantic load as our *abyss*)—Ea, "lord of the deep waters." It is difficult to tell exactly whether Gilgamesh, in seeing the *nagbu*, has seen the source of waters or "everything." Our guess is that the term is used precisely to capture these multiple meanings. And Gilgamesh is said to have discovered "secrets" of the gods and to have brought back news from before the Flood. The very opening of the poem announces, then, that the major achievement of the hero is also the end of his journey outward. He meets the "lord of the *nagbu*" only indirectly, through the sage Utnapishtim. What is clear is that the episode is dominated by the cunning of the one who dwells in the depths.

In two ways this is a journey into the archaic. First, Gilgamesh crosses back through time. Human history was thought to have changed profoundly with the event of the Flood. Gilgamesh finally pushes beyond the waters of death to speak to the only human to escape death, the sage Utnapishtim. Before the Flood, the land was ruled by the sages, men who, according to legend, were instructed in the arts of civilization by Ea. Utnapishtim, who lived through the Flood, is the last of the sages. In meeting Utnapishtim and returning with the story of the Flood, Gilgamesh has recovered his historical roots. In another sense, though, the journey of Gilgamesh winds back through cosmic time. Ea is one of the old gods, the old Father who is the last resort when all else fails. At the heart of this ancient cunning is a kind of truth that dwells in indirection, virtually a *via negativa*.[69]

Utnapishtim's first bit of advice to Gilgamesh is, to be sure, direct: "From the beginning there is no permanence" (X.vi). But the Flood story (XI.i–iv) is a masterwork of cunning. The story was already old when Sîn-leqi-unninnī introduced it into the *Gilgamesh*.[70] So tempting is the desire to read this story in light of the much later biblical version of the Flood that it is easy to emphasize similarities at the expense of differences. The three speeches of Ea (XI.i.19–31; XI.i.36–47; and XI.iv.177–188) have only rough parallels in Yahweh's speeches to Noah (Genesis 6:13–7:5; 8:15–18; and 9:1–17).[71] While each of Ea's speeches emphasizes the kind of cunning one might expect from his servant, the sage Utnapishtim, such intellectual play is entirely absent from the biblical account.[72] The gods have been forbidden to inform humans that Enlil has decreed the destruction of all human life. Ea finds a stratagem to reveal the truth—not directly to Utnapishtim, but through a wall of reeds, behind which the sage listens. But Utnapishtim is then faced with a very difficult practical matter: how to get the people's help in building the boat. Ea, in a masterfully ironic and polysemous speech (the best-known example of figurative language in Akkadian literature), tells Utnapishtim exactly what to say to the people in order to trick them. The key is to tell them the truth, but in such a figurative way that they will totally misinterpret the words. They do, and mankind is saved—though everyone but Utnapishtim and his family is destroyed.

More important still for Gilgamesh, who is seeking an answer to the problem of death, is Ea's third speech. Ea's words resolve the conflict among the high gods, reconciling the powerful Enlil to mankind in the persons of Utnapishtim and his wife. Ea chides Enlil for bringing on the devastating Flood "without talking it through." He establishes a basic moral principle in the universe: "Punish the one who commits the crime; punish the evildoer alone." (The following line, however, is very tricky, and seems to qualify the principle in an important way.) Further, he sets the absolute devastation of the Flood against what will now characterize the life of mankind in the world:

> Instead of your bringing on the Flood, let lions rise up and
> diminish the people.
> Instead of your bringing on the Flood, let the wolf rise up and
> cut the people low.
> Instead of your bringing on the Flood, let famine be set up to
> throw down the land.

Instead of your bringing on the Flood, let plague rise up and
  strike down the people.

Instead of the comforting message of Yahweh, that man should re-estab-
lish dominance over the earth, should be fruitful and multiply without
fear of devastation by the Flood, the Babylonian message gives instead
the terrible message of death. From this time forth, nature will be hostile
to man (although no Mesopotamian version of the Flood makes man-
kind's moral lapses the cause of the Flood). The lion, the wolf, famine,
and plague are not removed from life; rather, they are confirmed. All are
better than the loss of life entirely from the earth. Little wonder, then,
that Utnapishtim tells Gilgamesh to think carefully about Ea's words.

THE TWO CENTERS

Gilgamesh is a collection of tales, mainly about Gilgamesh, of course, but
in the case of the Flood, a story that originally had nothing to do with
Gilgamesh has been patched into the larger work. The tales are, for the
most part, much older than the version of Sîn-leqi-unninnī; some were
at first told in the Sumerian language. Further, a collection of Gilgamesh
tales into a unified "epic" seems to have been completed by the Old
Babylonian period, although only fragments of the Old Babylonian Gil-
gamesh stories have survived.[73] What Jeffrey H. Tigay has been able to
demonstrate is the extent to which the late version shows the artistic
work of an author.[74]

We have suggested that there are two major phases in the narrative,
an Apollonian and a Dionysian, each with a characteristic narrative style
and mode of thought. Even without those narrative movements, though,
on purely formal grounds the overall unity of Tablets I–XI can be estab-
lished. The last lines of Tablet XI explicitly return to the opening lines of
Tablet I, effectively closing the work. This formal frame allows us to see
the symbolic importance of the walls of Uruk for the work—the man-
made outer limits of the city—and the sacred center of Uruk, the dwell-
ing-place of the goddess Ishtar. However discouraging the journey to the
nagbu has turned out for Gilgamesh, the solemn return to Uruk and to
Ishtar is an artistic achievement in symbol-building that is all the more
remarkable for its terse, impersonal character.

The artistic integrity of Sîn-leqi-unninnī's version leads us to related
questions. Although the answers are quite speculative, brief mention
should be made of them, since they guided us in the translation of the
work. If *Gilgamesh* has a clear beginning and ending, does it have an
explicitly marked center? And if the narrative is effectively closed at the

end of Tablet XI, why is there a Tablet XII? We believe the two questions are related.

Tablet VI is not a long six-columned text, but it is internally coherent, and it occurs exactly at the center of *Gilgamesh* I–XI. After the victory over Humbaba, Ishtar offers herself to Gilgamesh. For his love, Ishtar is ready to offer him a great chariot and life in the house of Ishtar. With Ishtar come power and wonderful fertility. She offers, in short, the sacred marriage, hierogamy.[75] In one sense, Ishtar is offering the union that is the most sacred duty of the *en* of the city, a role in which priestly and kingly functions cannot be separated. Not surprisingly, Gilgamesh begins and ends his list of Ishtar's lovers with his predecessor, Tammuz, a human made divine, and Ishullanu, who uses cultic language in *his* rejection of the goddess.

The sacred marriage involves the goddess and a mortal, and Gilgamesh rejects it for three reasons. As a human, what could he give to Ishtar? More important, she is not what she appears to be; what she offers turns to destroy the one who accepts her favors. And finally, she has had a long history of transforming her lovers, destroying their lives. Gilgamesh's speech to Ishtar (VI.i–ii) is brilliantly contrived. So effective is the insult to Ishtar that many readers see in Tablet VI the complete rejection of the Great Goddess, a virtual break with a long religious tradition. We think this only partly correct. By explicitly identifying the goddess in the Flood story as Ishtar, Sîn-leqi-unninnî balances this rejection of Ishtar by revealing her most motherly, compassionate side. It is Ishtar who laments the terrible loss of her children in the Flood and vows it will not happen again. And it is to Ishtar that Gilgamesh returns after his lonely pilgrimage. But it is true that in Tablet VI her least attractive features are emphasized. She is insulted and, more, she is defeated by humans in what is the most shocking portrayal of humans in the same frame with gods in all of Akkadian literature.

The heroes defeat the Bull of Heaven sent by Anu at Ishtar's request to punish them for their *hybris*. Enkidu, characteristically brutal, throws a thigh of the Bull into Ishtar's face. As she sets up a wailing, the men begin a great celebration. For Gilgamesh, the celebration finally brings rest, which has escaped him throughout the story. Then, in an ironic twist, in the midst of their sleep comes a dream of the great gods in council. The news brings Tablet VI to a shocking end. In the next tablet we learn just what this mad moment will mean: the death of Enkidu.

The challenge to Ishtar and the defeat of the Bull of Heaven is an extension of the heroic, intensely masculine ordeal of defeating the monster Humbaba. Where that had been motivated by Shamash, however, this is a purely human concern. Nowhere else in *Gilgamesh* are the claims of god and man so much at variance. (The injustice of the Flood is a different matter.) The men have gained their names, and now they play with them, forming riddles about themselves. This is not the end of the Apollonian phase, for that requires insight. But it is clearly the event that turns the whole narrative around. So beautifully integrated into the larger movements of *Gilgamesh* is Tablet VI that it seems almost natural that this old Sumerian story break up the story of the education of Enkidu and repeat an heroic task as a centerpiece.

About Tablet XII there is nothing sure except that it belongs to the version of Sîn-leqi-unninnī. We consider it the displaced center of *Gilgamesh*. Like Tablets VI–VIII, Tablet XII narrates the causes of Enkidu's death and the death itself, although the narratives are very different indeed. The author chose to include only part of a longer Sumerian work for Tablet XII, "Gilgamesh, Enkidu, and the Nether World." [76] Tablet XII is surprising in that it is such a close translation of the Sumerian original. It shows little of the innovation Sîn-leqi-unninnī brought to his rehandling of other Sumerian material.

Instead of the sequence followed in Tablets VI–VIII, Tablet XII attributes the death of Enkidu not to a decision of the great gods in council, or to offenses against the gods in defeating Humbaba and the Bull of Heaven, but to a failure to follow the ways of the underworld. Enkidu is ready to make the perilous journey, and Gilgamesh advises him on how to enter and leave the underworld safely. But refusing to follow Gilgamesh's advice, Enkidu is seized by the earth. Much is made of his strange death. The usual causes—Namtar (fate), the plague, demonic abduction, injury in battle—are not given. Rather, "earth seized him," an action imaged as a cry of the earth. The cry is like a lullaby sung by the mother (Ereshkigal) to bring her baby back to rest.

The picture of the underworld drawn by Enkidu is violent and depressing—much like the dream of the world of the dead he recounted in VII.iv. Those who have managed to leave loved ones on earth are, it is true, given a measure of dignity in the underworld. But Enkidu's report —which ends *Gilgamesh* abruptly—ends with the worst fate of all: leaving no one behind to care for the restless spirit. Very likely Sîn-leqi-unninnī, an exorcist (*mashmashshu*), had a professional interest in the ways of the underworld and in control over demons. Still, the narrative ends as abruptly as it begins.

We suggest, very tentatively indeed, that in putting together *Gilgamesh* from traditional materials, Sîn-leqi-unninnī had at least two works to place at the center, after the heroic exploit that established the heroes' names and before Gilgamesh's lonely pilgrimage. Gilgamesh's rejection of Ishtar fits the narrative well and makes the motivation at least consistent. But "Gilgamesh, Enkidu, and the Nether World" could not be abandoned. Why? The extreme fidelity to the Sumerian may furnish a clue. This was a sacred text. Within the advice Gilgamesh gives Enkidu may be found magical language—language that had to be reproduced exactly in order to be effective. A sacred, magical text, it could not be disturbed for artistic reasons.[77] *Gilgamesh* itself was not a sacred text; it took no part in liturgies or rituals. Nevertheless, Tablet XII may well have retained its sacral importance. Setting it at the end recapitulates many of the themes of *Gilgamesh* I–XI and ends the work on a particularly solemn note.

WHAT KIND OF POEM IS *GILGAMESH?*

It remains to say something of the genre of the poem. When it was rediscovered a century ago, the poem was often called a "legend," without any very precise significance. Paul Haupt called it *Nimrodepos*, in the hope that Gilgamesh might have something to do with the biblical Nimrod, and suggesting a connection with the Greek *epos*, in which the oral presentation of the poet is the defining characteristic.[78] The work has come to be called, conventionally, the *epic* of Gilgamesh. Colophons at the ends of various tablets of *Gilgamesh* refer to it in two ways. Mesopotamian literary catalogues often refer to works by their *incipit*, the beginning of the first line. In the case of *Gilgamesh*, this is *šá nagba imuru*, "Of him who saw the *nagbu*." A second way found in the colophons is to call it an "*iškaru* of Gilgamesh." The term *iškaru*, usually translated "series," has the semantic range of "work assigned to be performed," "materials or supplies for workmen," and "finished products," in addition to "literary work" or "collection of songs."[79] As "literary work," *iškaru* does not seem to indicate anything of the content, and is a designation often used for ritual texts. As it may also designate a collection of songs, however, the term does not shed much light on the genre of the work.

Although *Gilgamesh* has nothing of the length of the Greek epic and its many imitations in the Western tradition, "epic" is a useful concept here because, unlike "myths," of which we have some twenty in Sumerian alone, the epic deals with a human, not a divine, protagonist.[80] (The nine Sumerian "epics" run from some one hundred to six hundred lines in length. Akkadian "epics" are often longer, but still are slight as compared with the Western epic.) Since, further, the epic is associated in the mind with "heroic deeds," there is some relevance to *Gilgamesh*, at least in the first half of the work. If not pushed too far, then, "epic" is useful, but it does not translate a Sumerian or Akkadian term. Aristotle considered the epic second only to tragedy in the ranks of literary genres, and since then the prestige of epic has grown, not diminished. That prestige also captures the interest of modern readers and confers upon an ancient work a certain automatic status that has its utility. And since the Western epic has been subdivided along the lines of the *Iliad* and the *Odyssey*, between Achilles' deeds in battle and Odysseus' long and arduous journey, the two phases of *Gilgamesh* find apt counterparts in a long critical tradition.

Nevertheless, we have not called our translation the "epic" of Gilgamesh. The term has been overworked, but at the same time, rather ironically, its use in relation to *Gilgamesh* has not been subjected to critical examination. To what extent *is* the first part like the *Iliad*, the second part like the *Odyssey?* Are the "epic conventions" seized upon by imitators of Homer (thereby becoming one of the defining features of a long, highly conscious *literary* tradition) really indices of oral composition? [81] If so, what do parallel features in *Gilgamesh* represent? The debate regarding oral tradition, oral composition, and literacy is almost closed out in advance by too hastily applying the "epic" label.

The other reason for avoiding the term here is to call attention to the version of the Gilgamesh tales followed here. Although Sîn-leqi-unninnī made use of Sumerian and Akkadian materials that were in some cases a thousand years old when he took them up, the organization of the Gilgamesh stories into a larger composition was made before Sîn-leqi-unninnī recast them. The Old Babylonian version, then, perhaps better deserves the title of epic. With the late version we have something that begins to look more like the work of an "author" in the modern sense of the word, like a Chaucer who did not hesitate to change traditional works to suit his purposes. In any case, calling the work simply *Gilgamesh* after the Akkadian "series of Gilgamesh" will help us avoid the dangers of assuming a single, composite text showing no sign of "evolution" or authorship.

The second prestigious literary genre, ranked by Aristotle above the epic, is tragedy, whose importance and structural features he noted. We have suggested something of this prestige by referring to Nietzsche's redefinition of tragedy in "The Birth of Tragedy." Even as a dramatic form, tragedy may have relevance for Mesopotamian religion and literature, for the sacred marriage rite and what Thorkild Jacobsen has called the "Mourning Drama" show connections between ritual, literature, and drama. [82] There is no evidence that *Gilgamesh* itself was part of religious ritual (the way, e.g., the so-called Babylonian Creation Epic was recited during the New Year's Festival). Still, parallels between *Gilgamesh* and Ishtar/Tammuz rituals and, perhaps, shamanistic journeys to the underworld may allow a ritual background or counterpart of Gilgamesh to emerge.

Whatever its possible origins in ritual, tragedy is now considered a basic narrative pattern, so that works with no connection with the stage or with institutional religion are seen as tragedies: The Book of Job, for example, or *Middlemarch*. Roger Cox offers this definition of tragedy while attempting to show that the gospels are works of tragic literature: "A 'tragedy' is a literary work, predominantly somber in tone, in which the main character encounters some significant misfortune for which he himself is partly, though not wholly, responsible."[83] This pattern can be seen in both phases of *Gilgamesh*. It is particularly evident in the Apollonian phase, where the question of fate and individual responsibility is raised, where the downfall of Enkidu (and the suffering of Gilgamesh) is entwined in a complex question of *hybris* and *hamartia*. It is not necessary that the hero die in a tragic work; the key is suffering for which the protagonist is partly responsible. Nor does tragedy require, as Aristotle himself pointed out, that the hero be simply crushed in the end. The necessary suffering of Orestes is relieved in the third part of the Aeschylean trilogy, the *Oresteia;* and the enlightenment of Oedipus at the end of Sophocles' *Oedipus Rex* foreshadows the somber but glorious exaltation of Oedipus at the end of *Oedipus at Colonus*. The desperate journey of Gilgamesh in the Dionysian phase is marked by both arrogance and obsession. It is important to see that, however terrifying the view of existence embodied in Utnapishtim's fable of the Flood, the ordeal does not crush Gilgamesh. His return to Uruk, though not exactly joyous, is glorious in a manner consistent with tragic literature.

The many folklore elements in *Gilgamesh*[84] allow us to see the work in a larger milieu, one less dominated by a specific historical situation or by the intention of its author. Patterns that recur in very different historical places and situations—in dreams, myths, fairy tales, and the popular arts as much as in prestigious literary and religious traditions—need not be dominated by conscious intent. The "hero myth" in its various guises, so much loved by the Jungians, is to be found in *Star Wars* as well as *Jerusalem Delivered*, in the Lone Ranger and Popeye even more obviously, perhaps, than in *Paradise Lost*. The struggle of the protagonist to break loose from the unconscious, to establish a name for himself, to undergo the ordeal that brings dismemberment and death, the dark night of the soul—these need not depend upon learned traditions or the works of modern psychologists and anthropologists. We must be cautious in imputing these motifs to remote cultural artifacts, but they may help us see the larger patterns in a work. The two stages of the heroic quest in *Gilgamesh* would seem to be evident; yet even so, a great deal remains to be seen as to how the deeper patterns work against or with the conscious work of the artist in a very specific historical situation.

Of these "archetypal" patterns, the death-and-rebirth pattern has been extensively considered by Maud Bodkin[85] and, in a different way, by Northrop Frye.[86] In his "Theory of Myths," or narrative patterns, Frye distinguished four aspects of what he calls the "quest myth," and each aspect is related to the four principal narrative genres.

> First, the *agon* or conflict itself. Second, the *pathos* or death, often the mutual death of hero and monster. Third, the disappearance of the hero, a theme which often takes the form of *sparagmos* or tearing to pieces. Sometimes the hero's body is divided among his followers, as in Eucharist symbolism: sometimes it is distributed around the natural world, as in the stories of Orpheus and more especially Osiris. Fourth, the reappearance and recognition of the hero, where sacramental Christianity follows the metaphorical logic: those who in the fallen world have partaken of their redeemer's divided body are united with his risen body.[87]

The four basic myths, in Frye's view, are related to these four aspects. The *agon* is the archetypal theme of romance; *pathos* that of tragedy; *sparagmos*, of irony and satire; and *anagnorisis*, or "recognition," that of comedy.

We can find all of these aspects in *Gilgamesh*, and if we have emphasized the aspect of *pathos* and tragedy, it is perhaps better to correct this somewhat, the way Frye has himself adjusted the schema. He considers the *romance* to be, on the one hand, the first aspect of a larger quest-myth, and, on the other, a form that stands below the others while incorporating them all: a kind of primary or super-genre. The "complete form of the romance," he indicates in one place, "is clearly the successful quest, and such a completed form has three main stages: the stage of the perilous journey and the preliminary minor adventures; the crucial struggle, usually some kind of battle in which either the hero or his foe, or both, must die; and the exaltation of the hero."[88] This can be an inner struggle or an outer battle. What Frye understands as the romance is not found only in the medieval romance (which gives the genre its name), but in the epic as well. Television police stories, Westerns, cartoons, and fairy tales are just as much romances as are the monster-slaying tales of ancient myth. Even tragedy is drawn up into this quest-myth.

We suggest that the genre of *Gilgamesh* is the romance. The center is the heroic quest, which divides into an Apollonian phase and a Dionysian phase. The first phase includes both the romance interest in the birth and youth of the young hero (the education of Enkidu) and the battle with Humbaba, the *agon*. This is replicated in the battle with the Bull of Heaven, where the "name" of the heroes is again emphasized and where the heroes break with the Great Goddess. At the center, though, the interest shifts to *pathos*, the tragic turn, with the difficult questions of *hybris* and *hamartia*, the "tragic error." The first phase ends with the death of Enkidu—but not before Shamash has given the hero a way of understanding the civilized life that, ironically, it is no longer possible for him to enjoy. Enkidu's understanding, the first of the "recognition" scenes, is important—although it is soon overwhelmed by the terror of death.

The Dionysian phase of *Gilgamesh* begins in the horror of Enkidu's death. The story is increasingly dominated by irony. With every step on his mad journey, the bitter ironies are redoubled. The journey ends with his encounter with Utnapishtim, where each moment twists the irony a painful turn: there is no permanence; the "secrets" of the gods, especially the terrible news of the Flood; the test of sleeplessness, which mocks Gilgamesh's hope and brings him to complete despair; even the magical plant, snatched away before Gilgamesh can distribute its life-giving powers to the people. Only briefly do we see the *anagnorisis*, or "recognition." It is already implicit in Gilgamesh's casting off the skins, his purification, and his desire to use the plant, not for himself, but for the citizens of Uruk. It is explicit only in the solemn return to Uruk, to his duty, to Ishtar. Tablet XII recapitulates the movement in simpler terms, and the ironic ending again forces us to dwell on what most readers respond to throughout the work: *sparagmos*, the irony that tends to characterize Sumero-Akkadian literature as a whole.[89]

The recognition scenes, in which Enkidu is reconciled with the prostitute and Gilgamesh with Ishtar, point, in a strange way, to the other element we demand of romances today: love. Romantic love has maintained such a pull on romances that since the Middle Ages stories of heroic adventure seem strangely incomplete without a woman for the hero to rescue and, usually, marry. The 1982 film *An Officer and a Gentleman* is a contemporary example, adjusted to modern American social conditions and a modern interest in deep psychological changes in the hero. Early translators of *Gilgamesh* were convinced there was a romantic interest for Gilgamesh: Mua (or Ragmua). The most inventive of the early translators, Leonidas Le Cenci Hamilton, in *Ishtar and Izdubar* (1884), not only developed the love relationship, but thought that the hero had to make a choice in the end: stay with the woman in a land of beauty and contemplation or, like Aeneas, take up the burden of duty, leave her, and return to the grueling demands of the ordinary world.[90] It turned out that "Mua" was not a female character in *Gilgamesh* after all. A better text restored a broken fragment of text, and Mua was forever lost, a victim of good textual criticism.

Still, just as Enkidu and Gilgamesh are "doubles" virtually equal in strength and valor and yet are distinguished from one another along an heroic continuum—Enkidu representing the lower or "earthly" side and Gilgamesh representing the higher or "heavenly" side—the two females match that polarity. The prostitute who transforms Enkidu and is ultimately blessed by him is not exactly the heroine of popular romances. The reader has no way of finding an inner life for her; she is not at all a developed character in the narrative. And there is nothing subtle about her relationship with Enkidu. She is a servant of the Great Goddess, nothing more, her human representative. Ishtar, on the other hand, is the heavenly side, and it is Gilgamesh, not Enkidu, to whom she turns her favor. The love she offers Gilgamesh does have something of romantic love about it—it recalls the love of Ishtar and Tammuz, whose love-play was celebrated in song, story, and ritual in the Ancient Near East. In the primarily masculine world of *Gilgamesh*, though, there are no hymns to heterosexual love. The females remain psychological and religious archetypes, important only for symbolizing stages in the development of the heroes.

But in a different way, *Gilgamesh* is very much a poem of love. No sooner do the men fight than they become friends. *Gilgamesh* is perhaps the earliest of a very long tradition, most obvious to us in Greek and Roman works, of friendship literature. As in these later works, friendship in *Gilgamesh* is the love between equals. It is the paradigm of primary social relationships: male bonding, husband and wife, brother and brother. Much has been made of Gilgamesh's fear of death once its reality is made known to him. But the words of Gilgamesh always balance a concern for the self—his fear of dying—with a concern for the other. Gilgamesh's lament for Enkidu has the eloquence of the long tradition of the threnody, or elegy, again best represented in Greek literature and later in "Lycidas." The disintegration of Gilgamesh upon the death of Enkidu plays out the grief in narrative terms as well. Nowhere else is the identification between lover and loved so strong as in Gilgamesh's attempt to become Enkidu. When, in Tablet XII, Gilgamesh tries to embrace the ghost of Enkidu but cannot, the reality of death as separation settles in at last. The *participation mystique* is never fully possible. In *Gilgamesh*, the pain of love and loss is the defining feature of humanity.

NOTES TO THE INTRODUCTION

1. John Gardner, *The Sunlight Dialogues* (New York: Alfred A. Knopf, 1973), p. 533. For Gardner's use of Mesopotamian materials, see Maier, "Mesopotamian Names in *The Sunlight Dialogues;* or, MAMA Makes It to Batavia, New York," *Literary Onomastics Studies,* 4 (1977), 33–48; and "Gilgamesh—John Gardner's Supreme Fiction," *Aramco World Magazine,* 34 (July–August, 1983), 4–11.

2. See George Smith's account of the discovery of the tablets in *The Chaldean Account of Genesis,* 2nd ed., A. H. Sayce (New York: Charles Scribner's Sons, 1880), pp. 1–12.

3. Thorkild Jacobsen, *The Treasures of Darkness* (New Haven: Yale University Press, 1976), pp. 195–219.

4. Or "Bilgamesh," as the name is sometimes read today. The reading of the cuneiform signs that make up the name was in dispute from the first, yielding Izdubar, Gishdubar, and the like. An early edition of the text called the work *Nimrodepos,* from the belief that Gilgamesh was the biblical Nimrod. Since the 1890s, though, the hero and the work have carried the name Gilgamesh. Since the reading is now traditional, there is little reason to change it for this translation.

5. See I.iv.6. G. S. Kirk has emphasized the nature/culture theme in *The Epic of Gilgamesh,* in *Myth, Its Meaning and Functions in Ancient and Other Cultures* (Cambridge: Cambridge University Press, 1970), pp. 132–152. The Old Babylonian Period (ca. 2000–1600 B.C.), in which the Gilgamesh materials are thought to have been put together into a larger, unified work, was fascinated with the nature/culture (i.e., civilization) theme. Bendt Alster, for example, in *Studies in Sumerian Proverbs* (Copenhagen: Akademisk Forlag, 1975), p. 86, noticed that a traditional collection of Sumerian proverbs was transformed during the period through a new concern for civilization versus the barbarians.

6. See II.iv. The most powerful term used to express the relationship between Gilgamesh and Enkidu is *ibru*. The *Chicago Assyrian Dictionary* (CAD 7.6) cautions that the term was originally devoid of emotional

connotations, and denoted an "institutionalized relationship between free persons of the same status or profession which entailed acceptance of the same code of behavior and an obligation of mutual assistance." "Friend" is better for the term with which *ibru* is sometimes linked, *tappû*. That Enkidu is an "equal" to the great Gilgamesh only strengthens the whole range of mutual obligations and ties all the imagery of friend, brother, lover, comrade and even "wife" together.

7. A. Leo Oppenheim, "Mesopotamian Mythology II," *Orientalia*, n.s. 17 (1948), 17–48, pointed out the unprecedented arrogance of the heroes in this episode. Nowhere else in Mesopotamian literature are the divine beings so slighted by mere humans.

8. Samuel Noah Kramer, *History Begins at Sumer*, 3rd ed. (Philadelphia: University of Pennsylvania Press, 1981), pp. 259–270, emphasizes the competitive strain in Sumerian life; and Thorkild Jacobsen, *Treasures*, pp. 226–239, points out the increasingly grim and vicious practice of the late Babylonian and Assyrian empires (First Millennium B.C.).

9. As an example, consider Hektor's killing of Patrokles in *Iliad* XVI.726–861 (e.g., in Richmond Lattimore's translation [Chicago: University of Chicago Press, 1961]).

10. Jeffrey H. Tigay, *The Evolution of the Gilgamesh Epic* (Philadelphia: University of Pennsylvania Press, 1982), p. 13. The locale has been changed as well. In the Sumerian Early Dynastic period, the chief source of valuable wood was in the east, the highlands of what is now Iran; later, the now almost completely deforested areas of northern Syria and southern Turkey were the chief sources of wood and seem to be the location of the cedar forest in this version.

11. Tigay, pp. 76–81, points out the important change in the role of Shamash as the epic developed. At first he is but the protector of Gilgamesh. Only in the late version is Shamash the *instigator* of Gilgamesh's designs upon Humbaba.

12. In this way, at least, the situation resembled that of the Greeks. Mesopotamian religion presents extraordinary questions—enough to move A. Leo Oppenheim to declare that a "Mesopotamian Religion" should not be written (*Ancient Mesopotamia* [Chicago: University of Chicago Press, 1964], pp. 172–183)—and even the reduction of the thousands of divine beings to a small group of high gods is a difficult

development to follow. A fourfold of deities—Sumerian An, Enlil, and Ninhursag, the mother goddess (who appear in the *Gilgamesh* as Anu, Enlil, and the Great Goddess), and Enki (appearing here as Ea)—appeared as high gods early in Sumerian literature. The mother goddess gives way in the pantheon to the powerful Inanna (the Ishtar of our poem). See Samuel Noah Kramer, "Sumero-Akkadian Interconnections: Religious Ideas," *Genava*, n.s. 8 (1960), 273–277.

13. For an introduction to the gods most important in Sumero-Akkadian myths, see Samuel Noah Kramer, *Sumerian Mythology* (New York: Harper, 1961), and Jacobsen, *Treasures*.

14. Thorkild Jacobsen has argued that the Battle Drama (a battle of a god against evil spirits—not necessarily the sun against the powers of darkness) was not important in the early Sumerian periods, but emerged only later, from Old Babylonian times to the First Millennium B.C.; "Religious Drama in Ancient Mesopotamia," *Unity and Diversity*, eds. Hans Goedicke and J. J. M. Roberts (Baltimore: Johns Hopkins Press, 1975), pp. 65–97. Bendt Alster, on the other hand, claims that the victory of the sun over the powers of darkness is a motif in archaic Sumerian literature; that the astral aspect of the Sumerian gods is as old as Sumerian literature itself; and that, against Jacobsen, Sumerian literature does not show a developmental or evolutionary transformation of the gods; "Early Patterns in Mesopotamian Literature," *Kramer Anniversary Volume*, ed. Barry L. Eichler (Neukirchen-Vluyn: Neukirchener Verlag, 1976), pp. 13–25.

15. See Joseph L. Henderson, "Ancient Myths and Modern Man," in *Man and His Symbols*, ed. Carl G. Jung (New York: Dell, 1964), pp. 95–119. The two-phase sequence in *Gilgamesh* might be characterized as Apollonian and Dionysian phases. While the importance of Shamash underscores the Apollonian character of Gilgamesh's battle with Humbaba, the Dionysian second-stage has not been recognized generally. See below.

16. For anecdotes about George Smith and the early years of Assyriology (from a man who was not terribly sympathetic to Smith), see E. A. Wallis Budge, *The Rise and Progress of Assyriology* (London: Martin Hopkinson, 1925), pp. 106–153. For a cautious view of the parallels between the biblical account of the Flood and the account in Tablet XI, see W. G. Lambert, "A New Look at the Babylonian Background of Genesis," *The Bible in Its Literary Milieu: Contemporary Essays*, eds. John

Maier and Vincent Tollers (Grand Rapids: Eerdmans, 1979), pp. 285–296.

17. The *Gilgamesh* Flood is but one of a number that survive in cuneiform literature. See W. G. Lambert and A. R. Millard, *Atra-ḫasīs, the Babylonian Story of the Flood* (Oxford: Clarendon Press, 1969), which includes Miguel Civil's edition of the Sumerian Flood story. *Atra-ḫasīs* ("excessively wise") is an epithet identifying the Noah-like sage, called Utnapishtim in the *Gilgamesh*.

18. On Ea (Sumerian Enki), see Kramer, *Sumerian Mythology*, pp. 53–75, and his "Enki and His Inferiority Complex," *Orientalia*, n.s. 39 (1970), 103–110; see also Jacobsen, *Treasures*, pp. 110–121.

19. Tigay, p. 49, concludes that Tablet XII was not part of the Old Babylonian version and is a late addition. The colophon to Tablet XII of the late version makes it clear that it belongs to the Gilgamesh "series" and completes it.

20. Tigay argues the point in impressive detail in *The Evolution of the Gilgamesh Epic*, a development of his 1971 Yale dissertation, "Literary-Critical Studies in the Gilgamesh Epic: an Assyriological Contribution to Biblical Literary Criticism." Largely because of his analysis, it is now possible—and mandatory—to focus on one or the other version of *Gilgamesh* and to avoid a text patched together with fragments from different periods.

21. For this reason, other versions, especially the Old Babylonian version so carefully distinguished from the Middle Babylonian and later versions by Tigay, will be cited in the notes when they illuminate the late version or fill a gap in the text.

22. Sîn-leqi-unninnī is thought to have lived in Uruk during the Middle Babylonian Period (ca. 1600–1000 B.C.). That he was an exorcist-priest may account for the great emphasis on ritual in the late version. What Tigay calls the "standard" version texts are the standardized First Millennium texts best exemplified by the *Gilgamesh* found at Nineveh; Tigay, pp. 10–13.

23. A. Shaffer, "The Sumerian Sources of Tablet XII of *The Epic of Gilgamesh*" (Ph.D. dissertation, University of Pennsylvania, 1963), presents the evidence.

24. One striking change, in view of the importance of Shamash in the first half of *Gilgamesh*, is that Shamash (Sumerian Utu) is removed from the story at this point and replaced by Nergal.

25. Modern accounts of Mesopotamian beliefs in an afterlife emphasize the doleful character of life there—dark, with batlike souls eating only dust. The accounts are strongly colored by details from Tablet XII and from "The Descent of Ishtar" (which offers a picture much like Enkidu's dream in VII.iv). While it seems clear that Mesopotamian thought always considered that *something* of the human survived death and entered an underground place, the beliefs about life in the underworld may have shifted quite a bit in different periods. There is little or no evidence that the underworld was specifically a place for punishment. On the other hand, Tablet XII makes it clear that one's fate in the underworld is tied directly to the number of sons produced in life and the survival of loved ones on earth.

26. On Ishtar (Sumerian Inanna), see Samuel Noah Kramer, "Adoration: a Divine Model of the Liberated Woman," in *From the Poetry of Sumer* (Berkeley: University of California Press, 1979), pp. 71–98; and Jacobsen, *Treasures*, pp. 135–143.

27. Tigay, pp. 66–71.

28. Or the god and high priestess, if the major deity of the city was male. On the rite, see Samuel Noah Kramer, *The Sacred Marriage Rite* (Bloomington: Indiana University Press, 1969).

29. Consider the semantic range of *gipāru*, which we take as a parallel to *supūru*. The *gipāru* was the residence of the *enu*-priest (and of the female counterpart, the *entu*-priestess), whose cultic function at least originally involved the Sacred Marriage; pasture; and its original meaning, "storehouse (for food)" (CAD 5.83–84). The CAD comments that "as storehouse the *gipāru* served as the place of the fertility rite of the sacred marriage" (p. 84).

30. Tigay, p. 68.

31. Mircea Eliade, *The Sacred and the Profane*, tr. Willard R. Trask (New York: Harcourt, Brace, 1959), p. 122. Tigay points out, p. 71, that by the Old Babylonian Period, Eanna *is* Ishtar's; the cult of Anu virtually disappears until very late, Seleucid times. In the introduction to *Gilga-*

mesh (I.i.14), Eanna is described simply as "the dwelling of Ishtar," without mention at all of Anu.

32. Tigay notes that Anu is exempted from blame in the Flood story, a theological modification of Anu's participation in the Old Babylonian *Atra-ḥasīs*, p. 231.

33. Although he presents impressive evidence to the contrary, Tigay still holds the belief in the poem's antagonism to Ishtar. His major interest is rather in trying to discover why she is ignored in the Old Babylonian version, pp. 70–71.

34. Tzvi Abush, in "Ishtar's Proposal and Gilgamesh's Refusal: an Interpretation of *Gilgamesh* VI 1–79," given in Baltimore (March, 1983) at the American Oriental Society Meeting, has analyzed the great complexity of this exchange.

35. Note the hypnotic repetition in the first line of the song: *ša ṣallat ša ṣallat ummu* ^d*Ninazu ša ṣallat* (XII.i.29). The goddess is no literal "mother of birth and death" but the "mother of the god Ninazu." According to J. J. M. Roberts, *The Earliest Semitic Pantheon* (Baltimore: Johns Hopkins Press, 1972), p. 44, the mother goddess, *Mama*, was the mother of Ninazu; Ereshkigal, goddess of death and sister-rival to Ishtar, was wedded to Ninazu. We have rendered this wife-mother connection with the complex "mother of birth and death" to capture the conflation of Ereshkigal and the Mother. Ninazu, according to Knut Leonard Tallqvist, *Akkadische Götterepitheta* (Hildesheim: Georg Olms Verlag, 1974 [orig. 1938]), pp. 214, 398, is a chthonic god of death. Roberts has shown that *Mama* is "mother earth," associated with birth and death (pp. 43–44, 344–358). After illustrating the "infinite variety" and contradictory qualities that characterize Inanna (numen of the storehouse, rain goddess, goddess of love and war, goddess of harlots, the morning and the evening stars), he stresses that Inanna is never portrayed in Sumerian myths as a mother. But *Gilgamesh* identifies the mother goddess in the Flood squarely with Ishtar (Inanna)—a departure from the Old Babylonian *Atra-ḥasīs* version of the Flood, where the mother is identified as *Mama;* cf. Tigay's parallel texts, pp. 224–225.

36. Erich Neumann, in *The Great Mother*, tr. Ralph Manheim (Princeton: Bollingen, 1963), taking a Jungian approach, has attempted to relate the manifold characteristics (Terrible Mother/Good Mother, Witch/Virgin, Whore/Muse, negative/positive polarities) of the Great Goddess to

the structures of the unconscious. He cites Mesopotamian examples often, especially Ishtar. See p. 80, passim.

37. *The Nag Hammadi Library*, gen. ed. James M. Robinson (San Francisco: Harper & Row, 1981).

38. For the implications for ecclesiastical polity, see Elaine Pagels, *The Gnostic Gospels* (New York: Vintage, 1981), pp. 57–83.

39. "The Thunder, Perfect Mind," tr. George W. MacRae, in *The Nag Hammadi Library*, pp. 271–272.

40. For an overview of the feminine element in the concept of God, see Marvin Pope, tr., *Song of Songs* (Garden City: Doubleday, 1977), esp. pp. 153–179.

41. The translation is from *The Jerusalem Bible*, Reader's Edition, ed. Alexander Jones (Garden City: Doubleday, 1966), p. 1132.

42. Robert Graves, *The Greek Myths* (Baltimore: Penguin, 1960), I, 16, sees the dethroning of the Great Goddess as the major element in Greek myth, which "is concerned, above all else, with the changing relations between the queen and her lover," a reference to the Sacred Marriage, and "with her eclipse by an unlimited male monarchy." Simone de Beauvoir, *The Second Sex*, tr. H. M. Parshley (New York: Alfred A. Knopf, 1952), p. 70, makes a larger claim. The dethroning of the Great Mother is a consequence of man's discovering his power as *Homo faber*. The whole concept of the universe is challenged by a world of tools, including rational thought, logic, and mathematics. "The peoples who have remained under the thumb of the goddess mother, those who have retained the matrilineal regime, are also those who are arrested at a primitive stage of civilization. Woman was venerated only to the degree that man made himself the slave of his own fears, a party to his own powerlessness: it was in terror and not in love that he worshipped her. He could achieve his destiny only as he began by dethroning her. From then on, it was to be the male principle of creative force, of light, of intelligence, of order, that he would recognize as sovereign."

43. On the character of Apollo in Greek religion, see W. K. C. Guthrie, *The Greeks and Their Gods* (Boston: Beacon Press, 1955), pp. 73–87, 182–204.

44. Guthrie, p. 87.

45. Guthrie, p. 184.

46. Graves, I, 76–80, recounts the stories and comments on their significance.

47. "The Gospel of Philip," tr. Wesley W. Isenberg, in *The Nag Hammadi Library*, p. 138.

48. Sam Keen, "The Cosmic Versus the Rational," *Psychology Today* 8 (1974), 56–59.

49. Keen, p. 59.

50. Keen, p. 59.

51. Friedrich Nietzsche, "The Birth of Tragedy," in *The Philosophy of Nietzsche* (New York: Modern Library, 1954), p. 966.

52. Nietzsche, p. 967.

53. Nietzsche, p. 1039.

54. Nietzsche, p. 1039.

55. Tigay, pp. 76–81.

56. Joseph L. Henderson, "Ancient Myths and Modern Man," in *Man and His Symbols*, ed. Carl G. Jung (New York: Dell, 1964), p. 110.

57. Henderson, p. 112.

58. The speech is analyzed in the Appendix.

59. This should counter the tendency to see in anything pre-Greek only the "primitive" or "pre-logical" mind. Julian Jaynes, who believes that consciousness itself was born in the breakdown of the bicameral mind only about three thousand years ago, claims *Gilgamesh* was dated too early because a passage showed Utnapishtim too far in advance of the civilization that produced him! See *The Origins of Consciousness in the*

Breakdown of the Bicameral Mind (Boston: Houghton Mifflin, 1976), pp. 251–253.

60. Nietzsche, p. 1000.

61. Giorgio de Santillana and Hertha van Dechend, *Hamlet's Mill* (Boston: Gambit, 1969), chs. xxii–xxiii (pp. 288–325).

62. He may have met someone in the heart of darkness; there is a gap in the text just long enough for Gilgamesh's plaint and a response.

63. Henderson, p. 111.

64. Guthrie, pp. 145–182, esp. p. 177.

65. Henderson, p. 123.

66. Henderson, p. 124.

67. Giorgio Buccellati, "Wisdom and Not: The Case of Mesopotamia," *Journal of the American Oriental Society*, 101 (1981), 35–47, has distinguished two intellectual streams in Mesopotamian thought opposed to one another regarding religious concepts of the absolute (fate/polytheism), the attitude toward the absolute (critical evaluation/revelation), the measure of personal enrichment (experience/success) and on certain aspects of knowledge (lyric introspection/narrative), including the disposition of the knower (skill and humility on the one hand/self-assertion on the other) and the nature of the object studied (universal principles/particular events). The first he considers a "wisdom" tradition (embodied in disputations, dialogues, and theodicy), the second an "other" tradition (often associated with myth and epic literature). In our terms, the Apollonian expresses this "wisdom" world view (Shamash), while the Dionysian expresses the "other" (Ea's cunning).

68. *Chicago Assyrian Dictionary* 10.2.109–111.

69. Wolfram von Soden, "Licht und Finsternis in der sumerischen und babylonisch-assyrischen Religion," *Studium Generale*, 13 (1960), 647–653, has traced the metaphor light = truth in Mesopotamian religious literature. Less well studied is the truth that dwells in darkness. A regular characteristic of Enki/Ea is his dwelling below, where light does

not penetrate. This seems to us to point to a profound grasp of the negative way, the thinking that leads to what Martin Heidegger has called "unconcealedness," *aletheia*, unhiddenness, which itself remains hidden. See, e.g., his "The Origin of the Work of Art," in *Poetry, Language, Thought*, tr. Albert Hofstadter (New York: Harper & Row, 1971), pp. 51–56.

70. The Akkadian and Sumerian versions of the Flood story can be found in W. G. Lambert and A. R. Millward, *Atra-ḥasīs, the Babylonian Story of the Flood* (Oxford: Clarendon, 1969). Tigay, pp. 214–240, has a detailed study of the parallels. Tigay thinks that Gilgamesh's journey to Utnapishtim was included in the Old Babylonian epic of Gilgamesh, but that the Flood story itself was introduced only in the late version, pp. 237–238.

71. Norman Habel, *Literary Criticism of the Old Testament* (Philadelphia: Fortress, 1971), pp. 31–42, distinguishes two versions interwoven in the biblical account.

72. This is especially evident in the Priestly Writer's account of the Flood, as Habel distinguishes it from the Yahwist version, pp. 32–36. The role of Ea in the Flood is, however, not new with Sîn-leqi-unninnī; it is one of the major invariants in all Mesopotamian versions. For the translation of one of Ea's speeches, see the Appendix.

73. For the connection, see Tigay, pp. 39–109.

74. On the complicated problem of authorship in Sumero-Akkadian literature, see W. G. Lambert, "A Catalogue of Texts and Authors," *Journal of Cuneiform Studies*, 16 (1962), 59–77, and W. W. Hallo, "New Viewpoints on Cuneiform Literature," *Israel Exploration Journal*, 12 (1962), 13–26. It is not, strictly speaking, true that the literature is anonymous, although much of it is. The stream of tradition that carried along Mesopotamian literature is mainly owing to the scribal schools, where texts were copied and recopied for more than two thousand years. Authorship, where it is indicated, is often the authority for a work; hence works are attributed to the early sages or to the gods, notably Ea. A few authors, in the modern sense, are known, however. Enheduanna is the earliest (ca. 2150 B.C.) and best known. Sîn-leqi-unninnī is particularly important because so much of the earlier, traditional material he used is known.

75. On the Hieros Gamos, see Eliade, pp. 89, 145–146, and Kramer, *The Sacred Marriage Rite*, especially the final chapters; also Pope, pp. 69–85.

76. Kramer, *History Begins*, pp. 194–198.

77. The changes are mainly theological. Sîn is added to the list of gods Gilgamesh appeals to before he finds a solution in Ea. Shamash (= Sumerian Utu), on the other hand, is removed from the story; the netherworld god Nergal acts in his place to open a hole for Enkidu's spirit to pass through. See Aaron Shaffer, *Sumerian Sources of Tablet XII of the Epic of Gilgameš* (Ph.D. dissertation, University of Pennsylvania, 1963), and Tigay, pp. 105–107.

78. Northrop Frye, *Anatomy of Criticism* (Princeton: Princeton University Press, 1957), p. 248.

79. *The Chicago Assyrian Dictionary* 7.244–250. Note the reference, p. 249, to a line that distinguishes the *iškaru* as a *written* text from oral tradition.

80. On the genres of Sumerian literature, see Samuel Noah Kramer, "Sumerian Literature and the Bible," in Maier and Tollers, pp. 272–284. *Gilgamesh does*, however, show a number of the "epic conventions" so conspicuous in Homer and his imitators (stating the theme; beginning *in medias res;* using formulas, epithets, and the like). Most of these conventions are taken now as marks of oral tradition.

81. See Albert B. Lord, *The Singer of Tales* (Cambridge: Harvard University Press, 1960), and Berkley Peabody, *The Winged Word* (Albany: State University of New York Press, 1975).

82. Thorkild Jacobsen, "Religious Drama in Ancient Mesopotamia," in *Unity and Diversity*, ed. Hans Goedicke and J. J. M. Roberts (Baltimore: Johns Hopkins Press, 1975), pp. 65–97; S. H. Hooke, *Babylonian and Assyrian Religion* (Norman: University of Oklahoma Press, 1963), pp. 29–40, 63–70.

83. Roger L. Cox, "Tragedy and the Gospel Narratives," in Tollers and Maier, p. 302.

84. See Jack M. Sasson, "Some Literary Motifs in the Composition of the Gilgamesh Epic," *Studies in Philology*, 69 (1972), 259–279.

85. Maud Bodkin, *Archetypal Patterns in Poetry* (Oxford: Oxford University Press, 1963), chapters 1 and 2.

86. Frye, pp. 186–206.

87. Frye, p. 192.

88. Frye, p. 187.

89. Kramer in particular has noted the ironic tendency in Sumerian literature; see, e.g., *History Begins*, pp. 255–269.

90. Leonidas Le Cenci Hamilton, *Ishtar and Izdubar, The Epic of Babylon* (London: W. H. Allen, 1884); see Maier, "The File on Leonidas Le Cenci Hamilton," *American Literary Realism, 1870–1910*, 11 (1976), 92–99.

GILGAMESH

TABLET I

Column i

The one who saw the abyss I will make the land know;   1
of him who knew all, let me tell the whole story
. . . in the same way . . .
[as] the lord of wisdom, he who knew everything, Gilgamesh,   4
who saw things secret, opened the place hidden,
and carried back word of the time before the Flood—   6
he travelled the road, exhausted, in pain,
and cut his works into a stone tablet.   8

He ordered built the walls of Uruk of the Sheepfold   9
the walls of holy Eanna, stainless sanctuary.   10
Observe its walls, whose upper hem is like bronze;
behold its inner wall, which no work can equal.
Touch the stone threshold, which is ancient;
draw near the Eanna, dwelling-place of the goddess Ishtar,   14
a work no king among later kings can match.
Ascend the walls of Uruk, walk around the top,
inspect the base, view the brickwork.
Is not the very core made of oven-fired brick?
As for its foundation, was it not laid down by the seven sages?   19
One part is city, one part orchard, and one part claypits.   20
Three parts including the claypits make up Uruk.

Find the copper tablet-box,   22
slip loose the ring-bolt made of bronze,
Open the mouth to its secrets.
Draw out the tablet of lapis lazuli and read it aloud:

How Gilgamesh endured everything harsh,   26

overpowering kings, famous, powerfully built—   27

---

hero, child of the city Uruk, a butting bull.   28
He takes the forefront, as a leader should.
Still he marches in the rear as one the brothers trust,
a mighty trap to protect his men.
He is a battering floodwave, who knocks the stone walls flat.

Son of Lugalbanda—Gilgamesh is the pattern of strength,   33
child of that great wild cow, Ninsun,
. . . Gilgamesh, dazzling, sublime.

Opener of the mountain passes,   36
digger of wells on the hills' side,
he crossed the ocean, the wide sea, to where Shamash rises,   38
scouted the world regions: the one who seeks life,   39
forcing his way to Utnapishtim the remote one,   40
the man who restored life where the Flood had destroyed it,   41
. . . peopling the earth.

Is there a king like him anywhere?   43
Who like Gilgamesh can boast, "I am the king!"?

From the day of his birth Gilgamesh was called by name.   45

NOTES TO TABLET I, COLUMN i

For a detailed consideration of the Prologue, see Jeffrey H. Tigay, *The Evolution of the Gilgamesh Epic* (Philadelphia: University of Pennsylvania Press, 1982), pp. 140–160, 261–265, hereafter Tigay.

1. The Prologue to *Gilgamesh* falls into three main parts, 1–8, 9–26, 27–45 (and perhaps into the early lines of column ii; line 26 and the final line, 45, are transitional verses). The first twenty-six lines are particularly important for the "late" version of *Gilgamesh*, attributed to the exorcist-priest Sîn-leqi-unninnî, since the lines have been added after the Old Babylonian version. While the late, standardized version is known mainly from First Millennium B.C. manuscripts, it is thought to have been composed in the latter half of the Second Millennium, during the Middle Babylonian Period, when several versions of *The Epic of Gilgamesh* are known to date. The attribution of the late version to Sîn-leqi-unninnî is not certain, but very possible. It is clear, though, from the Prologue that the late version changes the focus of the story. The Old Babylonian version began with line 27, the part of the Prologue that concentrates on Gilgamesh the warrior-king. The first two parts of the Prologue, on the contrary, focus, first, on the experience and knowledge *(nēmequ)* Gilgamesh will achieve, on the way in which he discovered "secrets" and hidden places—especially "word of the time before the Flood." This suggests that the second part of the *Gilgamesh* was particularly in the mind of the poet, especially the reference to the Flood, which is treated in Tablet XI. That the poet had the larger organization of the story in mind is confirmed in the second section (9–21), six lines of which are repeated at the end of XI.vi, thus completing the frame of the story. There the speaker is Gilgamesh, who tells Urshanabi the Boatman to inspect the walls of Uruk. The lines are thus anticipated by the poet, who speaks only in the Prologue in the first person, suggesting that his role is like Gilgamesh's. The poet will let the land know of Gilgamesh, just as Gilgamesh "cut his works into a stone tablet" *(narû)*. The *narû* may be the same as the hidden lapis lazuli tablet of 22–26. What is important is the parallel between Gilgamesh the knower and teller of secrets and the poet, whose task it is to retell the story in the authority of Gilgamesh.

The composition was known in antiquity by its incipit, or first line, *šá nagba imuru*, and as the "series" *(iškaru)* of Gilgamesh. The great emphasis on seeing and knowing the opening lines suggests that *nagbu* is not simply a place (perhaps the dwelling of the sage Utnapishtim, near the waters of Ea) but also the gnosis gained by Gilgamesh: hence, "the abyss."

4. Gilgamesh, or Bilgamesh, the hero of the work, was thought to be king of Uruk between 2700 and 2500 B.C., Early Dynastic II, when the walls of the city of Uruk were first constructed. The historical period of Gilgamesh is, then, about six hundred years earlier than the texts we have about him in Sumerian literature (though these may go back to a time just after the time of Gilgamesh himself). Eight Sumerian Gilgamesh texts are known, presumably from the Ur III Period (twenty-first century); they are thought to be older than the first attempt to integrate the short Sumerian tales into an epic story with most of the parts we have in the late version. This first attempt to build a larger work is considered to have taken place in the Akkadian language at the height of creative Akkadian composition, the Old Babylonian Period (2000–1600). This late version is thus at least a thousand years later than the historical Gilgamesh.

Joan G. Westenholz, in "Cult of Dead Heroes," a paper read in Baltimore at the meeting of the American Oriental Society, March 20–23, 1983, has recently pointed out that of the five ancient kings celebrated in compositions (Enmerkar, Lugalbanda, Gilgamesh, Sargon, and Naram-Sin), only Gilgamesh had a cult grow up around his memory. Celebrated as a judge in the netherworld and deified, Gilgamesh was given a festival that lasted nine days and included wrestling events. That he left a *narû* (unlike Enmerkar, who inspired no cult and was not deified), or tablet telling of his works, appears to be the most important precondition for his deification.

Lines 1–8 emphasize Gilgamesh's knowledge and experience in the journey that is narrated in the second part of the story (Tablets VII–XI). The result of his experience is the authorship of the stone tablet.

6. The Flood is known from early Sumerian and Akkadian writings. The threat of devastating floods was great in the plain of southern Iraq the Greeks called Mesopotamia; it lay between two major rivers, the Euphrates and the Tigris. Maintaining the canals and irrigation lines that allowed Mesopotamia to develop a fertile agricultural economy was a constant preoccupation of the south. Irrigation depended upon wise use of the annual flooding of the rivers; violent flooding could destroy the best efforts of the people. The Flood was seen as dividing history. Before the Flood, the people had been taught by the sages (19), the last of whom was Utnapishtim, the object of Gilgamesh's quest (40). After the Flood,

kingship, which had been a pattern created by the gods, descended to mankind. Gilgamesh was one of the early Sumerian kings just after the Flood.

8. Gilgamesh inscribed his toils on a tablet, or stele *(ⁿᵃ⁴narû)*. This is the end result of his labors, and it ties together the first eight lines of the poem, which concern the secrets wrested from an agonizing quest. The *šupšuḥ* of the previous line could mean "at peace" (Tigay, 262), which would emphasize the recognition of Gilgamesh at the end of his journey ("at peace" after the great restlessness that characterizes him, I.ii.32), but we follow the CAD, I.2.102–103, in seeing Gilgamesh "in pain" and inscribing the tablet in these lines.

9–21. The second section of the Prologue emphasizes the city-state of Uruk (modern Warka) in what is now southern Iraq. The walls and the sacred precinct called Eanna ("House of An" or "House of Heaven") are the most striking features. The division of the city into three parts (city, orchard, claypits) concludes the image of the powerful city. Gilgamesh is credited in the poem with building the famous walls of the city. Excavations have shown that by the Early Dynastic period, that is, just about the time of the historical Gilgamesh, the walls of Uruk had a perimeter of six miles. The great area of the city at that time, the end of what archaeologists call the Uruk Period (ca. 3800 B.C. to about the time of the earliest pictographs, ca. 3000 B.C.), shows that the city was probably without equal in size and wealth. Within the walls, excavators have found, about a third of the area was occupied by public buildings and the dwellings of the wealthy, about a third by houses of the poor, and a third by gardens, open spaces, and cemeteries. See Charles Burney, *The Ancient Near East* (Ithaca: Cornell University Press, 1977), pp. 58–63. An Anu "ziggurat" had dominated the city before the Uruk Period, but by the Uruk Period the Eanna precinct "formed the very heart of the city" (Burney, p. 59). Eanna had been the sanctuary of An/Anu, god of "the above" and his consort, Antum, but was later dominated by the goddess Inanna, Ishtar of the poem. Sumerian tradition saw Uruk as the rival to the city of Kish, north of Uruk, near Babylon (which would dominate southern Iraq in later years), and knew of a time when Uruk dominated the land of small city-states, as had Kish earlier. The tradition that links the exorcist-priest Sîn-leqi-unninnī with composing the *Gilgamesh* also claimed that the author was a priest at Uruk—at a much later period, of course.

9. Uruk of the Sheepfold is the designation of Uruk in the late version. Old Babylonian Gilgamesh narratives use a different formula,

"broad-marted" Uruk. If the "Sheepfold" *(supūru)* recalls the tradition of the Sacred Marriage described by the Sumerian poets as a union in the sheepfold between Inanna/Ishtar and her shepherd-lover, Dumuzi/Tammuz, the change from "broad-marted" Uruk to Uruk of the Sheepfold would be consistent with imaging the city as the dwelling-place of the Great Goddess. The formula would then point to the sacred center of the city even as the walls point to the outer limits and the contribution of the human, Gilgamesh. Uruk is depicted in these very simple formulas as an *imago mundi,* what Mircea Eliade calls a "city-cosmos," *The Sacred and the Profane,* tr. Willard R. Trask (New York: Harcourt, Brace, 1959), pp. 47–62.

10. The section moves easily between inner and outer parts of the city. Eanna is, strictly speaking, the center of the city, the complex of temples dedicated to Anu and Ishtar; but "of holy Eanna" is a variation of "Uruk of the Sheepfold" in the previous line and so designates the whole of the city.

14. Eanna, the sacred precinct, is again named, this time with the additional phrase qualifying it as the "dwelling-place of the goddess Ishtar" *(šubat ilu ištar).* The qualifying phrase is typical of the late version of *Gilgamesh.* In Old Babylonian Gilgamesh texts, the temple is the abode of the god Anu. The late version either adds "and Ishtar" (I.iv.37) or drops Anu entirely, as it does here (Tigay, 60, 62). Tigay elsewhere (68–70) emphasizes the change, noting that by the Old Babylonian Period Eanna was already Ishtar's temple, and that ignoring her in the Old Babylonian version is therefore puzzling. Very likely, the additional emphasis on Ishtar in the late version (and the virtual disappearance of Anu, except for his role in the creation of Enkidu and in the story of the Bull of Heaven) is an important thematic change in the poem.

19. The perfection of the walls built by Gilgamesh—so impressive that even the inner core is made of oven-fired brick rather than the rubble that was normally used—is underscored by the reference to the seven sages *(VII mundalki).* The sages are the figures, instructed by the gods (especially Ea), who brought the arts of civilization to mankind before the Flood.

20–21. After the outside and inside of the city have been described, the areas within the walls are delineated. The end of line 20 is broken, and may include a specific reference to the temple of Ishtar. The lines bring to an end not only the sequence on the walls of Uruk, but a

sequence within the whole (16–21) that is repeated at the very end of
Tablet XI, when Gilgamesh returns to Uruk after his journey to Utnapish-
tim. There the lines are attributed, not to the poet, but to Gilgamesh
himself. These lines anticipate the end of the story and establish another
connection between the poet and Gilgamesh.

22–25. Just as the walls of Uruk are made of precious materials, the
copper tablet-box, the bronze ring-bolt, and the tablet inside, of precious
lapis lazuli, are well-formed artifacts. Figurines of the sages have been
found in the foundation deposits of temples, and it is possible that the
tablet-box with its secret contents is to be found in the foundation deposit
of the *temenu* mentioned above in line 17. (See D. J. Wiseman, "A
Gilgamesh Epic Fragment from Nimrud," *Iraq*, 37 [1975], 157–158.)
Wiseman suggests that the tablet's being of lapis lazuli may be symbolic
of the divine destiny of Gilgamesh. Lapis lazuli tablets were found in
foundation deposits in a number of places, including Uruk. The sequence
1–8, 9–21, and 22–25 seems designed to set the "walls of Uruk" seg-
ment within a framework of the secret knowledge Gilgamesh has to
impart, the results of his agonizing journey(s).

26. The line is the first of the account of Gilgamesh to be read from
the lapis lazuli tablet. The line brings to an end the part of the Prologue
added in the late version by Sîn-leqi-unninnī. It is clearly a transitional
line. On the one hand, it summarizes Gilgamesh's adventures as one
who has passed through all hardships. On the other hand, it leads into
the hymn which describes Gilgamesh in a string of epithets, followed by
some of his adventures. As a summarizing line, it emphasizes the shift
that, as Tigay (149) points out, characterizes the change from the Old
Babylonian *The Epic of Gilgamesh* and its *carpe diem* theme to the darker
late version, with its emphasis on the wisdom acquired by Gilgamesh
and an indirect immortality gained by the hero through his inscription
and his building project.

27. This line begins the Old Babylonian version, *šūtur eli* ("over-
powering . . ."). See Tigay (48–49).

27–32. The section is a string of descriptive phrases and epithets
typical of royal hymns and inscriptions (Tigay, 150). Except for specifying
the city of Uruk in 28, the epithets are not specific to Gilgamesh. Rather,
they combine to portray the ideal warrior-king in a very traditional way.

28. The hero is called "child" *(lil-lid)* of Uruk. In 33 he is the child of the hero Lugalbanda, and in 34, child of the goddess Ninsun. In each case a different synonymn for child is employed *(bukru, māru)*, an example of poetic variation common in Akkadian poetry. The second term, *bukru*, in particular, is used chiefly in poetic contexts, and rarely of human beings (CAD 2.309–310). Note the use of powerful animal imagery (Gilgamesh as "a butting bull" and his mother, Ninsun, a "great wild cow") in a positive way. The wild bull and cow are favorite images of the gods, and pictorial tradition in Mesopotamia marks gods and goddesses with horns.

33–35. The hymnic technique is much the same as in 27–32, but the references are specific to Gilgamesh, who is named twice in the sequence.

33. Lugalbanda is another famous Sumerian warrior-king, by tradition the father of Gilgamesh. In VI.v.174 Lugalbanda is called the "god" of Gilgamesh, and Gilgamesh makes an offering of ointment. The allusion may be to the "personal god" a person has, some trace of which is carried, as it were, through a line of ancestors. Tablet X.v.38–50, in a very broken passage, appears to tell the story of Gilgamesh's birth, a trick involving an exchange, in which the father of Gilgamesh is a *lillu*, "fool" or "moron" (CAD 9.189). The story, told by the sage Utnapishtim, seems to explain why Gilgamesh is both human and divine. The accounts are not necessarily contradictory, for paternity and maternity and sonship can exist on more than one level of meaning in the poem; there may, however, be more than one tradition of the birth of Gilgamesh conflated in *Gilgamesh*. Ninsun, a minor goddess in the pantheon, is consistently the mother of Gilgamesh in the poem. Here she is imaged as the "great wild cow." Elsewhere in the poem she is characterized by her wisdom (especially in interpreting dreams) and piety. Even so, I.ii.2 describes the "image of his body" coming from the Great Goddess.

36–42. The lines refer to certain of Gilgamesh's adventures. Surprisingly, there is no interest in the heroic tasks of the warrior (the battle with Humbaba, the defeat of the Bull of Heaven). Most, and perhaps all, are references to the second half of *Gilgamesh*, where the hero opens the mountain passes, crosses the wide sea, scouts the world regions, and, especially, makes his way to Utnapishtim, the story of which is told at great length in Tablets X and XI. The list of his activities is rather like the list Gilgamesh himself repeats later (VIII.ii.9–13 and other passages).

Mainly, the lines emphasize the restless quest of Gilgamesh and the Gilgamesh "who seeks life."

38. The line may mean simply "to where the sun rises," that is, the east. The sun is, however, the god Shamash (Sumerian Utu). In view of the increasing importance of Shamash in the Old Babylonian and late versions of the Gilgamesh stories, and in light of Gilgamesh's daring journeys, which take him beyond human limits to places where only the sun has penetrated, it is better to make the connection with Shamash explicit here.

39. Gilgamesh is the *muš-t[e-e]'-ú ba-lá-ṭi*, "who seeks life." This may anticipate the command of Ea to Utnapishtim in XI.i.25–26 to "Abandon riches. Seek life./ Scorn possessions, hold onto life," where a different word for "life" is used, *napištu*. The term used here, though, appears in a passage about standing in the Assembly of the Gods asking for "life." The term used here, *balāṭu*, may be "immortality," the life only the gods enjoy; but it also means "life," "vigor," and "good health (held and dispensed by the gods)" (CAD 2.46–52). The ambiguity of *balāṭu* and its connection with *napištu*, with which it is often linked (CAD II.2.300), seems deliberate in *Gilgamesh*. The second term has a range of meanings —"life" and "vitality," but also "body," "self," and "breath."

40. Utnapishtim, the name of the sage Gilgamesh visits in Tablets X and XI, is, like Noah, a survivor of the Flood. He is the last of the antediluvian sages. His name may mean "he found life" (Tigay, 25n.10), which would complete the play on *balāṭu* in the previous line and *napištu* in his name. In the Sumerian Flood story, he is called Ziusudra, "life of long days" (the ZI in his name being the equivalent of Akkadian *napištu*). The epic in Akkadian that includes the Flood, *Atra-ḫasīs*, calls the hero *Atra-ḫasīs* ("overly clever"), an epithet applied to Utnapishtim on one occasion in *Gilgamesh* (XI.iv.187). In *Gilgamesh* he is also regularly accorded the epithet *rūqi*, "the remote one." Gilgamesh forces his way to Utnapishtim, and, as the poem has it, no other humans will follow him.

41–42. The lines are broken, but the sense seems clear. Utnapishtim is the one who restored something that had been destroyed by the Flood. The result is a "numerous people," an epithet used of mankind, meaning "teeming" (CAD 1.2.168).

43–44. Gilgamesh is praised as the very pattern of kingship. The question-form may anticipate the boasts of Gilgamesh and Enkidu after they have killed the Bull of Heaven (VI.vi.182–185).

45. Another transitional line. The line emphasizes the special destiny of Gilgamesh, "important enough to be called by name" from his birth. The second column will follow this by pointing to the extraordinary situation of Gilgamesh, both human and divine.

Column ii

Two-thirds of him is divine, one-third human. 1
The image of his body the Great Goddess designed. 2
She added to him . . . 3

On the sheepfold of Uruk he himself lifts his gaze, 7
like a wild bull rising up supreme, his head high.
The raising of his weapon has no equal;
with the drum his citizens are raised.
He runs wild with the young lords of Uruk through the holy
    places.

Gilgamesh does not allow the son to go with his father;
day and night he oppresses the weak—
Gilgamesh, who is shepherd of Uruk of the Sheepfold.
Is this our shepherd, strong, shining, full of thought?
Gilgamesh does not let the young woman go to her mother,
the girl to the warrior, the bride to the young groom.

The gods heard their lamentation; 18
the gods of the above [addressed] the keeper of Uruk: 19

"Did you not make this mighty wild bull? 20
The raising of his weapon has no equal;
with the drum his citizens are raised.
He, Gilgamesh, keeps the son from his father day and night.
Is this the shepherd of Uruk of the Sheepfold?
Is this their shepherd and . . .
strong, shining, full of thought?
Gilgamesh does not let the young woman go to her mother,
the girl to the warrior, the bride to the young groom."

When [Anu the sky god] heard their lamentation   29
he called to Aruru the Mother, Great Lady: "You, Aruru, who
    created humanity,   30
create now a second image of Gilgamesh: may the image be
    equal to the time of his heart.   31
Let them square off one against the other, that Uruk may have
    peace."

When Aruru heard this, she formed an image of Anu in her heart.   33
Aruru washed her hands, pinched off clay and threw it into the
    wilderness:
In the wilderness she made Enkidu the fighter; she gave birth in
    darkness and silence to one like the war god Ninurta.
His whole body was covered thickly with hair, his head covered
    with hair like a woman's;
the locks of his hair grew abundantly, like those of the grain god
    Nisaba.   37
He knew neither people nor homeland; he was clothed in the
    clothing of Sumuqan the cattle god.
He fed with the gazelles on grass;   39
with the wild animals he drank at waterholes;
with hurrying animals his heart grew light in the waters.

The Stalker, man-and-hunter,   42
met him at the watering place
one day—a second, a third—at the watering place.   44
Seeing him, the Stalker's face went still.
He, Enkidu, and his beasts had intruded on the Stalker's place.
Worried, troubled, quiet,
the Stalker's heart rushed; his face grew dark.
Woe entered his heart.
His face was like that of one who travels a long road.   50

NOTES TO TABLET I, COLUMN ii

The hymnic section of the Prologue continues until line 7, when the narrative begins abruptly in the middle of things. The reasons for the citizens' complaints about Gilgamesh are still under intense debate, but the explanation involves Gilgamesh's activity in 7–17. The gods hear the complaints and address the highest god in the pantheon, Anu, who in turn instructs the mother goddess, Aruru, to create a rival for Gilgamesh. This she does in 33–41, producing Enkidu, who grows up among the animals in the wild. A hunter encounters Enkidu and is terrified at the sight. In his own way, Enkidu dominates the wilderness the way Gilgamesh dominates the city.

1–6. Although the last lines are broken (3–6b), the sense is clear: the Great Goddess has designed (?) the "image of his body," completes his form, makes him in some ways "beautiful," "glorious," and "perfect." The passage completes the Prologue and provides a transition to the narrative that begins with line 7. It takes up from the final line of column i, which speaks of Gilgamesh's birth. Compare the account of the formation of Enkidu below, 31–35.

1. The striking image of two-thirds god, one-third man is repeated in the second part of *Gilgamesh*. The one-third human dooms him to the fate of all humans. One of the lines that define Gilgamesh.

2. Another way of looking at the birth/formation of the hero: the Great Goddess *(DINGIR.MAḪ)*, who may be identified with Aruru and Ishtar in the poem, has given shape to Gilgamesh.

3–6b. Only a few signs remain, just enough to indicate that the work of the Great Goddess is completed.

7–17. The nature of Gilgamesh's oppression of Uruk is very problematic. That Gilgamesh uses his strength, power, and position in an excessive way is clear. "Their lamentation" in 18 may refer only to the women in 16–17. The oppression clearly has a sexual character, as Tigay points out (182–184), and may involve Gilgamesh's demanding the first-night privilege with all women of the city. The emphasis on the "sheepfold" of Uruk (7), (and possibly "holy places" in 11), and with Gilgamesh's "shepherdship" of the city (14–15) points to the king's participation in the "sacred marriage" rite. The bride becomes the representative of Ishtar, and the king, recalling the ancient Sumerian practice of the *en* of the city, sleeps with Ishtar to insure the fertility of the land and the good fate of the city. The oppressive character may not come from the sacred marriage itself, even if it should involve first-night privileges. (All children are, theoretically, offspring of the king.) What may cause the problem is that Gilgamesh, two-thirds divine, has no rival among the men of the city. In the contests that accompanied the sacred marriage rite (Tigay, 187, attested at Mari, a city on the middle Euphrates), especially wrestling contests, the bride may be won by the winner of the event. Perhaps Gilgamesh simply dominates the contests so thoroughly that no one else can win the women of the city. At any event, the solution is to create a rival for Gilgamesh, so that they will "square off one against the other, that Uruk may have peace" (32). Complicating the matter is the possibility that the late version, at least, recalls the Sumerian story, part of which is translated as Tablet XII. The Sumerian work is "Gilgamesh, Enkidu, and the Nether World." In it the heroes Gilgamesh and Enkidu do something with a *pukku* and *mikkû* (the nature of which is debated) which cause the women of the city to cry out in protest (Tigay, 189–190). There may have been confusion about the nature of the *pukku*. If it was taken, as it seems, as a cultic drum in line 10, "with the drum his citizens are raised" (and again, line 22), Gilgamesh's use of the *pukku* may symbolize the power over the entire population. Gilgamesh's tyrannical power may extend to taking the young men away from their families and into battle.

Although the meaning is elusive, the passage breaks into two well-designed sections, 7–11 and 12–17. The first plays on the raising of the weapon (9) and the raising of the citizens by the *pukku* (10). The second balances what Gilgamesh does to the young men (12) with what he does to the women (16–17). At the center is the play on shepherd/sheepfold.

18–28. The first speech of the poem has the gods addressing the high god Anu. The technique of exact repetition, using the exact sequence and terminology of the first passage (8–17, 20–28), is a characteristic of *Sumerian* poetry. It is also typical of the *late version* of *Gilgamesh*. The return to a Sumerian poetic style not found in the Old Babylonian Akkadian *The Epic of Gilgamesh* may, then, be a deliberate attempt to make the Akkadian have the look of a Sumerian composition. Tigay considers the repetitiousness and homogenized style a marked change in the late version from the Old Babylonian versions (102–103). The Sumerian style is evident in Gilgamesh's journey in the second part of the story and especially in Tablet XII, which is a close translation of a Sumerian original.

19. Gods of the above are sometimes distinguished from gods of the lower world, but the line does not call them by the proper name of the group. The "keeper" or "lord" of Uruk is Anu, the great god of the city.

20. The line begins the repetition of 8–17. It is the most modified, because of its function as a comment. Not all lines are repeated in the sequence that follows (11, 13–14), and some variation is evident, but the variation is very slight.

29–41. Anu has a solution to the dilemma: create a rival for Gilgamesh, Enkidu. Forming a living creature by the work of male and female deities is typical of Sumerian compositions, especially those involving the god Enki and the mother goddess (Ninhursag, Nintu). The goddess takes the image of Anu and presses it into clay to form the creature, and is said to give birth to it (35). Enkidu grows up with the animals.

The epithets of the deities in this passage were added for the translation in order to make the identification easy in the reading, Anu the sky god, Aruru the Mother, war god Ninurta, grain god Nisaba, and cattle god Sumuqan. Especially in the last two cases, the gods are the phenomena they name.

30. Aruru is one of the names of the Great Goddess in the poem. Here she is a mother goddess, consort of Anu, highest of the pantheon. She is called "great" *(rabītam)* and the one who has created mankind *(amēlūtu)*.

31. The meaning of *zikru* is problematic, but the line emphasizes the equality of Gilgamesh and Enkidu. One is the replica of the other. The two men will fight, ironically, to bring peace to Uruk (32).

33–35. Enkidu has the image of Anu in him. The emphasis is first on his character as a warrior (to fight Gilgamesh), and he is thus compared with the war god Ninurta.

37–38. Note the emphasis on the wild aspect of Enkidu, with his thick covering of hair and "dressed" in the skin of cattle. Yet there is nothing negative about the description. Enkidu is likened to the gods who were, as above, often imaged as animals.

39–41. The lines are linked together by the repetition of the first word in each case, *itti*, "with." Enkidu is innocent of prepared food and drink.

42–50. The Stalker, who appears only in I.ii–iv and later when he is cursed by Enkidu, is not given a proper name. He stands as a mediating figure between the wilderness and the city. His terror upon seeing Enkidu deepens into grief. The simile employed in the last line of the column, "like that of one who travels a long road," will be used of Gilgamesh in the second part of *Gilgamesh*.

42. The Stalker *(ṣajādu)* is called ḫabilu-amēlu, "hunter-man." Compounds with *amēlu* are a special stylistic effect in *Gilgamesh*.

44. The line ends with a ditto sign *(kimin)*, a practice not infrequent in cuneiform literature where there is exact repetition.

Column iii

The Stalker shaped his mouth and spoke, saying to his father   1

"Father, there is a man who has come from the hills.
In all the land he is the most powerful; power belongs to him.
Like a shooting star of the god Anu, he has awesome strength.   4
He ranges endlessly over the hills,   5
endlessly feeds on grass with the animals,
endlessly sets his feet in the direction of the watering place.
For terror I cannot go near him.
He fills up the pits I dig;
he tears out the traps I set;
he allows the beasts to slip through my hands, the hurrying
        creatures of the abandon;
in the wilderness he does not let me work."

His father shaped his mouth and spoke, saying to the Stalker:

"My son, in Uruk lives a man, Gilgamesh:
no one has greater strength than his.
In all the land he is the most powerful; power belongs to him.
        Like a shooting star of Anu, he has awesome strength.
Go, set your face toward Uruk.
Let him, the knowing one, hear of it.   18
He will say, 'Go, Stalker, and take with you a love-priestess, a
        temple courtesan,   19
[let her conquer him with] power [equal to his own].
When he waters the animals at the watering place,
have her take off her clothes, let her show him her strong beauty.   22
When he sees her, he will come near her.
His animals, who grew up in the wilderness, will turn from him.' "

He listened to the counsel of his father.
The Stalker went to Gilgamesh.

He mounted the road; he set his face in the direction of Uruk
[to speak to] Gilgamesh [the knowing].

"There is a man who has come from the hills.
His power is great in the land.
Like a shooting star of Anu, he has awesome strength.
He ranges endlessly over the hills,
endlessly feeds on grass with the animals,
endlessly sets his feet in the direction of the watering place.
For terror I cannot go near him.
He fills up the pits I dig;
he tears out the traps I set;
he allows the beast to slip through my hands, the hurrying
        creatures of the abandon;
in the wilderness he does not let me work."

Gilgamesh said to him, to the Stalker,

"Go, Stalker, and take with you a love-priestess, a temple courtesan.
When he waters the animals at the watering place,
have her take off her clothes, have her show him her strong beauty.
When he sees her, he will come near her.
His animals, who grew up in his wilderness, will turn from him."

The Stalker went, taking with him a love-priestess, a temple
        courtesan.
They mounted the road, went their journey.
On the third day, in the wilderness, the set time arrived.   48
The Stalker and the woman sat in their places and waited.
One day, a second day, they sat at the watering place.
Then the wild animals came to the watering place to drink.   51

NOTES TO TABLET I, COLUMN iii

The column has a simple, elegant structure. The Stalker tells his father about Enkidu, and the father advises him to go to Gilgamesh for help—but not without telling Stalker what Gilgamesh's advice will be. He goes to Uruk, and Gilgamesh does indeed give him the advice he needs: take a temple prostitute into the wilderness. She will alienate the animals with whom Enkidu has lived. The column ends on a moment of suspense, as the Stalker and the woman wait for Enkidu to appear.

The column is a good illustration of the style of expansion and repetition characteristic of the late version. The Stalker's speech to his father is repeated exactly, except for the vocative, "Father," that introduces the speech (2–12, 29–39). The father's response includes the advice Gilgamesh will give, again in exactly the same form (19–24, 41–46). The first two speeches are introduced by a formula typical of the late version (1, 13), while the last speech, Gilgamesh's response, is introduced by a formula unique to the Gilgamesh texts but found in Old Babylonian versions (40). When the Stalker goes to Gilgamesh, on the other hand, no explicit speech formula is employed (25–28). This may argue that the first two speeches are an expansion backwards of a shorter exchange in an earlier version. Having the father speak has the advantage of allowing another praise-poem to Gilgamesh (14–16). The father of the Stalker is otherwise unidentified, and he disappears from *Gilgamesh* entirely. It would appear that Sîn-leqi-unninnī, in order to give the episode greater weight and a texture like a Sumerian composition, added the father. Appealing to a "father" for advice is common in cuneiform literature, especially in the "Marduk-Ea Rituals." An example of the pattern is found in Tablet XII, based on a Sumerian original.

4. The *kiṣru* of the god Anu has been translated in various ways. The word means "knot," a "contingent of soldiers," and "meteorite" (CAD 8.441). It is taken here as a "shooting star," appropriate to the sky god Anu.

5–7. The triplet is tied together by the repetition of *kajānama*, "constantly" or "regularly," in each line. The lines are varied in that the word appears last in line 5, but first in lines 6 and 7.

18. Gilgamesh is described as *emuq-amēlu*, "the knowing one," in line with the emphasis on Gilgamesh's wisdom in the late version.

19. Like the Stalker, the woman is not given a proper name in the story, but one that indicates her profession. She is regularly called *ḫarīmtu* and *šamḫātu*, terms quite difficult to translate. The *ḫarīmtu* was a prostitute; so was the *šamḫātu*. It may be that the status of the two was different, but they appear to be used as synonyms. The terms are used as epithets of the goddess Ishtar, and the women were in the service of the temple. Temple prostitution was a widespread phenomenon in the ancient world, and prostitutes and sexual inverts of various sorts are frequently associated with the Great Goddess. Sacred prostitution may be yet another link in the poem to the complex involving Ishtar and the sacred precinct of Uruk. "Love-priestess" and "temple courtesan" attempt to avoid the very negative resonances of "prostitute," especially the latter, which may be the more poetic of the two terms used to describe the priestess.

22. "Her strong beauty" is an attempt to capture the vigor of the priestess' sexual attractiveness, *kuzbu* (CAD 8.614). The term is used as a divine attribute.

48–51. The column ends on a note of expectation. The "set time" in 48, *adannu* (a term used later in the Flood story), is the third day they waited in the wilderness. The three lines are linked together by the counting of the days and the references to the two sitting—an elegant variation that sets up the line which ends the episode.

Column iv

The animals came; their hearts grew light in the waters. 1
And as for him, Enkidu, child of the mountain,
he who fed with gazelles on grass,
he drank with the wild beasts at the watering place
and with the hurrying animals his heart grew light in the waters.

The woman saw him, the man-as-he-was-in-the-beginning, 6
the man-and-killer from the deep wilderness. 7

"Here he is, courtesan; get ready to embrace him. 8
Open your legs, show him your beauty.
Do not hold back, take his wind away.
Seeing you, he will come near.
Strip off your clothes so he can mount you.
Make him know, this-man-as-he-was, what a woman is.
His beasts who grew up in his wilderness will turn from him.
He will press his body over your wildness."

The courtesan untied her wide belt and spread her legs, and he
     struck her wildness like a storm. 16
She was not shy; she took his wind away.
Her clothing she spread out, and he lay upon her.
She made him know, the man-as-he-was, what a woman is.
His body lay on her;
six days and seven nights Enkidu attacked, fucking the priestess.

After Enkidu was glutted on her richness 22
he set his face toward his animals.
Seeing him, Enkidu, the gazelles scattered, wheeling:
the beasts of the wilderness fled from his body.
Enkidu tried to rise up, but his body pulled back.
His knees froze. His animals had turned from him.

Enkidu grew weak; he could not gallop as before.
Yet he had knowledge, wider mind.

Turned around, Enkidu knelt at the knees of the prostitute.
He looked up at her face,
and as the woman spoke, his ears heard.

The woman said to him, to Enkidu:

"You have become wise, like a god, Enkidu.   34
Why did you range the wilderness with animals?
Come, let me lead you to the heart of Uruk of the Sheepfold,
to the stainless house, holy place of Anu and Ishtar,   37
where Gilgamesh lives, completely powerful,
and like a wild bull stands supreme, mounted above his people."

She speaks to him, and they look at one another.
With his heart's knowledge, he longs for a deeply loving friend.   41

Enkidu says to her, to the temple whore: 42

"Come, courtesan, join with me, [travel]
to the stainless house, the temple, dwelling of Anu and Ishtar,
where Gilgamesh is, completely powerful,
and like a wild bull stands supreme mounted above the people.
I, I will call to him; I'll shout with great force."   47

NOTES TO TABLET I, COLUMN iv

1–5. The idyllic scene is described in terms of the triplet used in I.ii.39–41. The difference is the parallelism in lines 1 and 5 that frame the lines, marking the opening and closing of the sequence. In contrast to line 7 below, Enkidu is called *ilittašu šadumma*, "child of the mountain."

6. That the story of Enkidu is the story of the early life of mankind is suggested by the epithet given him here, *lullâ-amēlu*, another of the compounds favored in the poem like *ḫabilu-amēlu* to describe the Stalker (I.ii.42). The *lullû*, borrowed from the Sumerian *lú-u_x-lu*, is "primordial" mankind, before humanizing and civilizing habits are learned. See Tigay, 198–213, on the tradition in Sumerian and Akkadian literature. Hence "man-as-he-was-in-the-beginning" here and "man-as-he-was" in line 13 below.

7. The line could conceivably refer to the Stalker, not Enkidu, in which it would serve as a lead-in to the speech that follows, assuming the verb in line 6 governs this line as well. It is usually taken, however, as a reference to Enkidu. If so, the epithet, *eṭlu šǎggasâ*, "man of destruction" or "killer," is in sharp contrast to the epithet given him in line 2 above. From the point of view of the woman and the Stalker, he is a man of destruction, but the epithet ironically serves the Stalker as well; perhaps the line is ambiguous for that reason. Certainly the line prepares the reader for the violent imagery in the seduction of Enkidu that follows.

8–15. Even this rather direct rendering of the lines may be euphemistic. The first part of line 9 may be "open your vagina," and the second, "let him take your *kuzbu*," an overpowering erotic attraction or *fascinans*. "Take his wind away" tries to capture the force of the suggestion; "wind" for *napištu* ("life," "soul," and "breath") gives the life-force a very vigorous embodiment. Similarly "mount" in 12 and "press his body" in 15 attempt to capture something of the active force of the lines. The last line of the sequence involves a play on the "wilderness" theme. The phrase *eli ṣêriki* usually means just "over you" or "upon you." In the context that emphasizes the *ṣêru*, "steppe," or *edin*, the wilderness which spread beyond the city, as in the line before (14), the simple phrase takes on greater resonance.

16–21. In the actual seduction, the woman is called *šamhātu* in both first and last lines, rendered "courtesan" and "priestess." The phrase "struck her wildness like a storm" may be only "possessed her beauty," but it contains the same possibilities as line 9 above, with *kuzbu*. The understatement about showing Enkidu what a woman is (19, as also line 13) does anticipate the consequence of the seduction, that is, knowledge, or *gnosis*. The "six days and seven nights" motif appears again in the sleeping-test Gilgamesh goes through in XI.iv. The violence of the final line contrasts sharply with the euphemisms employed earlier.

22–29. The treatment of Enkidu's alienation from the wild animals is carefully expanded over seven lines. Then, in the kind of terse summary that is frequent in Akkadian poetry, the consequence is put in sharp focus: *ṭemû* and *ḫasīsu* that have suddenly transformed Enkidu, wisdom and understanding.

34. Enkidu listens to the woman, the sign of his *ḫasīsu*, or understanding, and she tells him his has become "wise" like a god's. If it is a form of *emqu*, "skilled," "wise," "wily" (CAD 4.151) at the beginning of the line, Enkidu now has a trait used before to describe Gilgamesh.

37. For the first time in the poem, the sanctuary of Uruk is called the place of Anu and Ishtar. Before (I.i.14), it was the place of Ishtar. In the Old Babylonian texts, on the contrary, the sanctuary is regularly just the place of Anu.

41. Enkidu's "heart's knowledge," *mudû libbašu*, immediately brings the yearning for an equal, the deeply loving friend, *ibru*.

42. The variant *ḫarimtu* is used for the woman in this line.

47. Enkidu's first speech, which indicates in a special way the humanity he has gained through the ministrations of the priestess, mainly repeats the priestess's speech before it—but with one major difference. The poet ends the column, again on a suspenseful note, with the first boast, emphasized by the first use by Enkidu of the first person pronoun, *anaku*. As in Homeric or Old English heroic poetry, the boast is appropriate to the hero.

Column v

"I will cry out in Uruk: 'I, I alone, am powerful.   1
I am the one who changes fates,
who was born in the wild, might of strength belongs to me.' "

["Let us go, then, that he may see] your face.   4
Whoever there is [to know] I know.
Come, Enkidu, to Uruk of the Sheepfold,   6
where people are resplendent in wide belts,
and every day there's a festival,
and where strings and drums are played   9
and the holy courtesans beautify their forms,
radiating sexual prowess, filled with sex-joy.   11
At night they force the great ones into their beds.
Enkidu, pleased with life-joy,   13
I will show you Gilgamesh the joy-woe man.
Gaze at him—observe his face—
beautiful in manhood, well-hung,
his whole body filled with sexual glow: 17
he is stronger than you,
endlessly active day and night.   19
Enkidu, make yourself an enemy to your anger.
As for Gilgamesh, the justice god Shamash loves him.   21
The sky god Anu, the storm god Enlil, and the word god Ea
    have widened his mind.
Even before you come out of the mountains
Gilgamesh, in the heart of Uruk, will have seen you in dreams."   24

Gilgamesh rises, speaks to Ninsun his mother to untie his dream.   25
"Last night, Mother, I saw a dream.
There was a star in the heavens.
Like a shooting star of Anu it fell on me.   28
I tried to lift it; too much for me.
I tried to move it; I could not move it.
Uruk, the land, towered over it;   31

the people swarmed around it;
the people pressed themselves over it;
the men of the city massed above it;
companions kissed its feet.
I myself hugged him like a wife,   36
and I threw him down at your feet
so that you compared him with me."

The mother of Gilgamesh, skilled, wise, who knows
     everything, speaks to her lord;   39
the goddess Ninsun, skilled, wise, who knows everything,
     speaks to Gilgamesh:

"The star of heaven is your companion,   41
like a shooting star of Anu he falls on you;
you tried to lift it; too much for you;
you tried to move it; you were not able to move it;
you lay him down at my feet
so that I compared him with you;
like a wife you hugged him."   47

NOTES TO TABLET I, COLUMN v

1–3. The boast of Enkidu, his first utterance, continues from column iv. Again the use of the first-person pronoun, *anakumi*, adds emphasis. The lines indicate an emergence of identity, self-knowledge on the part of Enkidu.

4–24. The woman's response opens abruptly, without an introductory formula. The first part describes Uruk, the second Gilgamesh. The heavily festal character of the city is dominated, appropriately for the speaker, by sexual joy. Gilgamesh, in turn, is described in much the same way, yet he is the "joy-woe" man and "endlessly active day and night," which have positive and negative resonances in the passage. The end of the speech turns to the intellectual features of Gilgamesh.

6–12. A description of Uruk of the Sheepfold in terms of festival. Although there is nothing specifically religious in the description (unless lines 9–10, which are rather broken, make reference to the *assinnu*-priests and the *šamhātu*-priestesses), the festival could be cultic as much as secular—a distinction almost impossible to draw in the poem in any event.

9. The drum, *alû*, is not the one mentioned in I.ii.10 or in Tablet XII.

11. The sexual prowess is *kuzbu*; sex-joy is *rišatum*. "Beauty" and *kuzbu* are not restricted at all to women; both are attributes of Gilgamesh (16–17) and of gods as well as goddesses.

13–14. The sharp juxtaposition of Enkidu and Gilgamesh in the two lines makes the unusual complex, "joy-woe man," stand out in a very strong light. Enkidu, following on the lines of festal joy, is *ihtedu balatu*, "pleased with life," while Gilgamesh is *hādi-ū'a-amēlu*, the man who is happy/unhappy. The first part of the compound is a form of the verb "to be happy" used of Enkidu, *ihtedu/hādi*.

17. Like the courtesans, Gilgamesh is full of *kuzbu*.

19. Another terse summarizing line: Gilgamesh literally is "not sleeping [*la ṣalilu*] day and night." The motif of sleep and rest becomes particularly important in Tablet VI and in the sleep-test of Tablet XI.

21–22. The attributes "justice god," "sky god," "storm god," and "word god" are added here to make the identification of the gods easy. Significantly, Shamash is mentioned first. Although he never achieved the status of the three gods mentioned in the next line, Shamash's role in the Gilgamesh stories increased in importance. In the late version, Shamash is particularly important in the first part, culminating in his speech to Enkidu in VII.iii. Anu, Enlil, and Ea are often linked together in a unit, representing the highest level of the Mesopotamian pantheon. Together with the Great Goddess, these gods are the rulers of the universe; they govern the three realms of "the above," "the land," and "the below," respectively. Enlil and Ea are often rivals, as they are in the Flood story, where Enlil is the impetuous strong god outwitted by Ea's cunning.

24. Dreams were already important in the Old Babylonian *The Epic of Gilgamesh*. The standard work on the subject is A. Leo Oppenheim, *The Interpretation of Dreams in the Ancient Near East* (Philadelphia: American Philosophical Society, 1956). The dreams in *Gilgamesh* are "symbolic" dreams, as a rule found only in literary texts of a special type. Recognition and interpretation of symbolic dreams depend upon the intelligence of the dreaming person. The message in symbolic dreams always deals with the future (pp. 197–209).

25–38. Gilgamesh's first dream. It is not unusual for women to be involved in the interpretation of dreams. Ninsun, mother of Gilgamesh, is a goddess who is noted for her wisdom. The narrative cuts sharply from Enkidu and the woman to Gilgamesh and his dream. Gilgamesh speaks to his mother "to untie" *(pašaru)* the dream. The verb is used in three ways: (1) the reporting of a dream to another person; (2) the interpreting of an enigmatic dream by that person; and (3) the dispelling or removing of evil consequences of a dream by magical means (Oppenheim, p. 219). Dreams are dangerous; and the "untying" of the dream is necessary to remove the dream itself, i.e., therapeutic. A detailed comparison of this dream and a parallel from the Old Babylonian *The Epic of Gilgamesh* is given by Tigay (83–86, 270–276). The late version expands the dream considerably, but keeps the same sequence for the most part.

28. The *kiṣru* of Anu is the same phrase the Stalker used of Enkidu in I.iii.4.

31–35. A typical expansion of the late version style. The Old Baby-lonian parallel has only two lines, corresponding to the first and last lines of this version. The last line may read, "Like a baby, an infant, they kiss its feet" (Tigay, 85).

36–38. Both loving like a wife (36) and comparing the two (38), which may mean "you made it compete with me" (Tigay, 85), are motifs added in the late version; they are placed on either side of the line about placing the meteor at Ninsun's feet. When Ninsun repeats the lines, bringing the column to a close (and emphasizing the motifs), the se-quence is changed. As is typical of the late version, the loving embrace is juxtaposed with competition.

39–40. A doublet with variation in names and epithets. The two lines expand one in the Old Babylonian version.

41–47. The lines are a great expansion of the Old Babylonian ver-sion, which moves directly to the interpretation (i.e., to the equivalent of vi.1). The expansion is much like the repetitive, Sumerian style, but not all lines of the dream are repeated. Note that the sequence in the last three lines, 45–47, is reversed. The competition-motif is set directly next to loving like a wife—but the emphasis is greatest on the last line of the column, presaging Gilgamesh's love for Enkidu.

Column vi

"This means: he is a powerful companion, able to save a friend;   1
his strength is great in the land.
Like a shooting star of Anu his strength is awesome,
whom you hug like a wife.
He is the one who will take leave of you.
This unties your dream."

A second time Gilgamesh speaks to his mother.   7
"Mother, I saw a second dream.
Over the assembly of Uruk of the Sheepfold an axe fell.
Uruk, the land, towered over it.
The people thronged before it;
the people pressed over it;
I lay him down at your feet
and I hugged him like a wife,
so that you compared him with me."

The mother of Gilgamesh, skilled, wise, who knows
        everything, speaks to her offspring;   16
the mother, wild cow, goddess Ninsun, skilled, wise, who
        knows everything, speaks to Gilgamesh:

"The axe you saw is a man.   18
You loved him and hugged him like a wife
and I treated him as your equal.
Go, [find him], I say; this is a strong companion able to save a
        friend,
strong in the land; power belongs to him.
Like a shooting star of Anu he has awesome strength."

Gilgamesh speaks to her, to his mother.   24
"May a great piece of luck fall to me.
May I acquire as my friend a counsellor.
[. . . Let me go], I, myself."

———

[Even as Ninsun untied] his dreams
the temple prostitute was casting her spell on Enkidu   29
where they two sat.

NOTES TO TABLET I, COLUMN vi

The column is only a little over half the length of the first five columns on the tablet. The break between v and vi comes at another moment of suspense. Gilgamesh's dream has been retold by his mother; now she interprets the dream. The dream sequence has interrupted the narrative of Enkidu and the priestess. The last lines of the column return the reader to that part of the story.

1-6. Ninsun interprets the dream as favorable. The first line links two terms for "friend" repeated in 21 and elsewhere in the poem, *tappû* and *ibru;* the second carries with it the sense of "equal," the first something like "comrade in arms." Line 5 is very broken, and could mean "And he will always rescue you" (Tigay, 86). We follow Thompson in reading "abandon" or "take leave"—seeing in the line a very striking anticipation of the death of Enkidu, even as the dream anticipates his coming.

7-15. The second dream of Gilgamesh is shorter, but clearly modelled on the first. The tendency to repeat lines and the tendency to expand the parallel Old Babylonian text are both characteristics of the late version. The dreams differ from one another only on the shooting star versus the axe (*ḫaṣṣinnu*).

16-17. The same introductory formula is used as in v.39-40, again varying and expanding the Old Babylonian parallel (Tigay, 86).

18-23. The interpretation is brief, and much like the interpretation of the first dream. Line 20 may be "And I shall make him compete with you," again juxtaposed to the motif of loving like a wife. In column vi, though, the competition-motif stands after the loving-motif, reversing the sequence in column v. The expansion in lines 19-23 appears to have no parallel in the Old Babylonian text.

24-27. Gilgamesh's brief speech brings to a close the dream sequence. It has no apparent parallel in the Old Babylonian text. Yet another synonym for friend *(ibru)* is introduced, *maliku,* "counsellor." The last line of his speech may just vary the line before it. Note that the last two lines use the first-person pronoun—again for emphasis.

29. The verb, *tamū,* is frequently used with *šamhātu,* in the sense of charming and bewitching, a sense appropriate to the transforming of Enkidu, and in a sense paralleling what Ninsun (juxtaposed to her in the previous line) is doing in "untying" the dreams of Gilgamesh.

TABLET II

Column i

Enkidu sat before her
. . . his . . .
. . . good luck . . .
. . . great . . .
. . .
. . .
. . . Enkidu
. . .
. . .
. . . king
. . .

NOTES TO TABLET II, COLUMN i

In sharp contrast to Tablet I, which has been restored almost completely, Tablet II of the late version is very broken, especially column i. The contents can be gleaned from an Old Babylonian parallel. Enkidu is introduced to the arts of civilized life by the priestess. The older version reads roughly:

> Enkidu sat before the woman.
> The two of them made love together.
> Enkidu forgot the hills where he was born.
> Six days and seven nights Enkidu was hard,
> mating with the [love-priestess].
> [The woman] opened her [mouth],
> saying to Enkidu:
> "When I look at you, Enkidu, you are like a god.
> Why do you range the wilderness
> with wild animals?
> Come, let me lead you
> into [Uruk] of the broad places,
> to the holy house, home of Anu.
> Enkidu, get up: I will lead you
> to Eanna, home of Anu,
> the place where Gilgamesh is completely powerful,
> and you [will embrace] him [like a wife].
> You [will love him like] yourself.
> Get up, rise from the ground,
> bed of shepherds."
>
> He heard her words and listened to what she said.
> The advice of a woman
> came into his heart.
> She took off a part of her clothing
> and covered him;
> another part
> she kept on herself.
> She took his hand
> and led him like a child

to the shepherd-house,
the place of the sheepfold.
The shepherds clustered around him.
. . .

Even though the Old Babylonian lines are shorter, taking two lines for one of the late version on the tablet, it is clear that the Old Babylonian is much more condensed in its narrative line than the late version. Contrast the late version I.iv–v, where the two are somewhat parallel. Note that Uruk is "of the broad places," not Uruk "of the Sheepfold," and that the sanctuary, Eanna, is regularly the "home of Anu," not of Ishtar in the Old Babylonian version.

The loss of Tablet II at this point is particularly keen, because the subject is the stages of the life of mankind. Enkidu is *lullû*, primal man, and he must be taught what it is to be human step by step. He must "rise from the earth." He is given clothing to wear, and he is led "like a child" to the place where the shepherds care for their flocks. The sheepfold, with its deep association of divinity and the sacred marriage, celebrated in poetry and ritual of Inanna (Ishtar) and Dumuzi (Tammuz), is the place of fertility and life, the natural place; but it is also the first step toward domestication. Mesopotamian thought did not credit the stages as discovered by the intelligence of man. The patterns we associate with human life were originally the gods' possessions, revealed by the gods to humans (mediated by the antediluvian sages). The Old Babylonian Period, in particular, seems to have become fascinated with this notion of man in his primitive state and the characteristics that distinguished the simpler state of nature from the life of civilized men.

Possibly the hunter/gatherer was already described in the Stalker of Tablet I. But Enkidu is brought into the nomadic life, and he learns to eat and drink. The Old Babylonian version continues:

The milk of wild cattle
he was used to sucking.
They set bread before him.
He gagged, gaped at it,
stared.
Enkidu had not known
about eating cooked food.
About drinking strong wine
no one had taught him.
The love-priestess opened her mouth,
said to Enkidu:

"Eat the food, Enkidu,
as life requires.
Drink the wine, as is the custom of the land."
Enkidu ate the food
till he was full.
He drank the wine,
seven goblets.
His brain became loose, he became childish;
his heart became light,
his face glistened.
He rubbed [the shaggy growth],
the hair of his body;
he was massaged with oil;
he became a man.

Prepared food and drink (in the late version, linked with the gods and kings) transforms him into a human being—and it is important to note that, like sexual intercourse, intoxication is one of the characteristics of the human situation. Like other traits, these belong first to the gods, who are described in some works as drunk on wine or beer. Many grades of beer, for example, were brewed, and the best, like the best breads and cakes, was offered to the gods.

Tigay (199–200, 276–277) points out a brief late-version parallel in which Enkidu is asked why he roams the wild with the animals. He is given bread and beer, but he does not know what to do with it. He squints at it.

Column ii

... his garment ... 1
... [catching] wolves ...
... [protecting] shepherds ...
Enkidu, the protector of herdsmen ...
... to the house of incantation ...
... Uruk of the Sheepfold ...
... 7

... in the streets of Uruk of the Sheepfold 35
... at the show of his strength ...
he blocked the road ...
Uruk-the-land stood [over him]
the country gathered [around him]
the artists gathered [around him]
young heroes heaping up around him.
They kiss his feet as they would the feet of an infant.
From afar a hero has arisen.
For Ishhara the bed [is laid out at night]
For Gilgamesh, like a god, his equal has come. 45

Enkidu, at the gate of the bride house, planted his feet. 46
He prevents Gilgamesh from entering.
They seized one another in the bride-house gate;
they fight in the street, through the city quarter;
[they broke down part of] the wall. 50

NOTES TO TABLET II, COLUMN ii

The beginning of the column is broken, but what remains is enough like an Old Babylonian text—the same cited for its parallels to the previous column—to show that the column deals at first with Enkidu's upbringing. The middle of the column (lines 8–34) is missing entirely. The last fifteen lines of the column have, however, survived and can be compared with an Old Babylonian parallel (considered at length by Tigay, 90–93, 278–281). It describes the entry of Enkidu into Uruk and his fight with Gilgamesh.

The Old Babylonian parallel to the beginning of column ii is this:

> He put on clothes;
> he was like a groom.
> He seized a weapon
> to hunt lions.
> Now the shepherds could sleep at night.
> He caught wolves,
> captured lions.
> Now strong shepherds could lie down;
> Enkidu would guard them,
> powerful man,
> hero like no one else.

The late version retains the importance of clothing as a distinctive feature of mankind. And it appears to keep the motif of Enkidu the slayer of predators and protector of shepherds and herdsmen.

What is missing in the break of column ii may be surmised from the Old Babylonian parallel text, where Enkidu and the priestess enter the city and speak to a man who complains about Gilgamesh.

> Making merry,
> he lifts up his eyes,
> he sees a man.
> He says to the love-priestess,
> "Woman, call the man near.

Why has he come?
Let me hear his name."

The priestess calls to the man,
going up to him, saying to him,
"Lord, where are you hurrying?
Why this laborious journey?"

The man opened his mouth
and said to Enkidu:
"He has [intruded] into the meeting place
that is set aside for the people
. . . for brideship.
He has heaped up [defilement] on the city,
imposing on the unlucky city strange customs.
The King of Uruk-of-the-wide-marketplaces
lets the drum of the people be beaten, banns of marriage;
Gilgamesh, King of Uruk-of-the-wide-marketplaces,
lets the drum of the people be beaten, banns of marriage,
so that men may mate with legitimate wives.
[But] he goes first,
the husband comes after.
So the gods have decreed it.
With the cutting of his umbilical cord
it was decreed for him."

At the words of the man,
[Enkidu's] face grew dark.

The man's complaint seems clearly to be Gilgamesh's taking the first-night privileges, *jus primae noctis*, a practice best known from the Middle Ages (Tigay, 182–184). The man describes "strange customs" the king has imposed upon the city, but declares that the gods have decreed it for Gilgamesh. It is possible that Gilgamesh is acting his role as the *en* of the city in the sacred marriage rite, with the bride acting for the goddess Ishtar (a suggestion that finds favor in the late version's reference, in line 44, to Ishhara, lady of love, a goddess in her own right but often identified with Ishtar). Why it would be a strange custom, then, needs to be explained. Because religious institutions may have brought about the redistributive economy of the Mesopotamian city-state, the role of king as high priest *(en)* may also involve the notion that through him the favors of the gods flow; all offspring are first offspring of the gods, and citizens.

The end of the column in the late version is also paralleled in the Old Babylonian. Enkidu's entry into Uruk is described the way Gilgamesh's dreams describe Enkidu (I.v–vi). Lines 38–42 are clearly based on the dream sequences. Line 42 may be "Like a baby, an infant, they kiss his feet" (Tigay, 91).

45. The second part of the line is difficult; perhaps something is set up for Gilgamesh, "as for a god" (Tigay, 91), which would support the idea that a sacred marriage rite is to be performed.

46–50. The two men fight. If this brief sequence were the whole of the fight scene, it would be in line with the tendency to pare down the Old Babylonian narrative—a tendency in the late version that seems evident in this column, but is quite different from the late version's usual expansiveness. More likely, the late version breaks the narrative at another suspenseful moment, with the outcome of the fight in doubt. The beginning of column iii is missing, and it may well have continued the narrative of the great fight.

46–48. The bride house may be "marriage chamber" (Tigay, 280).

50. The final line may mean "The doorposts trembled, the wall shook." The Old Babylonian parallel to this section does not emphasize the congruence of the entry of Enkidu and the dream as much as the late version does; and it does not expand the motif of the bride house. But the sequence of events is the same in both versions.

> [Enkidu] walks [in front],
> the woman behind him.
> When he came into Uruk-of-the-wide-marketplaces,
> the people swarmed around him.
> When he stopped in the street
> of Uruk-of-the-wide-marketplaces,
> the people gathered,
> saying about him:
> "He is like Gilgamesh in build.
> Though he is shorter in stature,
> he has stronger bones.
> . . .

[In all the land he is the most powerful]; power belongs to him.
The milk of wild cattle
he used to suck.
Now in Uruk [there will be] a constant [clang] of arms.''
The lords rejoiced:
''A hero has come
for men of decency.
For Gilgamesh the godlike,
his equal has arrived.''
For the love-goddess Ishhara,
the bed is laid.
Gilgamesh . . .
at night . . .
As he approaches,
[Enkidu] stands in the street
barring the way.
To Gilgamesh
. . . in his strength.

Column iii

In the land his monstrous power . . .
like a shooting star of Anu, his strength, his power
. . .

The mother of Gilgamesh shaped her mouth, spoke
to Gilgamesh, the wild cow Ninsun.
Wild cow Ninsun . . .
"My son . . .
loudly . . ."

NOTES TO TABLET II, COLUMN iii

Only a few fragmentary lines at the bottom of the column have survived. Probably the column narrated the great fight, which had begun at the end of column ii. The Old Babylonian parallel text describes the fight in a vivid way. It does not seem to share with the late version the exchange of Gilgamesh and his mother, however.

> Gilgamesh . . .
> in the wilderness . . .
> sprouts . . .
> He rose up and . . .
> before him.
> They came together in the land's market;
> Enkidu blocked the gate
> with his foot,
> not letting Gilgamesh in.
> They wrestled with one another,
> locked like bulls.
> They shattered the doorpost,
> and the wall shook.
> Gilgamesh and Enkidu
> wrestled with one another,
> locked like bulls;
> they shattered the doorpost
> and the wall shook.
> As Gilgamesh bent his knee,
> his foot on the ground,
> his anger abated
> and he turned away.

The association of Gilgamesh with athletics, especially wrestling, was strong and enduring. A First Millennium text, *Astrolabe B*, describes the month of Ab as the "month of Gilgamesh" and outlines the events of a festival in his honor: nine days of wrestling and athletics in the city quarters (Tigay, 186). Perhaps more surprising is the connection between the sacred marriage rites and athletic competition, especially wrestling.

Samuel Noah Kramer, *History Begins at Sumer* (Philadelphia: University of Pennsylvania Press, 1981), pp. 281–282, emphasizes the importance of courage and a powerful physique for the Mesopotamian king; and elsewhere he characterizes the Sumerians as "ambitious, competitive, aggressive" (*The Sumerians: Their History, Culture, and Character* [Chicago: University of Chicago Press, 1963], p. 264). Tigay, following him, suggests that Gilgamesh is the embodiment of the Sumerian character. Whatever the connection with the sacred marriage rite athletic competition may have, it is clear that the late version of *Gilgamesh* describes sexual activity in terms of great physical force and juxtaposes the embrace of love and the grappling of competition.

46–50. Ninsun's speech, which ends the column, is too broken for reconstruction.

Column iv

...   1
[Strong] prisoner . . .
He went up into the gate;
loudly [he (Gilgamesh?) speaks] . . .
"Enkidu has no match . . .
wraps up his hair . . .
In the wilderness he was born; no one stands against him."

Enkidu stood there, listening to his words.
They caused him to grow pale. He sat down, weeping;
his eyes filled [with tears],
his arms went slack, his strength left him.

They seized one another, embracing,   12
took one another's hands like [brothers].
. . .
Enkidu spoke words to Gilgamesh:
"[Friend] . . ."   16

                                                                                 50

NOTES TO TABLET II, COLUMN iv

Little remains of the column; two-thirds of it is lost. At the beginning, perhaps at the suggestion of his mother, Ninsun (end of column iii), Gilgamesh makes a public speech praising Enkidu. Gilgamesh has won the contest, though it was between men of almost equal strength. Enkidu weeps in joy at the words of Gilgamesh. They embrace, and Enkidu speaks his first words to Gilgamesh.

12–13. Note the play again of fighting and loving allowed by the Akkadian verb, ṣabātu, "to grasp."

The episode is paralleled in the Old Babylonian text. Gilgamesh has won the match, and his anger is abated. He turns away.

> When he had turned away
> Enkidu said to him,
> to Gilgamesh:
> "A man without match your mother bore you,
> the wild cow of the cattlefields, Ninsun.
> Your head is raised above other men's;
> kingship over the people
> the storm god Enlil has granted you."
> . . .
> . . .
> "[Why] do you wish
> to do [this thing]?"
> . . .
> They kissed one another
> and were friends.
> . . .
> . . .
> . . .
> . . .
> [Enkidu's] eyes [filled with tears].
> His heart [was sick],
> and he sighed [heavily].
> Enkidu's eyes filled with tears;
> his heart [was sick],

and he sighed [heavily].
[Gilgamesh] was patient.
[He said] to Enkidu:
"[Friend, why] do your eyes
fill with tears?
Why is your heart sick,
[and why do you sigh]?"
En[kidu opened his mouth],
saying to Gilgamesh:
"Friend, a wail
has choked my throat;
my arms are slack
and my strength has turned to weakness."

The Old Babylonian text contains the friendship, which has already become strong—and moves quickly to the matter frightening Enkidu: Humbaba.

Column v

"To guard the [cedar forest]   1
and to terrify mankind Enlil has appointed him,   2
Humbaba: his shout is the storm-flood, his mouth, fire, his
    breath is death.   3
He will hear the footsteps of a young man on the road [to the
    forest gate], anyone who goes up to the forest.   4
To guard the cedar [forest] Enlil appointed him, and to make the
    people fear.
Whoever goes up to the forest, weakness will come over him."   6

Gilgamesh speaks to him, to Enkidu:
"Friend . . . you speak . . .
. . . heart . . .
. . ."   10

          50

NOTES TO TABLET II, COLUMN v

The text is quite broken after the first seven lines of the column. Evidently the speaker is Enkidu. Gilgamesh's response is lost. Enkidu tells Gilgamesh about the terrifying guardian of the cedar forest, Humbaba.

1. The cedar forest to which the two men will travel is to be located in what is now Syria, probably the Anti-Lebanon range of mountains. This is the beginning of the adventure that is known also from the Sumerian poem, "Gilgamesh and the Land of the Living," from the Old Babylonian *The Epic of Gilgamesh*, and from a Hittite version of the story. The cedar forest was probably in the east, in what is now Iran, and may represent a precious commodity for the relatively treeless southern Mesopotamia. The story of Gilgamesh's heroism may well have had political, economic, and historical motives behind it. The Akkadian versions have shifted the action to the west. For background and a translation of the Sumerian poem, see Samuel Noah Kramer, *History Begins at Sumer* (Philadelphia: University of Pennsylvania Press, 1981), pp. 168–180. Tigay compares the Sumerian and Akkadian (and Hittite) versions, 23–38, 111–118.

2. Enlil, the powerful god, leader of the pantheon, is the one who has appointed Humbaba guardian of the cedar forest in other versions as well.

3. The Sumerian, Old Babylonian, and Hittite versions call him Huwawa. His roar is *abūbu*, the Flood. The striking triplet of metaphors is already found in the Old Babylonian version.

4. The line may mean, "He can hear a rustling in the forest from a distance of sixty *bēru*, or double-hours, marching distance."

6. This line, unlike the others, has no equivalent in the Old Babylonian version (Tigay, 94–95), but it is in line with what does happen to Enkidu in the later version (IV.vi.24–25).

The parallel account in the Old Babylonian version describes the incident in this way.

> Gilgamesh opened his mouth,
> saying to Enkidu:
> "[In the cedar forest] fierce Humbaba lives.
> [Let us kill him, you and me,
> and drive evil out of the land.]"
> . . .
> Enkidu opened his mouth,
> saying to Gilgamesh:
> "I found out in the hills, friend,
> when I was ranging with wild animals,
> that the forest [runs] for ten thousand leagues.
> [Who] would go up to it?
> Humbaba's roar is the deluge,
> his mouth is fire,
> his breath is death.
> Why do you wish to do this thing?
> It will be no equal match,
> [trying to stand against] the siege-engine Humbaba."

In the Old Babylonian version, Enkidu adds a second warning.

> Enkidu opened his mouth,
> said to [Gilgamesh]:
> "How can we go up
> to the cedar forest?
> Wer is its guardian,
> who is mighty, never sleeping.
> Humbaba, Wer, . . .
> Adad . . .
> He . . .
> To guard the cedar forest
> a sevenfold terror [Enlil gave him]."

Column vi

Were [born] . . .   1
Gilgamesh [shaped his mouth and speaks, saying to Enkidu]:
"Friend . . .
no sons were born [in my house]."

Enkidu shaped his mouth [and speaks, saying to Gilgamesh]:
"Friend, who would want to beget him,
Humbaba, who . . ."

Gilgamesh [shaped his mouth and speaks, saying to Enkidu]:
"Friend . . .
. . ."   10

. . . flood   21(?)
. . . brim . . .
. . . causes to pour . . .
stirs up the sea; transforms the land,
. . . makes war,
stirs up the deluge, stirs up the whole world
. . . whose anger is the flood.
Through the opening of his mouth, the heavens are entered.
The mountains give way; the mountains are transformed.
. . . takes cover in the recesses [of the forest]
Heaven and earth he made, the whole of . . .
[His mouth is the god] Gibil (fire); his breath is death.
. . .   32(?)

50

NOTES TO TABLET II, COLUMN vi

Only a few broken lines remain of the beginning of column vi. The small fragment after the opening (1–10) may not belong in the column. If it does, it comes somewhere in the middle of the column. It may be an extended description of Humbaba as the Flood (a metaphor used above, II.v.3; note also the last line of the fragment), perhaps Enkidu's further warning to Gilgamesh. The first part of the column is of particular interest because of its style, using a dialogue of very brief, two-line exchanges.

The subject of column vi is not clear from either fragment, but the Old Babylonian parallel text takes up at this point a very important exchange between the two men. The Sumerian version also preserves the theme. While Enkidu, who has had some knowledge of the dangerous Humbaba, is frightened, Gilgamesh is full of courage. And he insists on a campaign against Humbaba in order to establish his name. Death is of little concern to him at this point. The Old Babylonian contains this.

> Gilgamesh opened his mouth,
> saying to [Enkidu]:
> "Friend, who can scale [heaven]?
> Only the gods [live] forever under the sun.
> As for men, their days are numbered;
> their achievements are a puff of wind.
> Here you are, afraid of death.
> What of your great strength?
> Let me walk in front of you,
> and let your mouth call to me, 'Keep on! Fear nothing!'
> If I fail, I will have made myself a name.
> 'Gilgamesh,' they will say, 'went against fierce Humbaba
> and died.' [They will remember], afterward,
> the child born in my house . . ."
> . . .
> "[What you've said] to me grieves my heart.
> I will lift [my hand]
> and [fell] the cedars.
> I will make for myself a name that lasts.
> [From] my friend the smith I will order
> [weapons] cast in our presence."

. . . they [ordered] the smith [to make weapons].
The craftsmen sat down to consider.
They cast mighty adzes,
axes of three talents each they cast.
Heavy swords they cast,
the blades two talents each,
and the [knobs] on their [sheaths], thirty minas each,
[the hilts] of the swords, thirty minas gold each.
Gilgamesh and Enkidu carried, each of them, ten talents.
[In the] gate of Uruk with its seven bolts
. . . the people gathered.
. . . in the street of Uruk-of-the-wide-marketplaces.
. . . sat down before him,
speaking . . .
". . . Uruk-of-the-wide-marketplaces."
. . .

TABLET III
Column i

The old ones shaped their mouths and spoke, saying to Gilgamesh, 1
"Do not trust all that strength of yours, Gilgamesh.
Make sure your eyes are wide, your blow certain.

The one who walks in front guards his friend;
the one who knows the way safeguards his companion.

Let Enkidu go before you as you march;
he knows the way of the forest, to the cedars.
He has seen battle, understands warfare.
Enkidu will watch over the friend, make the way safe for his
    companion.
Over all pitfalls he will carry his body.
[Enkidu,] we in our assembly entrust the king to you;
you, in turn, return him to us again."

Gilgamesh opened his mouth
and spoke to Enkidu:
"Up, blood-brother. Let us go to Egalmah, the great temple,   15
to the presence of Ninsun, the great queen.
Ninsun the wise, who knows everything.
A wise path she will lay out for our feet."

They seized each other, hand in hand.
Gilgamesh and Enkidu went up to Egalmah,
to the presence of Ninsun the great queen.

Gilgamesh approached, entered the queen's presence:
"Ninsun, I [want powerfully] . . .
[to make] the long journey to the place of Humbaba.
[I shall face] a battle I cannot know about.
I am about to travel a road I cannot know

[until the day I go and return],
[until I reach the forest, the cedars],
[until I destroy Humbaba, who is called the ferocious one]   29
[and remove from the land any evil that Shamash hates].
. . . a garment
. . . in your presence before you."

. . . Ninsun, speaking words to her son Gilgamesh,
". . . listen to me . . .
. . ."

NOTES TO TABLET III, COLUMN i

Tablet III opens with the elders of the city giving Gilgamesh advice on the campaign against Humbaba. Gilgamesh and Enkidu go to the temple, Egalmah, to consult with Ninsun, mother of Gilgamesh. Much of the column is lost, including at least Ninsun's response to her son.

1–12. The elders' warning is mainly a praise of Enkidu as the guardian of Gilgamesh. In line 8 they claim that Enkidu has experienced combat, although there has been no indication of this, unless the protection he gave the shepherds from lions and wolves is behind the reference (II.ii.2). The gods meet in assembly (e.g., VII.i and the Flood story, Tablet XI); humans follow the divine pattern and meet in assembly as well (11).

15. Egalmah is a Sumerian temple name; the meaning of the name is "lofty-great-house," captured in the descriptive epithet added for ease of identification. "Blood-brother" translates *ibru* here, "friend" and "equal." As before, Ninsun is identified with her wisdom.

29–30. Gilgamesh's response is quite broken, but reconstructed from III.ii.12–18. In line 29, the epithet of Humbaba, *dāpinu*, "the ferocious one," is used of gods, kings, and battles; of itself it does not appear to have negative connotations. The verb, *nāru*, means "to kill" or "to destroy," but also just "to strike." In combination with line 30, though, the suggestion is that Gilgamesh intends to kill Humbaba—a point that becomes important later (VI.iv–vi). Gilgamesh's intention to kill Humbaba (and not just to establish his name) is not in the Sumerian sources, but it is clear in the Old Babylonian version, where Humbaba (Huwawa) is already a personification of "what is evil," *mimma lemnu* (Tigay, 79), a phrase that usually refers to supernatural evil, demonic beings who are harmful to man. The late version adds the important theological concern that the evil is what "Shamash hates." Since Shamash is the god of justice and light, the added qualification of *mimma lemnu* may give the concept a moral dimension it did not have originally. (For the very different meanings of "evil" in the ancient world, see Paul Ricoeur, *The Symbolism of Evil*, tr. Emerson Buchanan [Boston: Beacon, 1967], which touches briefly on *Gilgamesh*, pp. 171–191, esp. 187–188.) The added motif agrees well with the late version's increasing concern with Shamash.

The Old Babylonian version develops the role of the elders in the following way:

> The elders of Uruk-of-the-wide-marketplaces
> said to Gilgamesh:
> "You are young, Gilgamesh; your heart runs away with
>   you.
> What you seek to do you know nothing about.
> We've heard that Huwawa is terrible to look at;
> who is there who [dares to] face his weapons?
> The forest runs for ten thousand leagues.
> Who is there that would go up to it?
> Huwawa's roar is the deluge,
> his mouth is fire, his breath is death.
> Why do you wish to do this thing?
> It will be no equal match, trying to stand against the siege-
>   machine Huwawa."
> When Gilgamesh heard this advice of his counsellors,
> he looked, smiling, toward his friend:
> "Now, friend, thus . . ."
> . . .

Another time the elders address Gilgamesh in the Old Babylonian version:

> "May your god [protect] you
> [and lead you] on the road back, safe.
> To the landing-place at Uruk [may he bring you back]."

Column ii

Ninsun entered [her inner chamber],   1
... Tulal ...
[She put on a garment] right for her body;
[She put on an ornament] right for her breast;
put on her head a circlet.
She ... the earth ...
She climbed up the steps, went up to the parapet;
up on the roof she set out a smoke offering for Shamash,
set up a libation before Shamash, and lifted up her hands.

"Why have you raised up my son Gilgamesh and laid on him a
    restless heart that will not sleep?   10
Now you push him to go   11
on a long journey to the place of Humbaba,   12
to face a battle he cannot know about
and travel a road he cannot know
until the day he goes and returns,
until he comes to the forest, the cedars,
until he kills Humbaba the ferocious one
and has removed from the land any evil you hate.
On the day set as his limit,
if he fears you, may Aia your bride remind you,   20
and may she commend him to the watchmen of the night."
...   22

                                                                        50

NOTES TO TABLET III, COLUMN ii

The bottom of the column is missing. The beginning has Ninsun preparing herself for a ritual and address to the sun god, Shamash. Once she prepares herself, Ninsun offers incense and drink for Shamash on the roof of the sanctuary (1–9). Her prayer (10–21) makes explicit the role of Shamash in the first part of *Gilgamesh*.

10. Gilgamesh's heart is *la ṣalila*, as before (I.v.19), unable to sleep. Here Ninsun asks why Shamash had placed the restless heart in Gilgamesh, an ethical question.

11. The sun god had been a part of the Humbaba story in the Sumerian version, where the god is Utu. There he is the protector of the men, as he is in the Old Babylonian version. Only in the late version is Shamash the instigator of the campaign against Humbaba, a theological shift that agrees with the depiction of Humbaba as the personification of "any evil you hate" (18—as in III.i.30).

12–18. The sequence is used to reconstruct Gilgamesh's speech to Ninsun in III.i.24–30.

20. Aia is the consort of Shamash.

Column iii

The dead . . .

. . .

At the departure [of Shamash?] . . .

The Anunnaki . . .   4

. . .

. . .

expedition (?) . . .

damaged (?) . . .

because . . .

the road . . .

. . .

until [Gilgamesh goes and returns to the cedar forest (?)]

either [day] . . .

or [month] . . .

or [year] . . .

. . .

16

50

NOTES TO TABLET III, COLUMN iii

So little is left of even the beginning of column iii that its part in the preparation for the campaign against Humbaba is still unclear.

4. The Anunnaki were considered divine judges of the underworld, a judicial assembly sometimes presided over by the sun god, the moon god, the queen of the netherworld, or Gilgamesh (who became a judge of the netherworld after his death). They have a counterpart in the upper world of the gods, the Igigi. See Thorkild Jacobsen, *The Treasures of Darkness* (New Haven: Yale University Press, 1976), p. 228.

Column iv

1

|

|

|

Shamash, in the heavens, to the storm . . .   13
. . . Gilgamesh makes . . .
He was honored; incense was raised to him.

She called Enkidu to hear the news.
"Enkidu, strong one, you are not the child of my womb—you.
Now I adopt you,   18
along with the cultic lovers of Gilgamesh,   19
the high-priestesses, wives of Uruk's gods, the holy women,
        those who throw away the seed."   20

She places the jewels on the neck of Enkidu.
The women took him . . .
and the daughters of the gods [made him sexually great].   23

"I am Enkidu who has taken [in order to . . .]   24
Enkidu, in order to . . .
. . . love-making . . .
. . ."
until they went and returned, until they reach the cedar forest
either month . . .
or year . . .

NOTES TO TABLET III, COLUMN iv

The beginning is broken, and even what has been preserved is rather obscure. It would appear that a cultic act has been completed by line 15, probably to Shamash. The most coherent part of the text is the adoption of Enkidu (16–20). Jewels are placed around his neck, and the women of the temple do something with him. What looks like Enkidu's response is very broken.

18. The men became brothers in the eyes of the law as Ninsun adopts Enkidu.

19. Along with the female prostitutes of the temple are male prostitutes, *širqu*, "of Gilgamesh," though one might expect that they would be "of" the city god, as the women are of Ishtar.

20. The line appears to list three classes of ritual priestesses. The *entu*, or *ugbabtu*, was the priestly (feminine) remainder of the *en* priest-king role (feminine when the dominant god of the city was male); the cultic office disappeared during the Old Babylonian Period (CAD 4.173). "Those who throw away the seed" is a literal rendering of what may be an epithet of the second class of women mentioned, the *qadištu*. The CAD (13.49) translates lines 19–20, "I discussed you with the oblates of Gilgamesh/ with the *ugbabtu*, *qadištu*, and *kulmašītu* women." While there is no evidence that the *qadištu* was a prostitute, there is a text that tells of one who, "because of his love for her, he married her even though she was a *qadištu* woman" (CAD 13.147).

23. The women in 22 are the same as those in line 20, and "daughters of the gods" may be a synonym for the whole group. Whether this is part of an investiture (with the jewels) is not clear; possibly the women, involved with childbirth and fertility, perform with Enkidu a ritual of adoption as a kind of new birth.

24. "I am Enkidu" may be the beginning of his new identity, but the passage is too broken to tell.

Column v

1

[until they approach the] cedar forest,   49(?)
[until] they kill [Humbaba the ferocious one].

NOTES TO TABLET III, COLUMN v

Only two signs remain, at the very bottom of the column. The context is still the preparations for the campaign against Humbaba.

Column vi

"Enkidu will protect the friend, safeguard the companion;   8
he will carry his body over pitfalls.
We in our assembly entrust the king to you;
you, in turn, bring him back to us."

Enkidu shaped his mouth and spoke,
saying to Gilgamesh:
"Friend, turn . . .
the road . . .
. . ."   16

NOTES TO TABLET III, COLUMN vi

The few lines that remain can be reconstructed from III.i.9–14. They are enough to indicate that the preparations for the campaign are continuing, and that the elders are repeating their earlier concern about Gilgamesh. At the beginning of Tablet IV, the men have begun their journey. Tablet III.v–vi must then have dealt with the arming and final preparations for the campaign, such as is found in the Old Babylonian version:

> Gilgamesh kneels down [to Shamash],
> and speaks, saying . . .
> "I go, Shamash, with my hands [lifted in prayer].
> May all be well with my soul later.
> Bring me back safe to the landing-place at [Uruk];
> Set your protection [over me]."
> Gilgamesh called to his friend
> [and examined] the omen.
> . . .
> . . .
> Tears run down Gilgamesh's [face].
> ". . . a road I have never walked,
> . . . I know not.
> . . . I should fare well.
> . . . with joy in my heart.
> . . .
> . . . thrones."
> [They brought him] his war-equipment,
> . . . heavy [swords].
> [Bow] and quiver
> they placed in his hands.
> [He] took the adzes,
> . . . his quiver,
> [the bow] of Anshan.
> His [sword he placed] in his belt.
> . . . they could start on their journey,
> [the people] pressed close [to Gilgamesh]:
> "May you return [safely] to the city!"
> [The elders] pay him tribute

and advise Gilgamesh [about] the journey.
"Do [not] trust in your own strength, Gilgamesh.
Keep a clear eye; guard yourself.
Let Enkidu go ahead of you,
who knows the way, has travelled the road.
[In] the forest, down every passage
of Humbaba, let him go first.
[The one who goes] in front guards his companion.
Let him keep a clear eye; [let him guard himself].
Shamash grant you your wish.
What your mouth has said, may your eyes see.
May he open for you the barred path,
unclose the road for your footsteps,
unlock the mountain for your foot.
May the night give you things that please you,
and may Lugalbanda stand beside you
and satisfy your wish.
May you be granted your wish as a child is.
After the killing of Huwawa, the thing you strive for,
wash your feet.
At night, time of rest, dig a well,
so that the water in your waterskin is always pure.
Offer up cool water to Shamash,
and keep Lugalbanda always in your mind."
[Enkidu] opened his mouth, saying to Gilgamesh:
"[Since] you must fight, be on your way!
Make your heart fearless. Follow me.
. . . I know where he lives
[and the road] Huwawa travels."
. . .

. . .

[When the elders heard] these words of his,
they sent the hero on his way.
"Go, Gilgamesh, may . . .
May your god [stand beside you]."

TABLET IV

Column i

At twenty leagues they broke off a morsel.   1(?)
At thirty leagues they prepared for the night.
At fifty leagues they walked all day.
The distance of a month and fifteen days they traversed in three
    days.
Before Shamash they dug a well.
. . .   6(?)

NOTES TO TABLET IV, COLUMN i

Very little has been discovered of Tablet IV. If the two fragments that attest to the five lines here are correctly placed at the opening of Tablet IV, and the fragments of columns v and vi below are in their proper place, the whole of Tablet IV is devoted to the journey of Gilgamesh and Enkidu to the cedar forest. Here they have just begun the journey. In contrast to the Sumerian text, where the men are accompanied by troops, in this version only the two men make the hazardous journey. Providing them guidance is the god Shamash.

Nothing of columns ii–iv has been found thus far.

Column v

...   38

"which at the heart of Uruk you spoke.   39
[Rise] and stand [that you may kill him]."

... Gilgamesh, child of the heart of Uruk
... listened to the words of his mouth, was filled with courage.
"Hurry up, step up to him, do not let him go.
Climb to the woods, [do not be afraid].
[Humbaba] has clothed himself with seven cloaks.
He has put on one; six are not on him yet.
Like a raging wild bull ...
Once raised, his mouth filled ...
The guard of the forest cries out ...
Humbaba, like ..."   50

NOTES TO TABLET IV, COLUMN v

The end of the column has Gilgamesh, filled with courage at something Enkidu has said, urging on battle with Humbaba. The "seven cloaks" with which Humbaba arms himself are not on yet. It is the time to strike. The "guard of the forest" in line 49 is a synonym for Humbaba, who is mentioned in the last line of the column.

Placing this fragment in *Gilgamesh* has proven a difficult task. Paul Haupt thought it belonged in Tablet V (column ii), and now J. V. Kinnier Wilson, "On the Fourth and Fifth Tablets of the Epic of Gilgameš," *Gilgameš et sa légende*, ed. Paul Garelli (Paris: C. Klincksieck, 1960), p. 105, has argued that it is perhaps a different recension of V.i.

Column vi

. . .   22

Enkidu shaped his mouth and spoke to Gilgamesh, saying,   23
"[Friend, let us not go] up [into the heart of the forest].
[Opening] the gate [my hand] went weak."

Gilgamesh opened his mouth, speaking to Enkidu, saying,
". . . Friend, like one who is grieving,   27
[You] will surpass all of them
[who came] before us . . .
a friend who knows battle, understands fighting.
Touch [my heart], you will not fear death.   31
Shouting together we will rise up
like a kettledrum. The shout will pierce . . .   33
So the slackness of your arms, the weakness of your hands
      will leave you.
. . . Stand, friend, we will [go up] together.
Let your heart grow light in battle. Forget death, fear nothing.
With unwaning strength the wary man,   37
going in front, guards his body and protects his companion.
Even though they fall, they have made themselves a name."

They drew near the [gate]-bolt, the two of them together.
Brought to silence, they stood: 41
they entered the forest.   42

NOTES TO TABLET IV, COLUMN vi

The top of the column is missing. The contents of the bottom of the column are clear. Enkidu hesitates before entering the cedar forest, and Gilgamesh uses the occasion to spur Enkidu on. Gilgamesh's bold words will prove ironic once Enkidu is taken from him. "Forget death, fear nothing" (36), "Even though they fall, they have made themselves a name" (39) and the proverb of which it is a part (37–38) are the clearest possible statements of the heroic challenge. The brave "Touch [my heart], you will not fear death" (31) anticipates the moment over the body of Enkidu when Gilgamesh touches the still heart of his friend (VIII.ii.17).

As with the previous column, placing this column has been a problem. George Smith and Paul Haupt thought it belonged in Tablet V as column i. Campbell Thompson, on the basis of what we marked as line 42, placed it here. He took the line, which is probably identical with the opening line of Tablet V, column i, as a catch-line. J. V. Kinnier Wilson (see notes to Tablet IV, column v) thinks the column belongs in Tablet V, column ii, possibly a different recension. It would be typical of the late version to end the column with 41, at a moment of suspense. However, Kinnier Wilson maintains that there is no room at the bottom of the tablet for a colophon that would contain the catch-line for V.i.

27. What is usually taken as "weakling" or "coward" is probably "grieving one," *piznuqu.*

31. "Touch" is clear, but the beginning of the line is broken, where the object is indicated.

33. The drum in this case is the *lilissu,* "kettledrum" (CAD 9.186).

37. Another of the compounds with *amēlu: pitqudu amēlu,* the prudent man.

41. This line may be the end of the column, with the men standing silently.

42. A line drawn on the tablet separates this from the previous section. It could mean "They stood and examined the forest" if it is the same as the line that opens V.i.

TABLET V

Column i

They stood looking at the forest.   1
They saw the cedars' height;
they saw the forest gate.
Where Humbaba walked, a path was made.
The alleys were straight, the road good.
They saw the cedar mountain, home of the gods, throne-base of
    Irnini.   6
On the face of the mountain, the cedar lifts its seed.
Its shade is good, full of comfort.
The thorn is covered and hidden . . .
. . . the incense of the tree . . .   10
. . . one double-hour . . .
. . . again for two-thirds . . .
. . .   13

                                           50

NOTES TO TABLET V, COLUMN i

Only the beginning of the column has been recovered. Gilgamesh and Enkidu wonder at the entrance of the cedar forest. The forest may be described as a single tree, the world-tree.

6. The cedar mountain is the dwelling-place of the gods, *mušab ilāni*. Only one of the gods is mentioned by name—Irnini, a manifestation of the goddess Ishtar. Her *parakku*, or throne-base, is found there. One reason for the singling out of the goddess in her form as Irnini may be a play on the word for cedar, *erēnu*.

10. The *sim*ballukku* may be the tree, not the aromatic substance taken from it (CAD 2.64).

The texts placed as v–vi at the end of Tablet IV may be the bottom parts of Tablet V, i–ii. If so, there may be two recensions of the late version of *Gilgamesh* V. See notes to IV.v–vi.

Tablet V narrates three dreams Gilgamesh has as the men make their way into the heart of the forest. All are symbolic dreams. The first is not preserved in the late version; the second and third dreams are found in V.iii–iv. An Old Babylonian text treats the first of the dreams.

"Get up, look toward the mountain . . .
I am robbed of holy sleep.
Friend, I saw a dream—bad luck troublesome . . .

I took hold of a wild bull of the wilderness.
He bellowed and [kicked up] earth; dust made the sky [dark].
I ran from him.
[With terrible strength] he seized my flank.
He tore out . . .
He provided food . . . [I] drank, [he] gave me water from his
     waterskin."

"The god we go to, friend,
Is not a wild bull, though strange of form.

The wild bull you saw is bright Shamash.
When we are in trouble, he will seize our hands.
The one who gave you water from his waterskin,
he is your god, who brings you honor.
Let us be one with [and with] Lugalbanda
so that we can do this thing, a work that will not be
    diminished by death.''

Column ii

From afar, the sword . . .
of far powers . . .
. . . would touch . . .
. . . sword . . .
. . .
covered . . .
Humbaba . . .
did not come . . .
did not come . . .
. . .
. . .
. . .
. . .
. . .
. . .
. . .
Enlil . . .
Enkidu shaped his mouth to speak, saying to Gilgamesh: 18
". . . Humbaba . . .
One alone c[annot . . .]   20
Strangers . . .
Slippery ground can[not . . .]
Two . . . triplets [. . .]
A three-stranded towrope [. . .]   24
Strong . . . two lion [cubs . . .]
. . .
. . .   27

                                                             50

NOTES TO TABLET V, COLUMN ii

It is difficult to tell what this very broken text is narrating. On the basis of the reference to a "three-stranded towrope" in line 24, Tigay (165–167) suggests that Enkidu's speech urges the difference between a person acting alone (20) and two people acting together. The three-stranded towrope is a traditional image of the way two people can overcome problems that one cannot overcome by himself. Tigay cites a parallel use in the Sumarian "Gilgamesh and the Land of the Living" and a biblical parallel (Ecclesiastes 4:9–12).

The bottom of the column may be reconstructed from the fragment placed in IV.vi. See notes to that column.

Column iii

"The other dream I saw: 32
into mountain gorges
[a mountain] fell.
. . . like flies . . .

The one who was born in the wilderness   36
spoke to his friend; Enkidu untied the dream.
"Friend, your dream is good luck,
the dream is valuable . . .
Friend, the mountain you saw . . .
we'll seize Humbaba and throw down his shape,
and his height will lie prone on the plain."

On the next day . . .
At twenty leagues they broke off a morsel.
At thirty leagues they rested.
Before Shamash they dug a pit.   46
Gilgamesh rose over it . . .
He poured out food into the pit.

"Mountain, bring a dream . . .
Do it for him . . ."   50

NOTES TO TABLET V, COLUMN iii

The beginning of the column is lost. The end deals with a second dream
Gilgamesh has had and Enkidu's brief interpretation of the dream (32–
35, 36–42). The men then resume their journey. In language that repeats
IV.i.1–5, they make their way. Then (46–50) they dig a pit or well
(būru). Gilgamesh completes a ritual to secure yet another dream. Tigay
suggests (152) that the sequence may provide an etiology of the *namburi*
ritual to be performed when a well is dug.

A Middle Babylonian Period text describes the second dream in this
way:

> They embraced each other for their night's rest;
> sleep overcame them, surging night.
> At midnight sleep left him.
> He tells a dream to Enkidu, his friend.
> "If you did not wake me, why am I awake?
> Enkidu, my friend, I must have seen a dream.
> Did you wake me? Why . . .
> Besides my first dream, I saw a second dream.
> In my dream, friend, a mountain toppled.
> It laid me low and took hold of my feet.
> The glare was overpowering. A man appeared,
> the handsomest in the land; his grace . . .
> From under the mountain he pulled me out,
> gave me water to drink. My heart grew quiet.
> He set my feet on the ground."
>
> Enkidu said to him, to this god-[man],
> to Gilgamesh: "Friend, let us go . . ."

The beginning is rather like the beginning of Gilgamesh's third dream,
V.iv. See Tigay (121–123, 284) for a comparison of the two accounts.

Column iv

The mountain brought a dream,   1
did it for him.
A cold wind passed
and made him lie down . . .
. . . And like the grain of the mountain
Gilgamesh drew his legs to his chin.   6
Sleep came over him, rest of mankind.   7
In the middle of the night his sleep ended.
He rose up and said to his friend,

"Friend, you did not call me; why am I awake?   10
You did not touch me; why am I troubled?
No god passed by; why are my limbs paralyzed?
Friend, I saw a third dream,
and the dream I saw was in every way frightening.
The heavens cried out; earth roared.
Daylight vanished and darkness issued forth.
Lightning flashed, fire broke out,
clouds swelled; it rained death.
The glow disappeared, the fire went out,
[and all that] had fallen turned to ashes.
Let us go down to the plain and consider this."

When Enkidu heard the dream reported he said to Gilgamesh,
". . . Shamash, your lord, the creator . . .   23
. . . "   24

                                                               50

NOTES TO TABLET V, COLUMN iv

The bottom of the column is missing, but we can assume that it dealt with Enkidu's interpretation of Gilgamesh's third dream. In a comparison of lines 7–13 with the Middle Babylonian text cited in the notes to V.iii, Tigay (121–123) has noted that while no line is identical between the two, the differences are minimal.

1–2. The lines pick up the final two lines of V.iii.

6. Gilgamesh has prepared to receive a dream. When sleep comes to him he curls into a pre-natal position, drawing his knees to his chin.

7. Sleep is described as what is "poured on" mankind.

10–21. Gilgamesh introduces the dream in a striking way. The late version appears to expand the Middle Babylonian parallel by mentioning the "touching" in 11 and the god passing by in 12. The effects of the dream are themselves frightening, quite apart from the content, which is sketched in 13–20.

23. The line is very broken. It may not refer to Shamash, although Paul Haupt saw the signs thus; the reference may be to a technical term for dream interpretation, *šumḫuru* (Tigay, 275n).

Column v

1

. . .

. . .

. . .

. . . Gilgamesh Enkidu . . .

Enkidu shaped his mouth to speak, saying to Gilgamesh:

"Friend, I speak to you and . . .

in order to descend . . ."

44

49

NOTES TO TABLET V, COLUMN v

Only a few signs remain at the very end of the column, in which Enkidu speaks to Gilgamesh. The two-line speech (49–50) may indicate what will follow at the beginning of the last column of the tablet, but the lines are too broken to attempt a reconstruction.

Column vi

1

42

. . .
. . . road . . .
. . . a second time . . .
. . . threw down . . .
. . . Enkidu
They cut off the head of Humbaba.

47

NOTES TO TABLET V, COLUMN vi

Even less remains of this column than of the preceding one. Only one line is entirely legible (47), and though the beginning and end of the line are broken, the meaning seems clear: Humbaba has been slain.

In parallel accounts of the defeat of Humbaba, there is always a debate over whether Humbaba should actually be killed. Humbaba asks for mercy, and Gilgamesh is inclined to grant it. Enkidu, though, persuades him against granting mercy. In the Sumerian "Gilgamesh and the Land of the Living," Enkidu picks up the image of a bird used by Gilgamesh to argue that Humbaba be killed: "If the caught bird goes (back) to its place,/ If the caught man returns to the bosom of his mother,/ You will not return to the city of the mother who gave birth to you." See Samuel Noah Kramer, *History Begins at Sumer* (Philadelphia: University of Pennsylvania Press, 1981), p. 179. Humbaba is given a brief rejoinder, but then the two men cut off his head.

An Old Babylonian parallel describes the killing more vividly.

[Gilgamesh said to] Enkidu:
"We will arrive in . . .
The evil beams of light will vanish in confusion,
the evil beams of light will vanish and the glow become clouded."
Enkidu said to Gilgamesh:
"Friend, (first) catch the bird. Where can the young birds go?
Let us hunt down the lightbeams later:
like young birds they will run in the grass.
Kill [Huwawa], then kill his henchmen."

Gilgamesh heeded what his friend said.
He took the axe in his hand;
he drew the sword from his belt.
Gilgamesh struck [Huwawa] in the [neck].
Enkidu, his friend . . .
At the third [stroke, Huwawa] fell.
Confusion . . . dumbfounded.
[He struck] the guardian, Huwawa, to the ground.
For two leagues the cedars [resounded].

Enkidu kill with him . . .
Forest . . . cedars.
Enkidu killed [the guardian] of the forest,
at whose words Saria and Lebanon [shook].
The mountains became . . .
The hills became . . .
He slew the . . . cedars.
These destroyed . . . after he killed the seven.
The net . . . the sword of eight talents,
the . . . of eight talents—with these he [pressed on] into the forest.
He opened up the secret place of the Anunnaki.
While Gilgamesh chopped down the trees, Enkidu dug up the . . .
Enkidu said to Gilgamesh,
". . . Gilgamesh, the cedars are felled . . ."

For the Old Babylonian parallels to the first part of *Gilgamesh*, see E. A. Speiser and A. K. Grayson in *Ancient Near Eastern Texts Relating to the Old Testament*, ed. James B. Pritchard (Princeton: Princeton University Press, 1969), pp. 76–83 and 503–507.

Finally, a Hittite parallel (see *Ancient Near Eastern Texts*, p. 83) gives Shamash an active part in the defeat of Humbaba:

> Gilgamesh took the axe in his hand
> [and] felled the cedar.
> [When Huwawa] heard the noise
> he became angry. "Who has come
> and slighted the trees grown on my mountain
> and has felled the cedar?"
> Then down from the sky heavenly Shamash
> spoke to them: "Draw near,
> fear not, and . . .
> march, as long as . . .
> and into his house he does not [enter] . . .
> His tears [came down in] streams
> and Gilgamesh [said] to heavenly Shamash,
> ". . .
> but I have come to heavenly Shamash
> and have followed the road assigned [me] . . ."
> Heavenly Shamash listened to the prayer of Gilgamesh,
> and against Huwawa mighty winds

rise up: the great wind, the north wind . . .
the storm wind, the chill wind, the tempestuous wind,
the hot winds; eight winds rose up against him and
beat against the eyes of Huwawa,
and he was unable to move forward
nor was he able to move back.
Then Huwawa let up.
The Huwawa said to Gilgamesh:
"Let me go, Gilgamesh. You will be my master
and I your servant. And of the trees
which I have grown, I shall . . .
Strong . . .
cut down, and houses . . ."
But Enkidu said to Gilgamesh,
"The words Huwawa has spoken
do not hear, do not listen . . .
Do not let Huwawa . . ."

TABLET VI

Column i

He washed his grimy hair and cleaned his straps;   1
he shook out the braid of his hair against his back;
he threw off his filthy clothes and put on clean ones;
he covered himself with a cloak, fastened the sash;
Gilgamesh put on his crown.

To Gilgamesh's beauty great Ishtar lifted her eyes.
"Come, Gilgamesh, be my lover!
Give me the taste of your body.   8
Would that you were my husband, and I your wife!
I'd order harnessed for you a chariot of lapis lazuli and gold,
its wheels of gold and its horns of precious amber.
You will drive storm demons—powerful mules!
Enter our house, into the sweet scent of cedarwood.
As you enter our house
the purification priests will kiss your feet the way they do in
    Aratta.   15
Kings, rulers, princes will bend down before you.
Mountains and lands will bring their yield to you.   17
Your goats will drop triplets, your ewes twins.
Even loaded down, your donkey will overtake the mule.
Your horses will win fame for their running.
Your ox under its yoke will have no rival."

Gilgamesh shaped his mouth to speak,
saying to great Ishtar:
"What could I give you if I should take you as a wife?
Would I give you oil for the body, and fine wrappings?   25
Would I give you bread and victuals?—
you who eat food of the gods,
you who drink wine fit for royalty?
. . .

[For you] they pour out [libations];
[you are clothed with the Great] Garment.
[Ah,] the gap [between us], if I take you in marriage!

You're a cooking fire that goes out in the cold,
a back door that keeps out neither wind nor storm,
a palace that crushes the brave ones defending it,
a well whose lid collapses,
pitch that defiles the one carrying it,
a waterskin that soaks the one who lifts it,
limestone that crumbles in the stone wall,
a battering ram that shatters in the land of the enemy,
a shoe that bites the owner's foot!

Which of your lovers have you loved forever?
Which of your little shepherds has continued to please you?   43
Come, let me name your lovers for you."   44

NOTES TO TABLET VI, COLUMN i

The scene shifts back to Uruk. Gilgamesh purifies himself after the battle with Humbaba, cleaning his hair and exchanging his filthy clothes for new. The return to the city is complete as he puts on his crown. Ishtar is so taken with his beauty *(dumqu)* that she offers to make him her lover *(ha'iru,* line 7) and consort *(mutu,* line 9). Her offer brings with it precious objects, a cedarwood house where priests *(išippu,* line 15), kings and other rulers will show their respect. More than wealth and power, she offers those things over which she has special control: fertility and vigor in the natural world. A Sumerian tale which may have been the source of this episode, "Gilgamesh and the Bull of Heaven," is very poorly preserved. (See Samuel Noah Kramer, *History Begins at Sumer* [Philadelphia: University of Pennsylvania Press, 1981], pp. 189–190.) The Sumerian equivalent of Ishtar, Inanna, offers Gilgamesh gifts, though they are not the same as these. And there is some doubt as to whether the Sumerian version includes a proposal to Gilgamesh (Tigay, 24, 175). The proposal may be an innovation in the late version of *Gilgamesh*. Tigay points out that her proposal resembles the literature of the sacred marriage rite (174–176). The purpose of the rite is to promote fertility of the land and "life."

Gilgamesh immediately responds with a speech in three parts. What could he, a mortal, give to the Great Goddess (24–32)? In a clever string of insults, Gilgamesh claims she is not what she seems to be (33–41). The third and most crushing of the claims is only begun at the end of column i (42–44).

8. Literally, "Give me the fruit of your body." The "fruit" *(inbu)* also has a meaning of sexual attractiveness (CAD 7.147).

15. Aratta was a state in what is now Iran, a rival to Uruk in Sumerian times, as a number of literary pieces attest.

17–21. A good example of the technique of expansion in the poem. Note the variation (yield, goats, donkey, horse, and ox) within a simple, elegant design.

25–28. The same formula will be used later, indicating the gifts the prostitute has given Enkidu (VII.iii.36–39).

43. The "little shepherd" is the name of the *allallu*-bird.

44. Ending the column in this way (at least the A-text of R. Campbell Thompson) is characteristic of the late version.

Column ii

"...

for Tammuz, the lover of your youth.   46
Year after year you set up a wailing for him.
You loved the mauve-colored shepherd bird: 48
you seized him and broke his wing.
In the forest he stands crying, 'Kappi! My wing!'   50
You loved the lion, full of spry power;
you dug for him seven pits and seven pits.   52
You loved the stallion glorious in battle:
you ordained for him the whip, the goad, the halter.
You brought it about that he runs seven leagues;
you brought it about that he roils the water as he drinks.
For his mother, Silili, you gave cause for weeping.   57
You loved a shepherd, a herdsman,
who endlessly put up cakes for you
and every day slaughtered kids for you.
You struck him, turned him into a wolf.
His own boys drove him away,
and his dogs tore his hide to bits.

You loved also Ishullanu, your father's gardener,   64
who endlessly brought you baskets of dates
and every day made the table jubilant.
You lifted your eyes to him and went to him:
'My Ishullanu, let us take pleasure in your strength.
Reach out your hand and touch my vulva!'
Ishullanu said to you,
'What do you want from me?
Mother, if you don't cook, I don't eat.
Should I eat the bread of bad faith, the food of curses?
Should I be covered with rushes against the cold?'
You heard his answer.
You struck him, turned him into a frog.

You set him to dwell in the middle of the garden,
where he can move neither upward nor downward.

So you'd love me in my turn and, as with them, set my fate."

When Ishtar heard this
Ishtar was furious and flew up to the heavens
and went before Anu the father.
Before Antum, her mother, she wept.   83
"Father, Gilgamesh has insulted me."   84

NOTES TO TABLET VI, COLUMN ii

45. Line numbering in this column does not mean the top of the column is missing. By convention, Tablets VI, XI, and XII of *Gilgamesh* are numbered consecutively, without concern for the six-column organization of the tablets. Since scholarly commentary is keyed to the consecutive numbering, we have retained the numbering while restoring the six-column design. The division of the text into six columns may not be universal in all versions of the Gilgamesh stories, but the late version often uses the column division in an effective way. Tablet VI is divided here as it is in R. Campbell Thompson's A-text. The first line of the column is obscure.

46–79. Most of the column is devoted to Gilgamesh's speech, the third part of the address begun in column i. The speech is very carefully constructed. The list of Ishtar's lovers begins with the divine lover (a mortal raised to divine status through Ishtar), Tammuz, the very paradigm of the sacred marriage. Then the list moves from animals in the wild to domesticated animals, from an unnamed shepherd to the most detailed example, Ishullanu, the gardener, the case most like Gilgamesh's own. In each case, the "fate" of the creature is set by Ishtar.

46. Tammuz is perhaps the most famous and widespread of the Mesopotamian gods in literature and ritual. He is the Sumerian Dumuzi, about whose love affair with Inanna much has been written. In some ancient works he is clearly the substitute for Inanna/Ishtar herself, who had descended into the netherworld and died; her resurrection was possible only through seizing Dumuzi/Tammuz. For a time it was thought that he was not resurrected with her, but that eventually a substitute was found for him; he was thought to spend only half of each year in the netherworld, his sister spending the other half there. The annual wailing for Tammuz was very ancient and very widespread, even mentioned in the Bible (Ezekiel 8:14 and possibly Isaiah 17:10). In the Levant Tammuz was called *'adōnī*, "Lord"—hence the Greek Adonis. The myth of Aphrodite/Venus and Adonis would appear to owe much to the ancient god. See Samuel Noah Kramer, *The Sacred Marriage Rite* (Bloomington: Indiana University Press, 1969); Thorkild Jacobsen, *The Treasures of Darkness* (New Haven: Yale University Press, 1976), pp. 23–74, on the Dying Gods of Fertility; and S. H. Hooke, *Babylonian and Assyrian Religion* (Nor-

man: University of Oklahoma Press, 1963), "Excursus on Tammuz," pp. 29–40, for Tammuz as a *puhu*-substitute for the sick person; by sending the substitute to death, the sick person is healed.

48. The shepherd bird is the *allallu*, as in column i.43. A possible play on Tammuz as shepherd may influence the choice of bird in this situation.

50. Onomatopoeia: the bird's cry sounds like *kappi*, which means "my wing."

52. Seven and seven is an expression for "many."

57. The mother's name is written with the divine determinative. It is most important not to divide the world of the gods from the world of nature.

64–78. The longest and most clever of the examples cited by Gilgamesh. Ishullanu is the faithful gardener, offering his "fruit" to the goddess. In much the same way as she offers herself to Gilgamesh, Ishtar (67–69) reveals herself to the mortal. Ishullanu's reply is difficult; it resembles a lament in the search for Damu, which makes gruesome reference to the food customarily placed in the grave with a corpse (Jacobsen, *Treasures*, p. 65). Ishtar may be the "mother" mentioned here (72), and the "bread" and "food" in line 73 appear to involve puns on *pišāti/bišētu* ("bad faith" and "being") and on different senses of *irritu/erītu* ("curses" and "pregnant woman"). The question about rushes protecting the person against the cold (line 74) may be proverbial. In any event, as with the others, Ishullanu's "fate" is determined by Ishtar, who punishes his *hybris* in a very peculiar way. The *dallālu* in line 76 is usually taken as a small animal (appropriate to a garden) (CAD 3.52); but it appears that the creature is really a "hanging one," agreeing with the fate he has, suspended in the garden in such a way that he can move neither up nor down (77–78).

83. Antum is the consort of Anu. Before Inanna/Ishtar came to dominate the Eanna temple in Uruk, it had been a temple for Anu and his consort, identified here as the mother of Ishtar.

84. The A-text ends again on a moment of suspense.

Column iii

"Gilgamesh has spoken to me of bad faith,   85
my bad faith and my cursings."

Anu shaped his mouth to speak
and said to glorious Ishtar,
"Come, come. Didn't you yourself pick a fight with Gilgamesh,
and Gilgamesh recited your iniquities,
your bad faith and your cursings?"

Ishtar shaped her mouth, speaking,
saying to Anu the father,
"Father, make the Bull of Heaven. Let him kill Gilgamesh in the
     very place he lives;   94
let the bull glut himself on Gilgamesh.
If you do not give me the bull,
I will smash in the gates of the netherworld;   97
I will set up the [ruler] of the great below,
and I will make the dead rise, and they will devour the living,
and the dead will increase beyond the number of the living."

Anu shaped his mouth to speak to glorious Ishtar: 101/2
"If you ask me for the bull,
for seven years the land of Uruk will harvest only chaff. 104
Have you stored up grain for the people?
Have you grown grass for the animals?"

Ishtar shaped her mouth to speak,
saying to Anu the father:
"I have stored up grain for the people.
For the animals I have caused grass to be, for the animals.
If there must be seven years of chaff,
I have stored grain for the people;
I have provided grass for the animals.

. . . to him.

. . .

. . . of the bull."

Anu listened to the words of Ishtar.
[He created for her the Bull of Heaven (?)]
Ishtar drove [him (?) down to earth (?)]
. . . [approaching Uruk.]
. . .
He descends to the river . . .
At the snorting of the bull, a hole opened up:
two hundred of the men of Uruk fell into it.   124

NOTES TO TABLET VI, COLUMN iii

85. On the line numbering, see notes to VI.ii. The careful repetition of the words used at the critical moment in VI.ii.73 at the opening of this column suggests that punning of some sort is involved in the expression. The phrase is repeated yet again by Anu, line 91.

94. As in the Sumerian version, the goddess insists that the monstrous Bull of Heaven (or "Bull of An," i.e., the sky god Anu) be sent to punish Gilgamesh.

97–101. Ishtar's threat is a variant of one she used in "The Descent of Ishtar to the Nether World" (see *Ancient Near Eastern Texts Relating to the Old Testament*, ed. James B. Pritchard [Princeton: Princeton University Press, 1969], pp. 106–109; obv. 17–20). The lines exhibit her great power over life (but not death, which resides with her sister, Ereshkigal).

101/2. Our translation conflates lines 101 and 102.

104. Anu's concern suggests that the Bull of Heaven symbolizes destruction in the form of famine. Anu is concerned for life in the city during the ordeal, and Ishtar quickly agrees. She has already provided for the people. Nevertheless, when the Bull of Heaven descends, a hole opens up and men of Uruk are destroyed in it.

124. The column ends just as the devastation begins.

Column iv

... men.   125
At his second snorting a hole opened up: two hundred men fell
    into it.
Two hundred men . . . three hundred men . . .
Even three hundred men of Uruk fell into it, *etc*.   128
At the third snorting a hole opened before Enkidu.
Enkidu fell upon him.
Enkidu leaped up, seized the Bull of Heaven, took hold of
    his horns.
The Bull of Heaven threw spittle into Enkidu's face;   132
he threw excrement on him.

Enkidu shaped his mouth, speaking,
saying to Gilgamesh:
"Friend, we have made ourselves great . . .
How shall we overthrow him?
Friend, I see . . .
and strength . . .
Let us destroy . . .
I . . .
Let us be strong . . .
Let us fill . . .
. . .
and stick him behind the neck."   145
. . .
Enkidu circles him, chasing the Bull of Heaven.
He seized him and [threw his excrement],
. . .   149

NOTES TO TABLET VI, COLUMN iv

The column is a short one; there may be a few lines at the end of the column, but Campbell Thompson thinks it improbable. The fighting between the heroes and the Bull of Heaven, especially lines 130–131 and 147–148, suggests more an athletic contest, like the bull-leaping represented on Cretan art, than a simple attack on the Bull. (Recall that athletic competition was part of the Gilgamesh festival.) Enkidu urges Gilgamesh on, and the last part of the fight begins just at the end of the column.

128. In one text (KAR 115) the line ends with *kimin*, like our *etc*.

132. The spittle was thought to possess magic power, and is often used by demonic forces for that reason. At this point the second text (KAR 115) has two broken lines, "Enkidu escaped and . . ./ the Bull of Heaven [retreated] from him . . ."

145. The advice is fulfilled in VI.v.152.

Column v

And Gilgamesh, like a matador . . .   150
mighty and . . .
struck [with his sword] in the neck [behind the horns].

After they had killed the Bull they tore out his heart.
They set it before Shamash.   154
They withdrew and worshipped Shamash.
They sat down, blood-brothers, the two of them.   156

Ishtar went up on the walls of Uruk of the Sheepfold.
Disguised as a mourner she let loose a curse:
"Curse Gilgamesh, who has besmeared me, killing the Bull of
    Heaven!"

When Enkidu heard this, the words of Ishtar,
he tore out the thigh of the bull and threw it in her face.   161
"If I could reach you, as I can him,
it would have been done to you: 163
I'd hang his guts around your arm!"

Ishtar called together the hair-curled high priestesses,   165
the love-priestesses and temple whores,
and over the thigh of the Bull of Heaven she set up a wailing.

Gilgamesh called together [the city's] experts, the craftsmen,
all of them.
Young specialists examined the thickness of the horns.
Each was made of thirty minas of lapis lazuli,
and the plating of each was two fingers thick.
The capacity of the two was six measures of oil,
which he offered as a lotion to his god Lugalbanda.   174
He brought [the horns] in and hung them in the shrine of his
    ancestors.   175

———

They washed their hands in the Euphrates.
They embraced each other as they walked along.

Mounted they rode through the streets of Uruk,
and the people of Uruk gathered to look up at them.
Gilgamesh speaks these words to the people assembled,
to the women he says: 181

NOTES TO TABLET VI, COLUMN v

150. On the numbering of the lines, see notes to VI.ii. The first line is broken, but a professional name should follow in the break. "Matador" is suggested by the context.

154–155. Shamash is not otherwise mentioned in the episode. The Sumerian parallel, "Gilgamesh and the Bull of Heaven," apparently is not complete enough at this point to indicate if Utu/Shamash plays a role in the story.

156. "Blood-brothers" is a rendering of *aḫu*.

161. The *imittu* Enkidu throws in the face of Ishtar is the right side or shoulder; it can refer to a cut of meat; and it can be used in rituals (CAD 7.125). The gesture is as appropriate for Enkidu as the clever, insulting speech of Gilgamesh in VI.i–ii was for Gilgamesh. In both cases they are shocking, unparalleled violations of human/divine disparity.

163. Enkidu seems to be playing with the notion of fixing the destiny, as Gilgamesh had in his address to Ishtar.

165–166. Of the three classes of priestess listed, the latter two are the *šamḫātu* and *ḫarimtu* used to characterize the woman who seduced Enkidu. The first, *kezertu*, designates a prostitute (CAD 8.315) whose name is, literally, the woman with curled hair.

174. The precious horns yield oil or ointment, which Gilgamesh gives to "his god," Lugalbanda, earlier identified (I.i.33) as Gilgamesh's father.

175. The shrine of his ancestors is a bedchamber or bedroom.

181. The column ends just as Gilgamesh is about to deliver his great boast. The statement is carried over to a half line, which emphasizes the "words" he speaks. The "women" may refer to women playing the lyre.

Column vi

"Who is the best formed of heroes? 182
Who is the most powerful among men?
Gilgamesh is the best formed of heroes.
[Enkidu is] the most powerful among men.
. . . our strength
. . . [the final investment of lordship they have not.]
. . . [seal of] . . . [sickness].
In his palace Gilgamesh holds a joyful celebration.
[At last] the heroes lie down, sleeping at night in their beds.
Enkidu, lying down, sees dreams.
Enkidu jerked upright to set free the dream,
saying to his friend:

"Friend, why are the great gods in council?" 193

NOTES TO TABLET VI, COLUMN vi

The column is extremely short. Although a few of the lines are broken, there is no gap in the text. (KAR 115 has only four lines in the column, the last four lines as they appear in this text.) By grouping the lines within such a brief column, the poet intensifies the terrible irony of a reversal. At the very center of the poem as a whole, Gilgamesh utters his great boast. It has the form of a riddle, one of the oldest Sumerian literary forms yet discovered; the riddle, however, is immediately solved. In the break of line 185, "Gilgamesh" is sometimes placed; we feel that in view of the emphasis on the two-as-one, especially in the episode of the Bull of Heaven, the name in the break should be Enkidu.

After triumph and boasting befitting a hero—the "men" in lines 183 and 185 is not "mankind," but *zikāru*, male, with the implication of "warrior" (CAD 21.112)—Gilgamesh has a moment of joy and rest. The "joyful celebration" *(ḫidūtu)* in line 189 recalls the image of Gilgamesh as the "joy-woe" man (I.v.14). Lying down and sleeping in bed recalls the *la ṣalilu* of Gilgamesh, "endlessly active day and night" (I.v.19). No sooner does he lie down, though, than Enkidu sees a dream and starts up to relate it. The column, which actually ends with line 192, ends on a note of highest expectation.

193. The line at the end, "Friend, why are the great gods in council?" actually announces the first line of the next tablet. It appears below the text in the colophon, separated from the text by a line drawn in the clay.

TABLET VII

Column i

"Friend, why are the great gods in council?"   1

. . .   40(?)

"Because . . .
Now I have set down for you the day of fate,
I humbly . . . the desire of your heart.
Let the king who arises after me extend . . .
or [let] the god . . . your gates.
Let him change [my] name and take on his."
He tore off . . . threw down . . .
Listening to his words, quickly, speedily . . .
Gilgamesh listened to the words of Enkidu, the friend, and tears
    streamed.
Gilgamesh shaped his mouth and spoke, saying to Enkidu:

NOTES TO TABLET VII, COLUMN i

The first two columns of Tablet VII are quite broken. From the catch-line at the end of VI.vi, we know that Enkidu relates his dream about the great gods in council (line 1). The dream itself is missing. A very fragmentary text at the bottom of the column appears to show an angry or distraught Enkidu. Something about the "day of fate" (death) and changing one name for another seem to be part of the speech. Gilgamesh listens and then speaks, just as the column ends.

A Hittite tablet from the Middle Babylonian Period provides a context for this very wild swing, from the joy that characterized the end of Tablet VI to what looks like despair. Enkidu's dream of the gods in council presages his death. One of the two friends must die for having slain Humbaba and the Bull of Heaven. The most powerful of the gods, Enlil, who is depicted (especially in the Flood story, Tablet XI) as one who acts arbitrarily, insists that Enkidu die—not Gilgamesh. Disputes between Enlil and Ea are traditional, but the Hittite text indicates that the dispute is between Enlil and Shamash. Shamash claims Enkidu is innocent— both are innocent—because they acted upon Shamash's orders, a point in agreement with the late version of *Gilgamesh*, where Shamash's role is just so indicated. Enlil does not debate the issue. He simply speaks contemptuously of Shamash as one too much like the humans—and the dream ends. Because the treatment of Shamash is in agreement with the late *Gilgamesh*, especially as it treats of a profound moral issue and the arbitrary acts of the gods, the Hittite text is particularly important in giving us an understanding of the late version:

. . . Then daylight came.
[And] Enkidu said to Gilgamesh:
"Hear the dream I had last night:
Anu, Enlil, Ea, and heavenly Shamash [were in council],
and Anu said to Enlil:
'Because they have slain the Bull of Heaven, and Huwawa
they have slain, for that reason'—said Anu—'the one of them
who stripped the mountain of its cedar [must die].'
But Enlil said: 'Enkidu must die.
Gilgamesh shall not die.'
Then heavenly Shamash answered mighty Enlil:

'Was it not by my order
that they killed the Bull of Heaven and Huwawa? Should
     now innocent
Enkidu die?' But Enlil turned
in anger toward heavenly Shamash. 'Because, much like
one of their comrades, you went down to them daily.' "

Enkidu lay down [sick] before Gilgamesh.
Tears streaming down, [Gilgamesh] said:
"My brother, my dear brother! They would free me
at the cost of my brother!" And:
"Must I beside the shade [of the dead]
sit down, at the shadowy door,
never again [to see] my dear brother with [my] eyes?"

(Translation after *Ancient Near Eastern Texts Relating to the Old Testament,*
ed. James B. Pritchard [Princeton: Princeton University Press, 1969], pp.
85–86.)

Column ii

"... into wide Uruk of the Sheepfold.
[A wise friend may speak] strange things.
Why, friend, has your heart said strange things ...?
[The dream is] sound, but the fear is great.
[Your limbs] are paralyzed like [one who has seen a god go by].
... the dream is sound.
For the living man it brings sorrow:
the dream causes the living to mourn.
... I will pray to the great gods.
I will ... I will pray to the great gods.
I will search for and turn to your god,
... [to] the father of the gods ...
to Enlil and plead for you.
I will make your statue of gold beyond measure.
...
... do not complain, gold ..."
...
The words they spoke were not like battle ...
They spoke ... He did not turn, he did not [flinch].
They cast ... He did not turn, he did not flinch.
...
...
... to the edict of Shamash ...
...
...
...
Enkidu shaped his mouth, spoke,
saying to Gilgamesh,
"Get up, friend ...
to the [wisdom of Shamash] ...
the door ...
in the west ...
...

...
..."
Enkidu . . . lifted [his eyes];
to the door he speaks, as to a man: 37
"Door of the woods, empty of understanding—   38
power of hearing which you do not have—
at twenty leagues away I admired your good wood,
even before I saw the lofty cedars . . .
Nothing compares with your wood [in all the land].
Your height is six dozen cubits, your breadth, two dozen . . .
your doorpost, your hinges below and above—
your door-maker has made you in the holy city of Nippur. 45
Had I known, door, that it would come to this,
and this, the beauty of [your structure],
I would have raised your mouth [higher], I would have . . . 48
I would have set a reed frame on [you]."   49

Except for the end of the column, the contents of this fragmented piece are rather obscure. Gilgamesh, who sees from Enkidu's dream that there is much to fear, appears to console Enkidu. He will plead with the gods for Enkidu. (This is not narrated in the tablet before Enkidu dies, but there is a parallel in Tablet XII, where Gilgamesh goes before the great gods to plead for Enkidu.) Gilgamesh offers him some consolation in that the statue he makes of Enkidu will be of gold "beyond measure." Such a statue is crafted in VIII.iv.

The most coherent part of the column is an address to a door, as if it were human (line 37). The door is usually taken as the gate of the cedar forest, which had paralyzed Enkidu at his approach to it. The term in line 38, *giš dalat ḫalbi*, does not contain the usual word for "forest" in *Gilgamesh*, and is, perhaps, "door of the woods" or even "door of wood." There is no question that the excellence and beauty of the wood is described by Enkidu. What is difficult is the two-line close of the column. It may mean that Enkidu wishes he had taken an axe to it (line 48) and thrown a frame over it—if he had known what pain the cedars would cost him. It is also possible that the "door" is not in the forest but rather in Uruk, symbolizing the value of the precious wood the two had cut down and brought back for use there. If line 48 refers to the "mouth" and line 49 to the frame, the structure might look like an Arab *mudhif* or the entrance to a temple. The mood may not be one of anger.

45. Nippur, in southern Iraq, was a holy city in Sumerian times.

Column iii

"Make him lose his profit, weaken his power;   1
make the path in front of him [hate him];
[let the animals] escape from him;
[keep] the Stalker from the fullness of his heart."

[His heart] urged him to curse the temple prostitute, the woman.   5
"Listen, woman. I will decree your fate,   6
[a destiny] that will have no end and [will last] forever.
I will curse you with a great curse.
In a rush the throw-stick will strike you.
Your hungers will never be satisfied.
You will love the child who beats you.
. . . of slave women
. . . wallow in the mud
. . . pollute.
. . .
. . . being collected
. . .
. . . thrown into your house.
. . . the road will be your dwelling-place.
. . . [the shadow of the wall] will be your resting place.
. . . your feet.
[The drunk and thirsty will strike] your cheek.
. . .
. . .
. . .
. . .
. . .
. . .
. . .
. . .
because me . . .
and the paralysis-demon has been sicked on me."

Shamash heard, opened his mouth,   33
and from afar, . . . from the heavens called to him:
"Why, Enkidu, do you curse the love-priestess, the woman
who would feed you with the food of the gods,   36
and would have you drink wine that is the drink of kings,
and would clothe you in a great garment,
and would give you beautiful Gilgamesh as a companion?

Listen: hasn't Gilgamesh, your beloved friend,   40
made you lie down in a great bed?
Hasn't he made you lie down in a bed of honor,
and placed you on the peaceful seat at his left hand?
The world's kings have kissed your feet.

He will make the people of Uruk weep for you, cause them to
        grieve you,   45
[will make the women], the whole city, fill up with sorrow for
        your sake.
And afterward he will carry the signs of grief on his own body,
putting on the skin of dogs and ranging the wilderness."

Enkidu listened to the words of Shamash the warrior   49
[and] his angry heart grew still,
. . . grew quiet.

NOTES TO TABLET VII, COLUMN iii

The column opens abruptly with a curse upon the Stalker (lines 1–4), followed by a lengthy curse of the woman who had changed Enkidu, the temple priestess (5–32), much of which is fragmentary. Shamash speaks to Enkidu from the heavens (33–48), arguing that the woman has given him much, especially Gilgamesh, who will have the city grieve for him after his death and will range the wilderness himself. The column breaks away at the end, but not before the result of Shamash's persuasive speech becomes clear: Enkidu's anger is abated (49–51).

A Middle Babylonian text preserves a few more lines of Enkidu's curse of the Stalker. Note that Shamash is prominent.

> When daylight came
> Enkidu lifted his head, weeping before Shamash,
> Before the radiance of Shamash his tears pour down:
> "I pray to you, Shamash, concerning that hunter, that scoundrel:
> The no-hunter who did not allow me to find as much as my
>   friend, may he not find as much as *his* friend."

(Translation after *Ancient Near Eastern Texts Relating to the Old Testament*, ed. James B. Pritchard [Princeton: Princeton University Press, 1969], pp. 505–506.)

Enkidu's curse of the woman, though very fragmentary, contains lines that resemble Ereshkigal's curse of the creature, Asushunamir, in two versions of "The Descent of Ishtar to the Nether World." For a comparison of three versions of lines 6–9, see Tigay (170–173), where he concludes that the influence of *Ishtar* on *Gilgamesh* appears to have been reciprocal. The Middle Babylonian parallel mentioned above contains a version of Enkidu's curse:

> "You shall never enter the tavern of young women;
> your lovely breasts . . .
> the place of your festivities may the drunkard spoil with vomit,
> . . . all the troops.

The dust of the potter's crossroad will be your dwelling place,
the desert will be your bed,
the shadow on the wall will be your station,
thorn and bramble will skin your feet,
the besotted and the thirsty will hit your face."

(Translation after *Ancient Near Eastern Texts*, p. 506.)

1–4. Enkidu curses the Stalker.

5–32. Enkidu's curse of the temple prostitute. Decreeing the fate in
line 6 recalls Enkidu's early boast (I.v.2), "I am the one who changes
fates." Line 9 appears to mean "With great speed let my curses reach
you" (Tigay, 171). The paralysis-demon (line 32) is the *asakku* (CAD
1.2.325), a demon and the disease it causes. Because the disease is not
found in medical texts, it is taken as a poetic term to describe Enkidu's
condition. Note that Tablet XII.ii.51 specifically denies that the cause of
Enkidu's death is the *asakku*-demon.

33–48. Shamash's important speech to Enkidu. See Appendix for
text, transliteration, translation, and commentary on the passage. When
Enkidu is persuaded by Shamash and his anger abates, he is most like
his double, Gilgamesh (who will, in his turn, become almost identical
with Enkidu). Note that Shamash speaks from the heavens (and that he
does *not* make a similar plea for the Stalker). Because the curse is not
just idle words but has the power to effect the change of fate, the curses
stand. Both the Stalker and the woman are representatives of a class of
persons, the woman in particular, and the curse indicates what terrible
conditions such women must put up with. The curse is not simply erased.
In the next column, Enkidu blesses the woman, giving her a good fate to
balance the evil. (No such blessing is given to the Stalker, note.)

The Middle Babylonian parallel to Shamash's rebuke of Enkidu is
fragmentary, but it appears to include the Stalker. The late version men-
tions only the harlot, and the wording is very different (Tigay, 128). Tigay
thinks Shamash's arguments are "forced," and that the emphasis on
Gilgamesh is "not directly to the point." In the Appendix we argue a
different position; but the passage remains, as Tigay points out, a good
example of the process of expansion and assimilation characteristic of
the late version. Note that Gilgamesh himself will cite part of the passage
later (VIII.iii.1–7). While the rebuke Shamash speaks is at least as old as
the Middle Babylonian Period, the treatment of the theme indicates the
care with which the late version expands the role of Shamash.

The rebuke falls into three parts (36–39, 40–44, and 45–48), with Gilgamesh subtly interwoven into each section. The reference to "ranging the wilderness" in line 48 is an echo of Enkidu in I.iv.35. It will be repeated often after this (VIII.iii.7, IX.i.2,5, X.i.38,45, X.iii.14, X.v.5). Tigay (7) points out the motif as an example of the thematic and structural integrity of the poem.

Column iv

"May [you, priestess] return to your [rightful] place.   1
May gods, kings, and princes love you.
Let no one strike his thigh because of you.
Let it be that no old one shakes his hair because of you.
Let the one who embraces you uncover his treasure for you,
[he will give you] carnelian, lapis, and gold.
[May the one who] sleeps with you pay [you well],
. . . jism out his storehouse.
[May] you enter [the presence of] the gods.
May the mother of seven be abandoned [for your sake]."

. . . Enkidu, [whose] body is sick
. . . lies down, all alone.
[He went] at night [to tell] his friend what he was thinking.
"[Friend,] I saw a dream in the night.   14
The heavens groaned; earth resounded.
Between them alone I stood.
[There was a man], his face was dark.
His face was like the face of Anzu.   18
The paws of a lion were his paws; the talons of an eagle were his
     talons.
He grabbed a tuft of my hair and overpowered me.
. . . up he leaps;
. . . he bore me down,
. . . upon me
. . . my body
. . .
. . .
. . .
. . .
. . .
. . .
. . . he transformed me

. . . like [the wings of] a bird, my arms.
He seized me and led me down to the house of darkness,
    house of Irkalla,   33
the house where one who goes in never comes out again,
the road that, if one takes it, one never comes back,
the house that, if one lives there, one never sees light,
the place where they live on dust, their food is mud;
their clothes are like birds' clothes, a garment of wings,
and they see no light, living in blackness:
on the door and door-bolt, deeply settled dust.   39a

In the house of ashes, where I entered,
I saw [the mighty], their crowns fallen to the dirt.   41
I heard about crowned kings who ruled the lands from days
    of old,
worldly images of Anu and Enlil, waiting table with roast meats,
serving baked goods, filling glasses with water from cool steins.

In the house of ashes, where I entered,
there lives the funereal priest who brings together gods and
    men, and the funereal wailing priest;   46
there lives the purification priest and the ecstatic shaman;   47
there live the *pashishu*, priests of the great gods;   48
there sat Etana, the human taken to the sky by an eagle; and
    there sat Sumuqan the cattle god.   49
There sits the queen of below-earth, Ereshkigal: 50
Belit-tseri, tablet-scribe of the underworld, kneels before her.   51
[She holds a tablet] and reads aloud to her.
Lifting her head, [Ereshkigal] looked directly at me—*me:*   53
'[Who] has brought this one here . . . ?' "

NOTES TO TABLET VII, COLUMN iv

The column has a number of broken lines, but the main design and much of the detail are clear. A short section (1–10) completes the sequence of Enkidu, Shamash, and the woman by blessing the woman. As Enkidu's condition becomes worse, he relates a dream to Gilgamesh, and the remainder of the column (14–54) recounts the dream. Enkidu's dream of the terrifying world of the dead should be compared with the account he gives to Gilgamesh in Tablet XII.iv–vi. In both cases, the depiction of the world of the dead is exceedingly grim. It is true that in the midst of the most desultory "life," a few figures exist in their old identity—mostly gods, but also priests and one man famous in history, Etana (49).

1–10. The blessings of the woman establish the fate of prostitutes, but they do not countermand the curse in VII.iii. Lines 5–8 seem to play on "treasure" and payment from the body of the lover. The key term in line 5, *misirrašu*, is really "his girdle" or "belt" (CAD 10.2.111), but the context draws in *mašrû*, "wealth" (CAD 10.2.385); and Enkidu asks that the lover "pour out his storehouse" in line 8. Note that it is not just humans who will be influenced by the power of the woman; the gods, too, will love her, and she will enter into the presence of the gods (2, 9). The last line (10) is the strongest: even the mother of seven, the perfect number, will be abandoned because of her allure.

14–20. For a comparison of these lines with two other Gilgamesh versions, see Tigay (124–125, 285–286). The other texts are Middle Babylonian. Although the texts are quite close to one another, the late version expands the others in its characteristic way.

18. Anzu (sometimes read ^{d}Zu) is a terrifying demonic being, depicted in much the same way as the man is here, with lion paws and eagle talons.

33–39a. The depiction of the netherworld is identical to passages in "The Descent of Ishtar to the Nether World" and "Nergal and Ereshkigal" (Tigay, 125). Line 39a follows Campbell Thompson's suggestion; the line is not found in the main text.

41–44. There is no indication anywhere in *Gilgamesh* that the netherworld, to which all humans are sent at death, distinguishes between a place of punishment for evildoers and a place of happiness for the morally upright. In XII.iv–vi, the fates of humans differ in the netherworld, but the difference is that some have left loved ones on earth to maintain them; others live like the spirits depicted in 33–39a. Of particular importance in this sequence is the fate of the great ones, great kings who now wait upon tables; once they were "images" of the great authorities in the universe, Anu and Enlil. Of course, the cool water is served in skins, not steins, literally.

46–50. Some of the epithets have been added to make identification easy.

46. The *ēnu*-priest is a high priest, originally the *en* who combined political and religious leadership in the community (hence our addition of "who brings together gods and men"). The second mentioned is the wailing-priest, *lagaru*.

47. The two priests are the purification priest, *išippu*, and the ecstatic, *lumaḫḫu*, whom we have called a shaman.

48. The *pašišu*-priest and the highest of his office, *gudapsû*, are called "of the great gods" in the text.

49. Etana was a human "taken to the sky by an eagle," which we have added; and Sumuqan we identify as "the cattle god," as before (I.ii.38).

50. Ereshkigal is the queen of the netherworld, and is so called in the text. She is usually considered the sister of Ishtar.

51. Bēlit-ṣeri is described in the text as tablet-scribe of the netherworld. (Note ts = ṣ.)

52–53. The feminine forms could refer to either Ereshkigal or Bēlit-ṣeri, but the terrifying question is appropriate to the queen, Ereshkigal.

53. The use of the first-person pronoun is emphatic here.

Nothing of column v has been found.

Column vi

. . .

. . .

. . . "Your weapon, let me look at it.   3
Trouble . . . wherever I go.
Friend, I have seen a dream which was not good."

The day he saw the dream is over.
Enkidu is thrown down, a first day, a second,
Enkidu is lying on his bed;
a third day and a fourth day, Enkidu on his bed;
a fifth, a sixth, a seventh, an eighth, a ninth [and a tenth day]
Enkidu lies sick . . .
An eleventh and a twelfth day
Enkidu [lay down] in his bed.

He called Gilgamesh . . .
"Friend, [some god] is angry at me.
Not like the one who falls in battle will I die.   16
I feared the battle . . .
Friend, the one who [falls] in battle [is blessed].
As for me, though . . .
. . ."

20

50

NOTES TO TABLET VII, COLUMN vi

Little remains of the final column of the tablet. It is clear from what is here that Enkidu is failing, and death is very near. At the beginning of Tablet VIII, Gilgamesh is already addressing him as if he were dead. It is likely, then, that the death of Enkidu was narrated at the conclusion of Tablet VII.

Since column v is missing, the reference to the dream in lines 3–5 is obscure. From what little remains, the most important point Enkidu makes is his bitterness that he was not given an heroic death in battle (line 16). The strange nature of Enkidu's death, including the point that it was not in battle, is emphasized in Tablet XII as well.

TABLET VIII
Column i

When something of the beginning of light came, 1
Gilgamesh spoke to his friend.

"Enkidu, . . . your mother is a gazelle, 3
and . . . your father who created you, a wild ass.
[You were] raised by creatures with tails,
and by the animals of the wilderness, with all its breadth.

The paths going up to and down from the forest of cedars 7
all mourn you: the weeping does not end day or night.

The elders of wide Uruk of the Sheepfold bewail you:
they bless us, waving their fingers after us
[as we move up the slope] of [the] mountain, Kur; 11
. . . our ascending.

The meadows weep; they mourn you like your mother.
. . . cedar trees
. . . among whom the bear, the hyena, the panther mourn you.
The bear, the hyena, the tiger, the deer, the lion,
the wild bull, the ibex—all the animals of the plain [cry for you].

The river Ulaj, on whose banks we walked, laments you; 18
we travelled its banks. The pure Euphrates bewails you 19
[where we filled the] waterbag.
  The men of wide Uruk of the Sheepfold— 20
we looked at [the walls], we killed the bull of the city—
  the men of [Uruk] bewail you,
and those who praised your name in Eridu, may they bewail you;

the people who have not yet exalted your name, may they
    bewail you.

The woman who placed food in your mouth, may she bewail
    you;   24
the one who set butter before you, *etc.*
who placed beer in your mouth, *etc.;* the prostitute
. . . [who] anointed you with sweet oil, she will weep [for you] . . .
[The house] of the husband you gave advice about a ring, a wife . . .
like brothers they weep for you—like sisters.
They will tear out their hair for you."

NOTES TO TABLET VIII, COLUMN i

The column contains much that resembles the Western "pastoral elegy," known to English readers in works like John Milton's "Lycidas." The tradition is Greek, but the elements of the genre here are a good deal older than Greek literature. The lament intensifies in the next column.

1. The formula opening the column, "with the first glow of dawn" *(mimmû šēri ina namāri),* with its vaguely Homeric ring, is used later on in exactly the same form (VIII.ii.28; VIII.iii.8; VIII.v.45; XI.ii.48; XI.iii.96). The formula may be unique to the Gilgamesh series (Tigay, 9, 231).

3–6. A good example of poetic variation, using different animals in different relationships along with variation in word order. The animal in line 5 may be the onager, which raised Enkidu "with their milk" (Tigay, 200).

7. Even more than the animals in the first group of lines, the motif of paths, meadows, and rivers mourning the death of Enkidu illustrates the "pathetic fallacy," common in the pastoral elegy. Of course, it is particularly appropriate to Enkidu, who not only was a shepherd (or guardian of shepherds) at the beginning of his human education, but was one with nature before that.

11. It may be that the reference is not to Kur ("mountain," often with mythological associations), but "grain of the hills" (reading *še* with Paul Haupt rather than *kur,* the usual reading today). Possibly it is an image that relates to the elders moving their fingers in a blessing, from the previous line.

18. The Ulaj is a river in Elam, that is, Iran. Since the poem does not feature a journey to the east, into Elam, the line may recall the earliest Sumerian Gilgamesh stories set there.

19. Pairing the Ulaj with the famous Euphrates, which winds down from Turkey, through Syria and through Iraq, may be a poetic expression for all the lands, east and west, the men had dominated.

20. The Sultantepe text followed in this passage is full of scribal errors (Tigay, 132), but the use of enjambed or run-on lines may be a deliberate poetic variation on the usual end-stopped lines.

24–30. The last lines are rather obscure, but the woman who offers prepared food and drink and anoints Enkidu with oil (in the manner of a cultic treatment of images) appears to be identified with the prostitute who gave Enkidu the capacity to experience human life. Note the use again of the *kimin*-sign, *etc.*

Column ii

"Listen to me, Elders. Hear me out, *me*.   1
I [have been] to [you], Enkidu, your mother, your father; I will
    weep for you in the wilderness.   1a
For Enkidu, for my friend, I weep like a wailing woman,   2
howling bitterly.
[He was] the axe at my side, the bow at my arm,
the dagger in my belt, the shield in front of me,
my festive garment, my splendid attire . . .

An evil has risen up and robbed me.

Friend, you chased the driving mule, the wild ass of the
    mountain, panther of the steppe.
Enkidu, you chased the driving mule, the wild ass of the
    mountain, panther of the steppe.   9
Then we came together, we went up into the mountains;
we caught the Bull of Heaven, we killed it;
we brought down Humbaba who lived in the cedar forest.

Now what is this sleep that has taken hold of you?   13
You've become dark. You can't hear me."

And he—he does not lift his head.   15
"I touched his heart, it does not beat."

He covered the friend's face like a bride's.

"Like an eagle I circled over him."   18

Like a lioness whose whelps are lost
he paces back and forth.
He tears and messes his rolls of hair.

He tears off and throws down his fine clothes like things
    unclean.   22

Then Gilgamesh issued a call through the land: "Artisan!
Metalworker, goldsmith, engraver! Make for my friend . . ."

Then he fashioned an image of his friend, of the friend's own
    stature.

"[Enkidu], of lapis lazuli is your chest, of gold your body."
————

When something of light had dawned, Gilgamesh   23
. . .

NOTES TO TABLET VIII, COLUMN ii

The column breaks off after line 23, which begins a new episode. (A line divides lines 22 and 23 on the tablet. The formula used in VIII.i.1 is used again to signal a narrative break.)

1–14. The elegy begun in VIII.i continues to this point. The personal pronoun is stressed in line 1. The term for "friend" in line 2 is *ibru*, the most important of the synonyms.

9–12. In Gilgamesh's summary of Enkidu's life, note the reversal of sequence, citing the Bull of Heaven first—as if interposing line 11 between the frame of the mountains/cedar forest, chiasmus rather than an error in the narrative.

13. The motif of sleep is literalized in the sleep-contest in XI.v.199–vi.228. Note the explicit comparison of sleep and death in X.vi.33.

15–16. The Su'tantepe text so varies the lines, from third person to first person.

18–22. First through language, which associates Gilgamesh with an animal, and then gesture, likening Gilgamesh to an animal grieving, the identification of Gilgamesh and Enkidu becomes increasingly evident. Messing the hair and ripping off clothes—traditional gestures of mourning in the Ancient Near East—literalize the association between grief and a return to the wild. Numbering lines after 22 is tricky, since a second text has been patched in at this point.

23. A line drawn on the tablet would seem to indicate a new episode begins at this point.

Column iii

"In a bed of honor I will give you rest.   1
I've placed you on a [peaceful seat on the left].
The princes of earth are [commanded to kiss your feet].

I will have the people [of Uruk] weep, [mourning you].
Whores and heroes [will weep].

And after you, I [will cover my body with unshorn hair]:
I will put on a dog-skin [and roam the wilderness]."

When something of the beginning of light came, [Gilgamesh] . . .
He loosened his wide belt . . .
. . . effigy (?) . . .
. . .

NOTES TO TABLET VIII, COLUMN iii

Little remains of the column. Gilgamesh commits himself to do what Shamash had told Enkidu he would do (VII.iii.33–48). Another episode begins in line 8, but the column breaks off. The mourning of Enkidu continues.

1–7. The lines recall VII.iii.41–48.

Column iv

. . .   38
. . . his heart is not sick   39
. . .
. . .
. . . land of Shamash, exposed to the sun
. . . world-wide (?)
. . . he will go by his side
. . . alabaster
official exposed . . . before wide-ranging Shamash,
official . . . putting (something) out on the ground
. . . may he go by his side
. . . whose [chest?] is of lapis lazuli
. . . inlaid with carnelian.   50

NOTES TO TABLET VIII, COLUMN iv

Only isolated words are visible until the end of the column: "for my friend," "your sword," "like [stone]," "for Bibbi" (the planet Mercury), "he saw the tools"(?), "alabaster," "his garment," "for his friend." Then a list with the specifics missing, but including the notation "amount of gold, ditto." Presumably the passage deals with the funereal statue of Enkidu. The bottom of the column appears to deal with rituals concerning the statue.

Column v

. . .

. . . his name we . . .   41
. . . judge of the Anunnaki . . .

Gilgamesh, when he heard this,
he fashioned an image of the river . . .

When something of light had dawned, Gilgamesh formed . . .
He brought out a large table of *elammakum*-wood,
filled a lapis lazuli bowl with cream.
. . . he decorated it and offered it to Shamash.   49
. . .

NOTES TO TABLET VIII, COLUMN v

All but the last few lines (41–49) are lost. Someone is speaking, and Gilgamesh fashions an image. Then the opening formula (45) is used to move to the next episode. Gilgamesh forms something, takes out a table of precious wood, and makes an offering of cream to Shamash.

One line at the bottom of the column is missing. Column vi is missing entirely. Apparently the rituals and mourning for Enkidu end in column vi, for in Tablet IX Gilgamesh begins his journey.

Nothing of column vi has been found.

TABLET IX

Column i

Gilgamesh for his friend Enkidu
bitterly cried. He roamed the hills.   2
"Me! Will I too not die like Enkidu?
Sorrow has come into my belly.
I fear death; I roam over the hills.
I will seize the road; quickly I will go
to the house of Utnapishtim, offspring of Ubaratutu.   7
I approach the entrance of the mountain at night.
Lions I see, and I am terrified.
I lift my head to pray to the moon god Sîn: 10
For . . . a dream I go to the gods in prayer:
'. . . preserve me!' "

. . . though he lay down [to sleep], the dream did not come.   13
. . . he loved life.

Gilgamesh takes up the axe in his hand;   15
he drew [the weapon] from his belt
[and] like an arrow . . . he fell among them.
He struck . . . smashing them,
. . . [enjoying] it.
He threw . . .
he [guarded] . . .
Second . . .
He lifted . . .
. . .   24

                                                                     50

NOTES TO TABLET IX, COLUMN i

The beginning of the column is the conclusion of the mourning for En-kidu. Gilgamesh is increasingly bitter, and he sees that he too will die. The passage in which he states his intention to see the sage Utnapishtim will be repeated at each stage of the journey he begins here. The frustration of Gilgamesh leads him to act in an increasingly violent way, a characteristic that will be marked by others on the journey. Unfortunately, the middle of the column is quite broken, and the end of the column is lost.

2. Tigay (7) has noted the thematic unity of the late version in the use of the motif of "roaming the steppe" *(ṣēra rapādu)*. It was used first of Enkidu when he lived in the wild (I.iv.35), then predicted of Gilgamesh (VII.iii.48), confirmed as a commitment by Gilgamesh (VIII.iii.7), begun here and repeated later (in line 5; X.i.38, 45; X.iii.14; and X.v.5). The expression is a way of indicating his identification with the dead Enkidu.

7. For Utnapishtim, see I.i.40. He is identified in the text as the son of Ubaratutu.

10. We add the epithet to the god Sîn for ease in identification; he is the moon god (Sumerian Nanna). The name forms the first element in the poet's theophoric name, Sîn-leqi-unninnī. The moon god is rarely mentioned in *Gilgamesh*, though he is introduced into Tablet XII.iii.62–69 in one of the striking departures from the Sumerian original of that tablet.

13–14. The lines are unfortunately quite broken. If, as seems to be the case, Gilgamesh asks the gods, especially Sîn, for a dream (10–12) to advise him, and no dream comes to him, the violence that follows (15–20) makes sense. Gilgamesh's frustration is the reason for it. (Note his terror of lions in line 9.) Line 14, which returns to an earlier motif, "enjoying life" *(iḫtedu balaṭu)*, if it refers either to Gilgamesh or Enkidu, is strikingly ironic, considering the slaughter that follows. It may even be that Gilgamesh enjoys the slaughter (19). The passage thus pursues the identification of Gilgamesh and the violent Enkidu. (Some think, however, that in line 13 a dream *does* come to Gilgamesh.)

Column ii

[Gilgamesh] came to the mountains whose name is Mashu;   1
approached the twin peaks
which guard each day the coming and going of Shamash.
Their tops reach the vault of heaven;
below, their feet touch the underworld.   5
Scorpion-people guard the gate,   6
whose terror is awesome and whose glance is death:
their grim aura is cast [up the slope of] the mountains.
In the going of Shamash and in the coming of Shamash, they
    guard him.
When he saw them, the face of Gilgamesh went dark at their
    dreadfulness.   10/11
He took hold of his wits and went up to them.

The Scorpion-man calls to his woman: 13
"The one who has come to us, his body is the flesh of gods."   14

The woman said to the Scorpion-man:
"Two-thirds of him is god, and one-third human."   16

The Scorpion-man calls to Gilgamesh—
to the part-god he speaks [these] words:
["Why have you undertaken] this long journey?   19
[Why have you] come here before me,
[to this place] whose crossings are troublesome?
[The purpose of your journey] I wish to penetrate;
[how] your . . . is established
. . . I would want to know.
. . . "   24

     50

NOTES TO TABLET IX, COLUMN ii

Gilgamesh's long and strange journey is under way. At the gate of the twin mountains he encounters the scorpion-people, who inquire about him. The end of their address to Gilgamesh and the beginning of his response to them are lost. In the next column, Gilgamesh's response ends.

1. The twin mountains—the name means "twins"—are described in the text. Already Gilgamesh has penetrated beyond the world appropriate to humans. Note the importance given Shamash in the description, for Mashu is the mountain of the rising and setting sun.

5. A special, poetic term for the netherworld is used here, Arallu.

6. The compound making up "Scorpion-man" is like the ones used earlier of Enkidu, the Stalker, and others ([noun] + "human"), *aqrabu-amēlu*, though it is read *girtablilu*.

10. Our line conflates a line and a half-line usually numbered 11.

13. Note that the guardians are paired male and female (as later Utnapishtim and his wife). Although usually identified as the "wife" of the Scorpion-man, the term used, *sinništu* ("woman"), is unusual. Elsewhere other terms are used for "wife" in *Gilgamesh*: *ḫīrtu*, *aššatu*, and *marḫītu*. This term would seem to be characteristic of the late version. On the significance of the term in *Gilgamesh*, see Tigay (232–233).

14. The phrase *šēr ilāni zumuršu*, "his body is the flesh of the gods," is another of the expressions indicating Gilgamesh's unique status as god and man.

16. The line recalls the earliest (I.ii.1) description of Gilgamesh in these terms.

19. The question underscores what the late version sees as the most significant of Gilgamesh's adventures, this perilous journey (I.i.6).

Column iii

...
...
"I have come on account of Utnapishtim, my elder,   3
who stands in the assembly [of the gods, and has found life].   4
Death and life [I wish to know]."   5

The Scorpion-man shapes his mouth and speaks,
saying to Gilgamesh:
"Never has a mortal man done that, Gilgamesh.
Over the mountain, no one has travelled the remote path,
for twelve double-hours it takes to reach its center,
and thick is its darkness; there is no light.   11
To the going out of Shamash . . .
To the entering in of Shamash . . .
To the entering in of Shamash . . .   14
I cause to go out . . .
I cause to [enter] . . ."
...   17

                                                                                                             50

NOTES TO TABLET IX, COLUMN iii

The end of Gilgamesh's response to the Scorpion-man has survived. The column has something of the Scorpion-man's description of the harrowing journey Gilgamesh is attempting, one that no mortal has ever accomplished (line 8). The rest of the column is broken. At the beginning of column iv, however, Gilgamesh and the Scorpion-man are still speaking with one another.

3. Literally "Utnapishtim, my father." The purpose is already to reach Utnapishtim, who is allowed into the assembly of the gods.

4. "And has found life" is something of an explanation of the sage's name.

5. In the simplest possible way, the poet points the theme: to know life and death *(mutu u balāṭu).*

11. As the Scorpion-man describes the journey, it is much like the first part of the longer journey (IX.iv–v).

14. Note that the rising and setting of the sun are the primary means of describing the journey. The prominence of Shamash is underscored by the exact repetition here of the previous line.

Column iv

. . .
"Because of pain [in my belly] . . .   33
[Though my face is wasted] by cold or [heat] . . .
I will go, sighing . . .
Now [therefore open the gate of the mountain]."

The Scorpion-man [shaped his mouth, saying]
go Gilgamesh [the king] . . .
"Go, Gilgamesh; [enter into]
the mountains, the twins . . .
the mountains, hills [of Shamash] . . .
Go safely . . .
[For you] the gate of the mountain [is open]."

When Gilgamesh heard this,
[he gave heed] to the word [of the Scorpion-man];
[he took] the road of Shamash, the sun.   46

When he had gone one double-hour,   47
thick is the darkness, there is no light;
he can see neither behind him nor ahead of him.

When he had gone two double-hours,   50

NOTES TO TABLET IX, COLUMN iv

The first part of the column is missing, but it is clear that the exchange between the Scorpion-man and Gilgamesh continues. Finally, Gilgamesh persuades the Scorpion-man to open the gates to the mountain, and Gilgamesh enters into a terrible darkness. The journey has only begun when the column ends.

46. The path he takes is the sun's road, *harran* *ilušamaš*.

47–50. The journey is described in stages of *bēru* or "double-hours," all of which is travelled in darkness until the nearing of eleven double-hours, when light begins to shine into the darkness. At each stage the poet marks the movement by exact repetition, without variation (except for the number). The technique is that of Sumerian poetry. It is characteristic of the late version to reintroduce such ancient Sumerian practice, as if he were aware of the archaizing involved. The column ends just as the second stage is being described.

Column v

[thick is the darkness, there is no light;   1
he can see neither behind him nor ahead of him.]
. . .   3

. . .   22
When he had gone four double-hours,   23
thick is [the darkness, there is no light];
he can see [neither behind him nor ahead of him].

[When he had gone] five double-hours,
thick is the [darkness, there is no light];
he can see neither behind him nor ahead of him.

When he had gone six double-hours,
thick is the darkness, there is no light;
he can see neither behind him nor ahead of him.

When he had gone seven double-hours,
thick is the darkness, there is no light;
he can see neither behind him nor ahead of him.

At eight double-hours . . . heat flares up in him;   35
thick is the darkness, there is no light;
he can see neither behind him nor ahead of him.

At nine double-hours . . . the north wind   38
[bit into] his face:
thick is the darkness, there is no light;
he can see neither behind him nor ahead of him.

———

At ten double-hours
. . . approaches
. . . of the double-hour.

At the nearing of eleven double-hours, light breaks out.   45
At the nearing of twelve double-hours, the light is steady.   46
He sees the grove of stones and heads for [it].   47
Carnelian it bears as its fruit,
[and] vines hang from it, good to see,
leaves formed of lapis lazuli,
the fruit it bears alluring to the eye.   51

NOTES TO TABLET IX, COLUMN v

The strange thing about this column is the long gap at the beginning. IX.iv.47–50 begins a sequence that uses triplets of exact repetition to describe the stages of Gilgamesh's journey. The first, probably the second, fourth, fifth, sixth, and seventh stages are identical. Only in eight (line 35) does the pattern break, and only there for one line. Then the pattern quickly breaks down: nine (38–41) adds a line; ten is broken, but clearly different from the rest; eleven and twelve are marked by only one line each (45–46). With such effective use of exact repetition (followed by the elegant breaking of the pattern in the late stages), the question poses itself: why is there a gap of twenty-two lines at the beginning of the column? Paul Haupt's (pp. 62–63, #32) and R. Campbell Thompson's (Plates 36 and 37) handcopies of the tablet (K2360 + K3060) show the situation clearly enough. If only the second stage (two lines) and the third stage (three more lines) are described, what happens in the gap? There is only one conspicuous and baffling episode missing in the late version that is recounted in the Old Babylonian texts of Gilgamesh's journey: a dialogue with Shamash (Tigay, 99). In Gilg. Me. i (Tigay, 97–98) an unknown speaker addresses Gilgamesh, and then Shamash speaks to him before he encounters the Barmaid and the Boatman. There is no evidence of this in the late version, and it would seem unlikely that he would encounter Shamash in the heart of darkness. But an encounter with some figure at this point in the late version would be a possibility. Expanded second and third stages would be another possibility.

35. Gilgamesh becomes feverish. The pattern is retained in the second and third lines of the triplet.

38. The north wind chills Gilgamesh. The pattern is expanded to four lines, but the last two lines are identical with earlier stages.

45. Light appears at the eleventh double-hour, literally the "shadow of Shamash," *ṣilām ilušamaš.*

46. At the twelfth and last station, light, *namirtu,* is established brightly, *šaknat.*

47–51. Gilgamesh enters a garden of precious stones, like an earthly paradise.

Column vi

NOTES TO TABLET IX, COLUMN vi

No single line can be reconstructed from the fragmentary remains of the column. The subject is apparently still a description of the Garden of the Gods. R. Campbell Thompson, *The Epic of Gilgamesh, A New Translation* (London: Luzac, 1928), p. 43, suggests a parallel Old Babylonian version in which "warrior" Shamash tells Gilgamesh that the life he seeks cannot be found, and Gilgamesh asks,

> "Shall I, after I roam up and down o'er the waste as a wand'rer,
> Lay my head in the bowels of earth, and throughout the years
>   slumber
> Ever and aye? Let mine eyes see the Sun and be sated with
>   brightness,
> (Yea, for) the darkness is (banish'd) afar, if wide be the brightness.
> When will the man who is dead (ever) look on the light of the
>   Sunshine?"

The identification of light with life is intriguing indeed. Tigay (98) adds a note from another Old Babylonian Gilgamesh text that says, "only the gods [live] forever with Shamash." Tigay points out that the Old Babylonian dialogue with Shamash is not to be found in Tablet X of the late version, and there is no room for it here in Tablet IX (99).

TABLET X

Column i

Siduri the Barmaid, who dwells at the lip of the sea 1
and sits . . .
For her is made the jug; for her is made the mashing-bowl
    of gold.
She is veiled with a veil . . .

Gilgamesh made his way to her . . .
dressed in skins . . .
possessing the flesh of the gods in [his body]; 7
sorrow is in his belly; 8
his face like that of a man who goes on a long journey.

The Barmaid looked into the distance. 10
She talked to her heart, said these words—
she took counsel with herself—
"Possibly this one is a killer.
Where is he headed . . . ?"

Seeing him, the Barmaid barred her door.
Her gate she closed; she shot [the bolt].

And he, Gilgamesh, at hearing her,
lifted his pointed staff, set [himself before the door].
Gilgamesh spoke to her, to the Barmaid.
"Barmaid, what do you see [that you bar your door]?
Your gate you shut. You've shot the bolt.
I will smash down your door, [break the gate down] . . ."
. . .
. . .
. . .
. . .
. . .

. . .
. . .
. . .
. . .

The Barmaid says to him, to Gilgamesh: 32
"Why is your strength wasted, your face sunken?
Why has evil fortune entered your heart, done in your looks?
There is sorrow in your belly.
Your face is like that of a man who has gone on a long journey.
Your face is weathered by cold and heat
because you roam the wilderness in search of a wind-puff."

Gilgamesh spoke to her, to the Barmaid.
"Barmaid, it is not that my strength is wasted, my face sunken,
not that evil fortune has entered my heart, done in my looks.
It is not the sorrow in my belly,
not that I look like a man who has gone on a long journey,
nor that cold and heat have weathered my features—
not for that do I roam the wilderness in quest of a wind-puff,
        but because of
my friend, companion, who chased the wild ass, the panther of the
        steppe—
Enkidu, friend, loved-one, who chased the wild ass, panther of the
        steppe.
We overcame everything: climbed the mountain,
captured the Bull of Heaven and killed him,
brought Humbaba to grief, who lives in the cedar forest;
entering the mountain gates we slew lions.   51

NOTES TO TABLET X, COLUMN i

The first line of the column is known from the colophon at the end of IX.vi. This is the first of three meetings Gilgamesh has in Tablet X. After the Barmaid, he will encounter Urshanabi the Boatman, and finally Utnapishtim. All will give him the same advice: his search is futile. The Old Babylonian parallel contains an encounter with Shamash before this one as well. (See notes to Tablet IX.v–vi.) Tigay (95–100), who has compared versions of Gilgamesh's encounters on his journey very carefully, points out the high degree of homogenization in the late version, where one encounter echoes the others, rather than maintaining their individuality as they do in the Old Babylonian parallels.

1. Siduri, whose name is written with the divine determinative, is called a *sabitu*, or "barmaid," throughout the episode. She is a manifestation of Ishtar.

7. A repetition of IX.ii.14.

8–9. Another of the sequences that show the thematic unity of *Gilgamesh*. Variations of this doublet appear in I.ii.49–50, IX.i.4–5, and five other places in Tablet X.

10–13. The manner in which the Barmaid sees Gilgamesh is almost identical to the way Utnapishtim spots him (X.iv.12–14). Possibly the Urshanabi episode contained the same repeated lines (Tigay, 99). Note that she worries that he may be a killer, *muna'iru*.

32–38. This passage shows the highly stylized, repetitive composition typical of the late version. Gilgamesh's response to her does as well.

51. Note the motif of Enkidu and Gilgamesh slaying lions, an episode not narrated in *Gilgamesh*.

Column ii

"My friend whom I love dearly underwent with me all hardships.   1
Enkidu whom I love dearly underwent with me all hardships.
The fate of mankind overtook him.
Six days and seven nights I wept over him
until a worm fell out of his nose.   5/6
Then I was afraid.
In fear of death I roam the wilderness. The case of my friend lies
      heavy in me.
On a remote path I roam the wilderness. The case of my friend
      Enkidu lies heavy in me.
On a long journey I wander the steppe.
How can I keep still? How can I be silent?
The friend I loved has turned to clay. Enkidu, the friend I love,
      has turned to clay.
Me, shall I not lie down like him,
never again to move?"

Gilgamesh spoke to her, to the Barmaid:
"Now, Barmaid, which is the way to Utnapishtim?   16
What are its landmarks? Give them to me. Give its signs to me.
If it is possible, let me cross the sea;
If it is possible, let me traverse the wilderness."

The Barmaid spoke to him, to Gilgamesh.
"Gilgamesh, there has never been a crossing,   21
and none from the beginning of days has been able to cross
      the sea.
None but Shamash crosses the sea; apart from Shamash, no one
      crosses.
Painful is the crossing, troublesome the road,
and everywhere the waters of death stream across its face.
Even if you, Gilgamesh, cross the sea
when you arrive at the waters of death, what would you do?

There, Gilgamesh, lives Urshanabi, boatman to Utnapishtim. 28
The things of stone are with him. In the heart of the forest he
    picks up the Urnu-snakes. 29
Show him your face.
If it is possible, cross with him. If it is not possible, come back." 31

Gilgamesh, hearing this,
lifted the axe in his hand,
drew the dagger from his belt. He crept along the path and went
    down to them.
Like a lance he fell on them;
in the heart of the forest he beset himself.
Urshanabi saw the flash of the dagger,
heard the axe . . .
Then Gilgamesh hits its head . . .
seizes its wings, [presses down on] its chest,
and the stone things [he loaded] in the boat,
[the stone things] without which [there is no crossing death's
    waters],
[no crossing] the broad sea
on the waters [of death] . . .
. . . to the river
. . . the boat
. . . on the bank
. . . the boatman
. . . descended (?)
. . . your . . . to him. 50

NOTES TO TABLET X, COLUMN ii

Like Circe, the goddess who gives Odysseus advice on crossing the river of death to consult with the prophet (*Odyssey*, X.503–540), Siduri dispenses the advice Gilgamesh will need to find Utnapishtim. What is missing from the column is advice of a very different sort, quite appropriate to the Barmaid (and to Circe, note *Odyssey*, X.455–465), advice conspicuous in an Old Babylonian parallel and conspicuously absent in the late version:

> 6. As for you, Gilgamesh, let your belly be full,
> 7. Make merry day and night.
> 8. Of each day make a feast of rejoicing,
> 9. Day and night dance and play!
> 10. Let your garments be sparkling fresh,
> 11. Your head be washed; bathe in water.
> 12. Pay heed to a little one that holds on to your hand.
> 13. Let a spouse delight in your bosom,
> 14. For this is the task of [woman].

(Translation: Tigay, 168)

Tigay (95–103) emphasizes, by comparing parallel accounts, the tendency in the late version to reduce the individuality of the scenes along Gilgamesh's journey. Everywhere the late version prefers homogenization and repetition. (Note the doublets 1–2, 7–8, 18–19; wherever Gilgamesh mentions "the friend," he repeats the line or half-line, as in 11, with the variation, "Enkidu.") The poem gains in solemnity with this Sumerian-style echoing, but it may, as Tigay suggests (100–103), lose something of the vigor of, especially, the Old Babylonian *The Epic of Gilgamesh*.

Typical of the late version also, the column concludes one episode in the middle of the column and begins another. (One wonders why the journey from the Garden of the Gods to the dwelling-place of the Barmaid is not narrated in the short column, IX.vi, the way the journey from her place to Urshanabi's is in this column.) The Barmaid's advice includes not only the necessity of finding Utnapishtim's boatman, Urshanabi, but also refers to "things of stone" and "Urnu-snakes," obviously needed in some way either to force Urshanabi to take Gilgamesh across the waters or to serve as magical tokens on the journey. The nature of these objects is not known completely.

1–14. Gilgamesh will repeat his lament in exactly the same terms to Urshanabi and Utnapishtim. Death is "the fate of mankind," *šimāt amē-lūtim,* in line 3. Line 5 actually conflates 5 and 6 here.

16–19. Tigay (96) points out the exact repetition of the lines in X.iii.33–35.

21–31. The Barmaid's advice. Note that no one crosses the sea but the sun; no human has made the passage. Passage involves crossing the waters of death, *mē muti* (25). Tigay (115) compares lines 26–27 and a Hittite parallel.

28. Urshanabi is identified in the text as the boatman to Utnapishtim.

29. In an Old Babylonian parallel, the Boatman explains that the "Stone Things" carried him across the waters so that the waters of death would not touch him (Tigay, 114); in a Hittite parallel they are identified as "stone images."

31–50. Much of the column is broken at the end, and many of the details are obscure. In 34, Gilgamesh goes down to "them," and he attacks "them." Line 36 may refer to Urshanabi's dwelling in the forest, or it could be something else dwelling there. Gilgamesh attacks "its head" and pins back "its wings" (39–40). Are these references to the *urnu*-snakes? to Urshanabi? to protective guardians of the "things of stone"? The violence is characteristic of Gilgamesh in this phase, but the details are not clear; and as the next column opens, Gilgamesh is speaking to Urshanabi.

Column iii

Urshanabi spoke to him, to Gilgamesh:
"Why are your cheeks wasted, why is your face sunken?
Why has evil fortune entered your heart, done in your looks?
There is sorrow in your belly.
Your face is like that of a man who has gone on a long journey.
Your face is weathered by cold and heat
because you roam the wilderness in search of a wind-puff."

Gilgamesh spoke to him, to the Boatman.
"Urshanabi, it is not that my strength is wasted, my face sunken,
not that evil fortune has entered my heart, done in my looks.
It is not the sorrow in my belly,
not that I look like a man who has gone on a long journey,
nor that cold and heat have weathered my features—
not for that do I roam the wilderness in quest of a wind-puff, but
    [because of]
my friend, companion, who chased the wild ass, the panther of
    the steppe—
Enkidu, friend, loved-one, who chased the wild ass, panther of
    the steppe.
We overcame everything: climbed the mountain,
captured the Bull of Heaven and killed him,
brought Humbaba to grief, who lives in the cedar forest;
entering the mountain gates we slew lions;
my friend whom I love dearly underwent with me all hardships.
The fate of mankind overtook him.
Six days and seven nights I wept over him
until a worm fell out of his nose.
Then I was afraid.
In fear of death I roam the wilderness. The case of my friend lies
    heavy in me.
On a remote path I roam the wilderness. The case of my friend
    Enkidu lies heavy in me.
On a long journey I wander the steppe.

How can I keep still? How can I be silent?
The friend I loved has turned to clay. Enkidu, the friend I love,
    has turned to clay.
Me, shall I not lie down like him,
never again to move?"

Urshanabi spoke to him, to Gilgamesh:
"Your heart is filled with sadness, your features are worn;
there is sorrow in your belly.
Your face is like that of a man who has been on a long journey.
With cold and heat your face is weathered.
You roam the steppe in search of a wind-puff."

Gilgamesh said to him, to Urshanabi,
"Why should my cheeks not be wasted, my face shrunken,
my heart sad, features worn?
Why should there not be sorrow in my belly?
Now, Urshanabi, what is the road to Utnapishtim?   33
What are its landmarks? Give them to me; give me the signs.
If it is possible, let me cross the sea; if it is not possible, let me
    roam the land."

Urshanabi said to him, to Gilgamesh,
"Your own hands, Gilgamesh, have hindered the crossing.   37
You have destroyed the stone things and have picked up the
    Urnu-snakes.
The stone things are broken; the Urnu-snakes not [in the forest].
Lift up, Gilgamesh, the axe in your hand: 40
go down to the forest, [cut] poles of sixty cubits;
paint bitumen on the sockets; bring them to me."

Gilgamesh, when he heard him,
lifted the axe in his hand, drew the dagger from his belt,
went down to the forest [and cut] poles of sixty cubits.
Bitumen he applied to the sockets, [then] carried them to him.
Gilgamesh and Urshanabi boarded the boat.
The boat went out, they threw it on the waves.
A voyage of a month and fifteen days they had travelled by the
    third day.
Urshanabi arrived at the waters of death.   50

NOTES TO TABLET X, COLUMN iii

The column, in stately repetition of the encounter with the Barmaid, brings to a conclusion the encounter with Urshanabi in the forest. With Urshanabi's advice, Gilgamesh cuts poles to help in crossing the waters of death.

33–35. Compare X.ii.16–19.

37–39. Note the point: ironically, Gilgamesh has hindered the crossing by destroying the stone things and picking up the Urnu-snakes. Possibly this means that a crossing such as Gilgamesh will make will never be made again.

40–50. Tigay (115–117) compares this passage with a Hittite parallel and a brief Old Babylonian text. The poles will be needed to cross the waters of death.

Column iv

Urshanabi spoke to him, to Gilgamesh.
"Take care, Gilgamesh . . .
Do not let your hand touch the waters of death . . ."

A second time, a third and a fourth, Gilgamesh heaves with the
poles.   4
A fifth, a sixth, and a seventh, Gilgamesh heaves with the poles.
An eighth, ninth, and tenth, Gilgamesh heaves with the poles.
An eleventh, a twelfth, Gilgamesh heaves with the poles.
In twice sixty times Gilgamesh had worn the poles to nothing.

He broke [Urshanabi's] belt, in order that . . .   9
Gilgamesh stripped off [Urshanabi's] covering.
He made him stand with his wings spread.

Utnapishtim looked on from afar.   12
He made his heart hear the words he spoke,
taking counsel with himself:
"Why have the stone things of the boat been smashed,
and one who is not its master rides in the boat?
The one who comes is not one of mine, and . . .
I see, but I do not . . .
I see, but . . .
I see . . .
. . . the animal (?) . . .
. . ."   22

                                                                           50

NOTES TO TABLET X, COLUMN iv

At least half of the column is lost. The first part continues the journey across the waters of death (1–11), and the men are within view of their destination. The sage Utnapishtim, in one of the shifts in point of view, sees the boat and notices the stranger aboard. He also notes that the "stone things" have been smashed.

4–8. The type of boat used, its size and the like, is not indicated. To get across the waters of death, Gilgamesh uses the punting poles he had cut and prepared in X.iii. Possibly the boat is like a *mushhuf* or a *tarada* used even today by the Marsh Arabs of southern Iraq to get through the shallow marshes. Often such punting poles are employed. See examples in Michael Spencer, "The Marsh Arabs Revisited," *Aramco World Magazine*, 33 (1982), 32–36.

9–11. The punting poles are not enough, and Gilgamesh uses a stratagem to complete the journey. The lines are rather obscure, and are usually taken to mean that Gilgamesh is wearing a shirt of some sort and uses it like a sail. The reference to wings in line 11 suggests to us that Urshanabi is depicted as winged, and that he is forced by Gilgamesh to use his wings as a sail. This is admittedly speculative; the only thing approaching evidence is the curious reference to wings in X.ii.40. We suggest that the attack Gilgamesh made in the forest was on Urshanabi himself, and that the stone things are not the only things violated by Gilgamesh.

12–14. The introduction is similar to X.i.10–12.

Column v

. . .

. . . "animal

. . . not like

. . . before me

. . . [one who] roams the steppe,

[chased] the panther of the steppe,

. . . *etc.*

we climbed the mountain,

captured the Bull of Heaven and killed him,

[brought Humbaba to grief], who lives in the cedar forest;

[entering the mountain gates we slew] lions;

[my friend whom I love dearly underwent with me all hardships.]

[The fate of mankind], *etc.*

[Six days and seven nights] I wept over him,

[not burying him]

[until a worm dropped out of his nose].

[I roamed the steppe]

[I put skins on] over me [and] set out on a long journey through the
     wilderness.

. . . my friend *(etc.);* the long road . . .

[How could I keep silent?]

[My friend,] the one I love dearly, has turned to dirt—Enkidu . . .

Me, will I not lie down like him and never move?"

Gilgamesh says to him, to Utnapishtim: 23

"I said, 'I will go to Utnapishtim, the remote one about whom
     they tell tales.'

I turned, wandering, over all the lands.

I crossed uncrossable mountains.

I travelled all the seas.

No real sleep has calmed my face.

I have worn myself out in sleeplessness; my flesh is filled with
     grief.

I had not yet arrived at the house of the Barmaid when my
     clothing was used up.
I killed bear, hyena, lion, panther, tiger, stag and [ibex]—wild
     beasts and creeping things of the wilderness.
I ate their flesh, covered myself with their skins.
She barred her gate against me. I slept in dirt and bitumen.
[I lay down with animals, I touched . . .]
[I am] the unlucky one, the fated . . . "

Utnapishtim says to him, to Gilgamesh: 36
"Why, Gilgamesh, are you full of woe?—
you who have been made of the flesh of the gods and man?
You, when your father and mother made you—
when [you], Gilgamesh, were [conceived] for the Fool—
in the Assembly of the Gods she lay down on the couch:
She was given to him, for mud is given butter,
good flour for poor, which like . . .
. . . swift like . . .
and he [clings to her] like a belt,
good flour given for poor . . .
. . . swift like . . .
like . . .
since there is no . . .
There is no word of advice . . ."   50

NOTES TO TABLET X, COLUMN v

1–22. Gilgamesh first tells Utnapishtim of his adventures with En-kidu and Enkidu's death, in much the same language as before.

23–35. Gilgamesh continues his account, in somewhat different terms. He tells of his intention from the start of his journey to reach Utnapishtim, describes his travels in a triplet using different verbs in each line (25–27), and emphasizes the sleep motif (28–29). Of his wanderings, only the encounter with the Barmaid is recalled by Gilgamesh (30–34), and his recollection is cast in terms more violent and savage than had been described in X.i. Killing animals, eating their flesh, covering himself with skins take Gilgamesh to the point of ultimate contact with the wild. He is forced to sleep in the dirt, to lay down with the animals. He calls himself *paddi'u*, the unlucky, the unfortunate one, fated *(išam-mat)* in some dreadful way.

38–50. In Utnapishtim's response to Gilgamesh, yet another version of Gilgamesh's conception is given, in response to Gilgamesh's concern for his fate. He has been made of *šīr ilāni u amēlūti*, "flesh of gods and mankind" (38). Utnapishtim's account is unfortunately much broken, but it seems to emphasize the enormous gap between the divine and human natures combined in the hero. The reference to the *lillu*, Fool, in line 40 may recall a tradition in which his human father is a fool, given to his goddess-mother in the Assembly of the Gods; or the exchange metaphors (mud/butter, good flour/poor flour) may simply indicate in a vivid way what a sacred marriage has produced. The account appears to end on a negative note.

Column vi

. . .   24

angry . . .

"Do we build a house forever? Do we seal a contract for all time?   26

Do brothers divide shares forever?

Does hostility last forever between enemies?

Does the river forever rise higher, bringing on floods?

Does the dragonfly [leave] its husk . . .

the face that looks at the face of Shamash?

From the beginning there is no permanence.

The sleeping and the dead, how like brothers they are!   33

Do they not both make a picture of death?

The man-as-he-was-in-the-beginning and the hero: [are they
      not the same] when they arrive at their fate?

The Anunnaki, in the Assembly of the Great Gods—

Mammetum with them, mother of Destiny—set the ends of things.

They settle death and life.

As for death, its time is hidden. The time of life is shown plain."   39

NOTES TO TABLET X, COLUMN vi

Whether Gilgamesh made a response to Utnapishtim's account of the hero's conception, or whether Utnapishtim continued his "advice" in the first half of X.vi is not known. The second half of the column brings the tablet to an end in a most decisive way with a terrible truth: there is no permanence. The questions Utnapishtim raises are in one sense rhetorical questions (26–29), but they indicate a kind of negative wisdom. Whatever humans may do to ensure a lasting condition (building houses, cutting contracts, dividing shares, even fighting), nothing lasts. The reference to floods (29) is particularly interesting, since it anticipates the great "secret" Utnapishtim will tell Gilgamesh, the story of the Flood. The following lines (30–31) may even suggest a kind of rebirth, but the key line is unfortunately broken.

33–39. The end of the short column makes the connection between the impermanence of things and death clear enough. The motif of sleep recurs in the comparison between sleep and death (33–34): they are like brothers, and they both draw the picture (ṣalmu) of death. Primal man, lullû, and the hero, eṭlu, illustrated in Enkidu and Gilgamesh, are alike subject to death (35). The universalizing character of Utnapishtim's wisdom is marked by the divine judges, the Anunnaki, who decree fate with the Great Goddess, Mammetum (37), who is called the maker or mother of fate, banat šimti. There is some question if the last line contrasts life and death, or if it is an ironic comment: "They hide the time of death— sometimes they do not." See Tigay (136).

A colophon after the last line of the column gives the catchline for Tablet XI, indicates that this is the tenth tablet of the Gilgamesh series; that it is not yet complete in ten tablets; that the text is written "according to its older version" and has been inspected and checked. The names of the scribes and a scribal tradition are then noted, as is the date of the copying of the tablets.

TABLET XI

Column i

Gilgamesh said to him, to Utnapishtim the remote one: 1
"I look at you, Utnapishtim.
Your features are no different than mine. I'm like you.
And *you* are not different, or I from you.
Your heart burns entirely for war-making,
yet there you are, lying on your back.
Tell me, how did you stand in the Assembly of the Gods, asking
     for life?"

Utnapishtim says to him, to Gilgamesh:
"I will uncover for you, Gilgamesh, a hidden thing,   9
tell you a secret of the gods.

In Shurippak—you know the city, I think—   11
set on the bank of the Euphrates—
the city was old and close to the gods.   13
The great gods stirred their hearts to make the Flood.
Mama was there, and the father, Anu,
and their counsellor, the warrior Enlil;
their throne-bearer Ninurta;
their inspector of canals Ennugi;
[and] Ea, lord of the clear eye, was present with them.

Their words he, [Ea,] repeats to the wall of reeds: 20
'Reed-wall, reed-wall! Wall, wall!
Reed-wall, listen! Wall, pay attention!
Man of Shuruppak, son of Ubaratutu,
Tear down the house. Build an ark.
Abandon riches. Seek life.
Scorn possessions, hold onto life.
Load the seed of every living thing into your ark,
the boat that you will build.

Let her measure be measured;
let her breadth and length be equal.
Cover it with a roof as the abyss is covered.'

I understood. I said to my lord, Ea,   32
'My lord, what you have thus spoken
I will do in praise of you.
As for me, I will need to answer the city, the people, and
    the elders.'

Ea shaped his mouth, saying,   36
saying to me, his servant,
'You, you may say this to them:
Enlil hates me—me!
I cannot live in your city
or turn my face toward the land which is Enlil's.
I will go down to the Abyss, to live with Ea, my lord.
He will make richness rain down on you—
the choicest birds, the rarest fish.
The land will have its fill of harvest riches.
At dawn bread
he will pour down on you—showers of wheat.' "   47

NOTES TO TABLET XI, COLUMN i

By convention, Tablet XI is lined consecutively, a practice followed here. But the division of the tablet into six major episodes of about fifty lines each, following Campbell Thompson's Plates 44–54, is also used here to indicate columns. Since scholarly discussions refer to the line numbers, for convenience the lines in this translation are numbered consecutively from 1 to 307, but with the addition of the column numbers.

1–7. Gilgamesh is astonished that the sage Utnapishtim looks no different from him, i.e., human (not necessarily that Utnapishtim retains a youthful look, although he lived before the Flood). Their limbs (3), *minītu*, are the same. The contrast between a heart given completely to battle (5) and lying on one's back (6) is tricky. It may refer to the warrior-hero as an image of "man" as opposed to the resting figures of the gods —and thus combine human and divine in Utnapishtim, the only man to live a life "like the gods" (XI.iv.193–194). (There is no indication in the story that Utnapishtim was known as a fighting man.) Standing in the Assembly of the Gods, seeking life, is precisely what Gilgamesh cannot do (XI.iv.197–198). "Seeking life" is probably a pun on the name Utnapishtim—if *balaṭa teš'u* continues the synonymy of *balaṭu* and *napištu*.

9–10. The lines recall the opening of I.i.4–6. Tigay points out that, while the Old Babylonian version contained Gilgamesh's journey to Utnapishtim, there is no evidence that it included a retelling of the Flood (214). The Flood narrative is one of the major additions of the late version to the *Gilgamesh*. The Flood itself has a complex history in Mesopotamian literature, for which see the Sumerian and Akkadian versions in W. G. Lambert and A. R. Millard, *Atra-ḥasīs; The Babylonian Story of the Flood*, with "The Sumerian Flood Story," by M. Civil (Oxford: Clarendon, 1969), and Tigay, esp. 214–240, which includes a number of parallel *Gilgamesh* and *Atra-ḥasīs* passages. The Flood narrative continues through XI.iv.196. Utnapishtim will tell Gilgamesh a hidden matter, *amat niṣirti*, and a secret of the gods, *pirišta ša ilāni*. Note the enjambment.

11. Utnapishtim's city is Shurippak (or Shuruppak, as it is spelled in line 23), modern Fara, a city located some seventy-five miles north and slightly west of Uruk and nearly one hundred miles south of Babylon. It

would not have been on the banks of the Euphrates (12) in the time of the late version. The lines suggest that ancient Shurippak no longer exists.

13–19. Note that the late version gives no reason for the Flood. The city is close to the gods (13), and ironically the "great gods" "moved their hearts" to bring on the Flood. Enlil will be blamed for it by Ishtar (XI.iv.167–168) and by Ea (XI.iv.179) as an irrational act. Tigay (231) notes that Anu is exempted from complicity in the Flood. Norman Habel, *Literary Criticism of the Old Testament* (Philadelphia: Fortress, 1971), pp. 31–42, distinguishes two accounts in the biblical Flood story, the Yahwist version and the Priestly Writer's version, both of which provide statements about the reason for the Flood (Genesis 6:5–8 and 6:9–13), the "wickedness of man" and the corrupt and violent earth. Of course, the monotheistic biblical account makes Yahweh/Elohim the only divine character in the narrative. Of the great gods who decide on the Flood, six are mentioned, but their degree of complicity is not indicated. Mama is mentioned with Anu (15), and she may be identified with Ishtar in the late version (XI.iii.16). Enlil is called both "counsellor" and "warrior," a combination used ironically by Ea later (XI.iv.178). Ninurta and Ennugi are identified in their traditional roles as throne-bearer and inspector of canals. The list ends with Ea, "lord of the clear eye" (19), said to be "present with them." Immediately he begins to subvert the plan.

20–31. Ea, whose name in Sumerian is Enki, speaks, not to Utna-pishtim but to the reed-wall—so as not to violate the agreement of the gods (XI.iv.186–187). Conflict between Enki and Enlil is a pattern found in Sumerian myths. In the biblical versions, the conflict is resolved within Yahweh/Elohim, who "remembers" Noah and has a change of heart at the destruction he has caused. Tigay (222–224) notes the way the late version of *Gilgamesh* expands this beyond the Old Babylonian parallel in *Atra-ḫasīs*. The late version adds the specific reference to Utnapishtim in line 23, makes explicit the order to carry the seed of all living things aboard the ship in line 27, and adds the comment on the "measure" of the ship in line 29. Otherwise the passage is very close to the Old Babylonian text. Ea's words may be proverbial and may establish an ethical norm, "Abandon riches. Seek life," and the like. But the instruction to dismantle the house and build a ship (24) (a change from the Old Babylonian, which has "Flee your house") may have a very practical purpose. Thor Heyerdahl, who built and sailed a 60-foot, 33-ton Sumerian boat made of reed-bundles, considered this to be advice on boat-building: use the technique and materials of building reed-houses, such as are found among the Marsh Arabs today, to build a great ship. See *The Tigris Expedition* (London: George Allen and Unwin, 1980), p. 34. The details of the ship are quite sketchy in this passage, as they are in the Old Babylonian parallel text. More is given in XI.ii.56—69, which has some parallels in common with the Priestly Writer's biblical account.

32—35. The late version does not ignore the problem that the community will be needed to build the boat, but the people must not know the secret that the Flood is coming. The ruse that follows, 36—47, is not found in the Old Babylonian parallel, and the motif is absent completely from the biblical accounts. See Tigay (224).

36—47. Ea's second speech to Utnapishtim includes the most famous examples of metaphoric language in Mesopotamian literature. The ambiguous language helps Utnapishtim tell the truth to the community without revealing the secret of the gods. The passage, especially the last lines, is richly ironic. The last two lines especially are metaphoric. Line 46 contains a pun on *kukku*, "bread," and *kukkû*, "darkness." Similarly *kibtu* in the last line can be "wheat" but also "misfortune." For a close analysis of the passage, see Appendix. The last two lines become the name of the event which they herald (see XI.ii.87 and 90).

Column ii

"When something of dawn appeared,   48
the people gathered about me,
. . .
. . .
. . . the young heroes
houses of . . . earthworks (?);
the little ones carried bitumen,
the strong brought in whatever else was needed.

On the fifth day I drew its plan.   56
One acre was its whole floorspace; ten dozen cubits the height
      of each wall;
ten dozen cubits its deck, square on each side.
I laid out the contours, drew it all.
I gave it six decks
and divided it, thus, into seven parts.
Its innards I divided into nine parts.
I struck water-plugs into it.
I checked the poles and laid in all that was necessary.
[For the hull] I poured 24,000 gallons of bitumen into the kiln;
the same amount I laid on the inside.
The basket-bearers brought on three *shars* of oil
in addition to the *shar* of oil consumed in the seed-meal
and the two *shars* of oil stowed away by the boatman.

I butchered bulls for the people   70
and killed sheep every day.
Drink, beer, oil, and wine
I gave the workmen to swill as if it were the water of a river,
so that they made festival as if it were the days of New Year's.
I opened the bowl of ointment and applied it to my hands.
On the seventh day the ark was completed.

———

The launching was not easy: 77
The hull had to be shifted, above and below,
until two-thirds of the structure had entered the water.
All I had I loaded into the boat:
all I had of silver I loaded,
all I had of gold I loaded,
all I had of the seed of all living creatures I loaded;
I made all my kin and family go onto the boat.
The animals of the fields, wild beasts of the fields, the children
    of all the craftsmen I drove aboard.

Shamash had set the time for me: 86
'When he orders *bread* at night, he will rain down *wheat*,
enter the boat and close your gate.'

The hour approached: 89
'When he orders *bread* at night, he will rain down *wheat*.'
I saw day coming on.
To look at that day filled me with terror.
I went into the ark and closed the gate.
For the caulking of the boat I gave to Puzur-Amuru, the
    shipbuilder,
my palace with all its goods."   95

NOTES TO TABLET XI, COLUMN ii

On the numbering of lines in Tablet XI, see notes to XI.i. The column is devoted entirely to preparations for the Flood. It ends at a moment of suspense, just as the closing of the ship is ordered.

48. The *Gilgamesh* formula for introducing an episode.

56—69. Details of the ark. The ship *(elippu)* is enormous, the size of the great ziggurat of Babylon known from biblical tradition as the Tower of Babel, and the amount of material used is vast. (The *ikû*-measure was 3600 square meters.) If the dimensions suggest something more like a ziggurat or temple than a ship, a number of the details are reflective of Sumerian shipbuilding. Thor Heyerdahl rediscovered, for example, the reason for oil as well as bitumen in caulking the boat: by itself, bitumen on reed-bundles will crack; together with oil, the bitumen will keep the reeds dry for months *(The Tigris Expedition* [London: George Allen and Unwin, 1980], pp. 64ff.).

70—76. Preparations include what look like cultic acts, but may be simply provisioning for the labor force. The cultic connection is suggested again, though, in the reference to the New Year's Festival, *akitu*, in line 74. The New Year's Festival was held throughout Mesopotamia for millennia and lasted ten days. It included reading of the so-called "Epic of Creation," scapegoat rituals, the burning of costly decorated figurines, and many other rituals. (See A. Leo Oppenheim, *Ancient Mesopotamia* [Chicago: University of Chicago Press, 1964], p. 178.) The motif is absent from the Yahwist version of the Flood, but a few of the details of the ark are given by the Priestly Writer (Genesis 6:14–22).

77—85. Launching and loading of the ship. It has been suggested by Harry A. Hoffner, "Enki's Command to Atrahasis," *Kramer Anniversary Volume* (Kevelaer: Butzon and Bercker, 1976), pp. 241–245, that the late version misunderstood what seems to be a clear command to "spurn property" in XI.i.26. (See Tigay, 292.) At any rate, Utnapishtim loads the boat with all he possesses, including silver, gold, the "seed of all living creatures," his kin, and animals.

86–88. The introduction of Shamash is an innovation of the late version, which elsewhere expands Shamash's role in the poem. It may be that Shamash is supposed to be speaking the two lines, but the first part is the name of the event, whose time, *adannu*, is set.

89–95. The time, again *adannu*, approaches, and its sign is mentioned again. Utnapishtim indicates his terror as the day approaches. The caulking is completed by Puzur-Amuru, the boatman *(malaḫu)*, cited in line 94.

Column iii

"When something of dawn appeared   96
a black cloud rose up from the horizon.
Adad the thunder god roared within it.   98
Nabû the god of despoilment and Sharru the god of submission
    rushed before it,
moving like heralds over mountains and land.
Nergal of the underworld breaks his doorposts.
Ninurta comes, making the dikes flow.
The Anunnaki lift up their torches:
the land glowed in their terrifying brightness.
The confusion of Adad sweeps the heavens
turning all that was light to blackness.
The wide land was smashed like a pot.

For one day the south wind blew: 108
it gathered speed, stormed, submerged the mountains.
Like a war it swept over everything:
brother could not see brother;
from heaven, the people could not be sighted.
The gods themselves were terrified by the Flood:
they shrank back, fled upward to the heavens of Anu.
Curled up like dogs, the gods lay outside [his door].

Ishtar cried out like a woman giving birth,   116
the sweet-voiced lady of the gods cried out,
'The days of old are turned to clay
since I spoke evil in the Assembly of the Gods.
How could I speak evil in the Assembly of the Gods?
How could I cry out for battle for the destruction of
    my people?
I myself gave birth to my people!
[Now] like the children of fish they will fill the sea!'

———

235

Even the Anunnaki wept with her;
the gods, humble now, sit weeping,
their lips drawn taut, . . . all together.   126

Six days and seven nights   127
the wind shrieked, the stormflood rolled through the land.
On the seventh day of its coming the stormflood broke from the
    battle
which had labored like a woman giving birth.
The sea grew quiet, the storm was still; the Flood stopped.
I looked out at the day. Stillness had settled in.
All of humanity was turned to clay.   133
The ground was like a great, flat roof.
I opened the window and light fell on my face.
I crouched, sitting, and wept.
My tears flowed over my cheeks.

I looked for a shore at the boundary of the sea,
and the twelfth time I looked, an island emerged.
The ark stood grounded on the mountain Nisir.   140
The mountain Nisir seized the boat; it could not rise.
A first day, a second day, the mountain Nisir seized the boat.
A third day, a fourth day, the mountain Nisir, *etc.*
A fifth, a sixth the mountain Nisir, *etc.*
A seventh day, when it arrived,"   145

NOTES TO TABLET XI, COLUMN iii

On the numbering of lines in Tablet XI, see notes to XI.i. The column narrates the Flood, from its beginning at dawn until the seventh day of the Flood's retreat.

98–107. The gods, who are closely identified with natural powers, produce the Flood. Epithets have been added in some cases to make identification easy: Adad, a storm god, is called here "the thunder god"; in line 101, the god's name is Erragal, identified with the netherworld god Nergal; Ninurta and the Anunnaki appear again. Nabû, or Shullat, and Sharru, or Hanish, paired in line 99, are virtually personifications: "despoilment" and "submission." The description is vivid and ends in a traditional simile: the land smashed like a pot.

108–115. The Flood becomes so terrifying that the gods themselves are frightened, and they flee upward into the highest heaven, the heaven of Anu, where they curl up "like dogs." A motif that is conspicuously missing in the late version of *Gilgamesh* but important in the Old Babylonian *Atra-ḥasīs* is the effect on the gods' existence. Since the gods depend upon mankind for food and drink, they suffer terribly from thirst and hunger when mankind is destroyed. In this version, though, the gods are simply frightened—and Ishtar becomes a spokesman for them. (See Tigay, 224–229.)

116–123. The speech is striking in a number of ways. By closely comparing Ishtar's speech with the parallel Old Babylonian *Atra-ḥasīs* III.iii.30–iv.23, Tigay (224–227, 293–295) noticed many significant departures in the late version of *Gilgamesh*. The late version style in the Flood narrative is quite different from the usual narrative style; there is little of the expansion and repetition that remind one of Sumerian compositions. The Flood is much in the style of Old Babylonian Akkadian compositions, but this speech is a fine example not of expansion but of abridgment. In the earlier version, the speaker is the mother goddess, Mami/Nintu; here it is, significantly, Ishtar. The character of Ishtar as a mother is emphasized, first, by having her cry out like a woman giving birth (line 116), and then lamenting that her evil advice is all the greater since it was she herself who "gave birth to my people" (line 122). Also, the late version uses the term *lemutta*, "evil," twice (119–120), where the Old Babylonian uses a term for "total destruction"—a significant shift in keeping with the addition of the motif of "evil" in the first part of *Gilgamesh* in the late version. Even parenthetically noting that the gods weeping with Ishtar are the Anunnaki (line 124) is a switch from the Old Babylonian. On the other hand, the most obvious feature is how much shorter Ishtar's speech is than its counterpart in *Atra-ḫasīs*.

126. The line may read, "Their lips burn, they have contracted fever" (reading *le-qa-a* in the break). Absent is the Old Babylonian emphasis on the gods' starving.

127–145. The Flood ends. The late version prefers the six/seven formula for noting the fulfillment of time. The quiet is described in great solemnity. At the very end of the column, the late version returns briefly to the repetitive style and again ends on a note of suspense.

133. Note the echo of line 118, where "the days of old are turned to clay." The term for humanity is not that used elsewhere in the poem, but a special word, *tenēšētu*, used at this special moment of stillness.

140. The mountain Nisir is modern Pir Omar Gudrun, south of the lower Zab in Turkey; sometimes it is identified with the biblical Ararat.

Column iv

"I sent out a dove, letting it fly up.   146
The dove went out and returned.
It could see no place to stand, and turned around.

I sent out a swallow, letting it fly.
The swallow went out and returned.
It saw no standing place, and turned around.

I sent out my crow, letting it fly.
The crow went out and, seeing that the waters had receded,
it ate, circled around, turned, and did not come back.

I sent them out to the four winds and offered sacrifice.   155
I sent out a drink offering upon the ziggurat of the mountain:
seven and seven cult-vessels I set up.
Beneath them I poured cane, cedar, myrtle.
The gods smelled the fragrance—
the gods smelled the sweet fragrance—
and the gods like flies gathered over the sacrificer.

From afar the lady of the gods came down.   162
[From the corpses] she raised up the [iridescent] fly which
      Anu made for love-making.
'Gods, let me not forget this, by the power of the lapis lazuli on
      my neck.
These [evil] days I will remember and never forget.
Gods, approach the offering.
But let Enlil not approach the offering,
for without discussion [in the Assembly of the Gods] he brought
      on the Flood,
and my people he numbered for slaughter.'

———————

As soon as Enlil arrived
he spotted the ark. Enlil was furious.
He was filled with the wrath of the gods, the Igigi.   172
'Has life-breath escaped? No man was meant to live through
    the devastation!'   173

Ninurta shaped his mouth to speak, saying to warrior Enlil,   174
'Who but Ea can create things?
Ea knows all the Word.'

Ea shaped his mouth to speak, saying to warrior Enlil:
'You, shrewd one of the gods, warrior,   178
how is it—how could you—without talking it through, send
    the Flood?
Punish the one who commits the crime; punish the evildoer
    alone.
Give him play so he is not cut free; pull him in, lest he be lost.

Instead of your bringing on the Flood, let lions rise up and
    diminish the people.
Instead of your bringing on the Flood, let the wolf rise up and
    cut the people low.
Instead of your bringing on the Flood, let famine be set up to
    throw down the land.
Instead of your bringing on the Flood, let plague rise up and
    strike down the people.

I, I did not unhide the secret of the great gods.
[Utnapishtim] the over-wise, a vision was shown to him; he
    heard the secret of the gods.'

Think about [Ea's] words, now, [Gilgamesh].   188

Enlil came up to the ark.   189
He seized my hand and picked me up,
and he raised my wife up, making her kneel at my side.
He touched our foreheads and, standing between us, he
    blessed us.

'Before this, Utnapishtim has been human.
Now Utnapishtim and his wife are transformed, being like
    us gods.
Let Utnapishtim live far off, at the source of all rivers.'

They took me far away, to live at the source of the rivers.

In your case, now, who will assemble the gods for you   197
so that the life you seek you may discover?

Test yourself! Don't sleep for six days and seven nights."   199

Even as he sat there on his haunches,   200
sleep like a wet haze blew over him.

Utnapishtim said to his wife,
"Look at this hero who asks for life!
Sleep has blown over him like a wet haze!"

His wife answers Utnapishtim the remote:
"Touch the man, so he'll wake up.
He'll take the road, return in peace.
He'll go out through the gate, returning to his land."

Utnapishtim says to her, his wife:
"A man who is trouble will give you trouble.
Come, bake bread for him, place it near him, by his head,
and the days he sleeps score on the wall."

She baked bread for him, set it by his head,
and the days he slept she scored on the wall.
The first wafer is dried out,
the second is leathery, the third moist, the fourth turned white,
the fifth had gray on it, the sixth was rotten,
the seventh—
          Suddenly as he touched the man he came alive.   218

NOTES TO TABLET XI, COLUMN iv

On the numbering of lines in Tablet XI, see notes to XI.i. The very long column concludes the Flood story (146–196) and narrates most of the Sleeping Test (199–218). Whatever "wisdom" is contained in the Flood, the test is designed to eliminate Gilgamesh's exhausting search for immortality. Once again, the poet breaks the text at a moment of suspense.

146–154. Like the Yahwist version of the biblical Flood, the late version of *Gilgamesh* includes the sending out of birds to test the waters. Where the biblical account has a raven sent once and a dove three times, *Gilgamesh* has a dove, a swallow, and a crow. The style, with its exact repetition, is Sumerian. (For the biblical account, see Genesis 8:7–13.)

155–161. Again like the Yahwist version of the biblical Flood, *Gilgamesh* has Utnapishtim make offerings to the gods. The gods, smelling the sweet fragrance, gather around Utnapishtim. (See Genesis 8:20–21.) Tigay (227–229, 296) compares the passage with the Old Babylonian parallel in *Atra-ḥasīs* III.v.29–36. Noteworthy is the absence of the starving gods eating and drinking; here they only smell the savor of the offering.

162–169. The lady of the gods is *DINGIR.MAḪ*, the Great Goddess, as earlier in I.ii.2. Where the Great Goddess is Ishtar here, in the Old Babylonian version, the goddess is Mami/Nintu. Ishtar raises up a fly-ornament, a pendant made of lapis lazuli (163–164). Like the Priestly sign, the rainbow (Genesis 9:13–17), the fly-ornament is raised in a solemn commitment not to forget the devastation of the Flood. Unlike the biblical account, though, one of the gods, Enlil, is accused of the deed. He brought on the Flood "without discussing it," *la imtalkuma* (168). The reference to the fly-ornament as something made by Anu "for love-making," *kî ṣuḫišu*, could be "for his making love" to the Great Goddess—but no such myth has been discovered yet to account for the reference.

172. The anger of the powerful Enlil is likened to that of the Igigi gods, like the Anunnaki a group of divine judges.

173. Enlil's remark again combines *napištu,* "life-breath," and *bal-āṭu,* here the verb "to live."

174–176. Ninurta's brief speech mainly points to the character of Ea, who can form *amatu*—words, news, secrets, plans, commands, matters, and affairs. Ea knows every *šipru*—matter, word, message. The lines show that with Ea, to speak is to make. The word/thing distinction is overcome in what approximates the *logos:* hence, he knows "all the Word."

178–187. Ishtar's recognition and repentance at being a party to the destruction of her "offspring" is one important aspect of the Flood "secret," and Ea's third speech is another. The "wisdom" is indeed a terrible one, charged with an idea of god and man far different from the Yahwist's conclusion to the biblical Flood (Genesis 8:20–22), or the Priestly Writer's version (Genesis 9:1–17). Both biblical accounts conflate the roles of Ishtar, Ea, and Enlil. True, Ea chides the angry Enlil for his irrational act, *la tamtalikma,* and thus demands something like reasonable behavior of the gods (179). Calling Enlil the "shrewd one of the gods," *apkalli ilāni,* is ironic. (Utnapishtim was, by tradition, one of the *apkalli,* or antediluvian sages.) What follows, though, in Ea's speech is a founding act—one filled with a bitter wisdom, indeed. The biblical accounts, with their promise to humanity and a covenant cut between God and man, are far more positive than this, the ideational climax of the Flood in *Gilgamesh* and, perhaps, the intellectual core of the work. (Certainly it is the wisdom Gilgamesh has been seeking, although he does not seem at once to grasp it.) "Punish the one who commits the crime; punish the evildoer alone" (line 180) is a variant on the Old Babylonian parallel's "On the criminal visit your penalty, on whoever disregards your command" (Tigay, 221). In one line, Ea establishes an ethical norm that rids mankind of the burden of collective responsibility. It is the counterpart of the promise never to destroy all humanity by the Flood. What the metaphor is in line 181 is not entirely clear; presumably the "evildoer" is likened to a fish on a line, with a paradoxical relationship between letting loose and pulling in, a metaphor that would be appropriate to the character of Ea, whose sign is the goatfish. The magnificent sequence in 182–185, in the Sumerian style, is something else. The four terrors of mankind—the lion, the wolf, famine, and plague—are not removed; indeed, they may be established here. (In *Atra-ḥasīs,* famine and plague are used before the Flood to reduce the "noise" of a teeming mankind, but Ea thwarts that stratagem as well.) Each line plays on "rising up" and "cutting low." The world after the Flood is a hostile world, where nature is the enemy of human life. Still, life—individual life, not the collective "mankind"—is better than the death of mankind; but the other side is the point Utnapishtim makes time and again: the individual must die. If the Old Babylonian Gilgamesh story emphasized a *carpe diem* theme, the later version's solemn counterpart is the inevitability of death. The final lines of Ea's speech (186–187) seal the wisdom in trickery. Ea's claim looks like a flat-out lie, but is not: Utnapishtim, called by his name *Atra-ḥasis*, "the over-wise," was given a dream *(šunatu)* by which he heard the secret of the gods.

188. The transitional sentence is clear—"Now, consider his advice" —but it is not entirely clear who is to consider, and whose advice it is. We take it to mean that Gilgamesh should pay close attention to Ea's words.

189–196. Utnapishtim concludes the Flood story with the description of the reconciliation with Enlil and the virtual deification of Utnapishtim and his wife. Utnapishtim's "wife" is really his "woman," *sinništu* (as in IX.ii.13 and 15), here; later she is identified as his "wife," *marḥītu*. (See Tigay, 232–233.) Enlil pronounces a special fate for the sage and his woman. Where Utnapishtim had been merely human, *amēlūtumma*, he is transformed into something "like us gods," *kî ilāni našima*. (Contrast Genesis 8:15–9:17, the Priestly Writer's conclusion to the Flood story.) They do not dwell with the high gods, but "far away," at the "mouth of rivers" (195).

197–198. Utnapishtim challenges Gilgamesh: who will stand for him so that he would attain the life, *balaṭa*, which is the life of Utnapishtim?

199. In view of the repeated concern with Gilgamesh's inability to sleep, Utnapishtim's challenge is ironic indeed.

200–218. The Sleeping Test is failed immediately. Utnapishtim's wife intervenes, as she will do later, but Utnapishtim figures a clever way to indicate the passage of time—through the natural process of decay. The decaying bread (211–218) is the very image of mortality. The seven days are marked by the changing character of the bread. The column ends abruptly with Gilgamesh rising at the touch of Utnapishtim, almost a parody of resurrection.

Column v

Gilgamesh says to him, to Utnapishtim the remote,   219
"As soon as I was ready to fall asleep,
right away you touched me and roused me."

Utnapishtim says to him, to Gilgamesh,   222
"Come on, Gilgamesh. Count your wafers.
I'll show you how many days you've slept.
Your first one is dried out,
the second is leathery, the third moist, the fourth turned white,
the fifth has gray on it, the sixth is rotten,
the seventh—suddenly as you were touched, you came alive."

Gilgamesh said to him, to Utnapishtim the remote,   229
"What can I do, Utnapishtim? Where can I go?
A thief has stolen my flesh.
Death lives in the house where my bed is,
and wherever I set my feet, there Death is."

Utnapishtim says to Urshanabi the Boatman: 234
"Urshanabi, [from now on] the harbor will reject you, the
      crossing will be hateful to you.
You have been coming to its shore. [From now on] its shore
      will be denied you.
The man you led here: matted hair covers his body.
Skins have hidden the beauty of his flesh.
Take him, Urshanabi, and lead him to the washing place.
Have him wash off the filthy body hair in water, become pure.
Let his skins be thrown off, have them carried to the sea; let the
      goodness of his body shine out.
Bind the hair on his head again.
Have him put on a garment, the robe of life,   243
so that he may go back to his city,
so that he may now go the rest of the way down his road.
Let him put on an elder's robe, and let it be always new."

———

Urshanabi took [charge] of him and brought him to the
    washing place.   247
He cleaned his filthy body hair in the water, made him pure.
He cast off the skins and carried them to the sea;
the goodness of his body shone out.
He bound the hair on his head again
and put a garment on him, the robe of life,
so he could return to his city,
so he could now go the rest of the way down his road.
He put on the elder's robe, always new.

Gilgamesh and Urshanabi boarded the boat.   256
They lifted the boat onto the waves and were carried away.

NOTES TO TABLET XI, COLUMN v

On the numbering of lines in Tablet XI, see notes to XI.i. After the lengthy episodes of column iv, column v is relatively simple.

219–221. Gilgamesh, as Utnapishtim had thought, thinks he has not slept at all.

222–228. In the repetitive style, Utnapishtim proves to Gilgamesh that he has indeed slept—and failed the test.

229–233. Gilgamesh's response is brief but simple and eloquent. There is nowhere else to go. Death is everywhere.

234–248. Although Gilgamesh's response had been cast in the form of a question to Utnapishtim, the sage does not respond to the question. Rather, he abruptly shifts to the Boatman, who is now forbidden to return to Utnapishtim's place beyond the waters of death. This suggests that by making the crossing, Gilgamesh has destroyed, ironically, the possibility of any future crossings. Only his message will remain. Utnapishtim orders the cleansing of Gilgamesh, binding of the hair, and a new garment, so that Gilgamesh may return to his city.

243–246. A beautifully designed quatrain. Utnapishtim refers to two garments in the first and fourth lines—garments which may be used synonymously for the revivified Gilgamesh. The first is the *ṣubat baltišu;* the second, *šiba*, appears to confirm Gilgamesh in his leadership role. That the garment shall always be new does not indicate personal immortality any more than the "garment of life" does, but it would seem to involve a commitment to "life" in the world. Between the two lines that frame the quatrain are two lines that open with the same term, *adi*, "so that" (as the frame lines open with *tediqi* and *tediqu*). The *adi*-lines establish a parallel between returning to his city and the completion of his journey, both with strong symbolic resonances in the poem. The shedding of old skin and the putting on of a new, ever-fresh garment anticipates the episode in column vi, when Gilgamesh is given a magical plant, which is stolen by a serpent.

247–255. In the repetitive style, what Utnapishtim has ordered is done.

256–257. The column ends with every indication that Gilgamesh is on his way back to Uruk—having been given, if not personal immortality, at least the symbols of "life."

Column vi

Then his wife said to him, to Utnapishtim the remote: 258
"Gilgamesh has come here—has strained, has toiled—
What have you given him as he returns to his land?"

At that Gilgamesh lifted his pole   261
and brought the boat close to shore again.

Utnapishtim said to him, to Gilgamesh: 263
"Gilgamesh, you came here; you strained, you toiled.
What can I give you as you return to your land?
Let me uncover for you, Gilgamesh, a secret thing.
A secret of the gods let me tell you.
There is a plant. Its roots go deep, like the boxthorn;
its spike will prick your hand like a bramble.
If you get your hands on that plant, you'll have everlasting life."

Gilgamesh, on hearing this, opened the conduit.   271
He bound heavy stones to his feet;
they dragged him down into the abyss, and he saw the plant.
He seized the plant, though it cut into his hand;
he cut the heavy stones from his feet;
the sea cast him up onto its shore.

Gilgamesh said to Urshanabi the Boatman: 277
"Urshanabi, this is the plant of Openings,   278
by which a man can get life within.
I will carry it to Uruk of the Sheepfold; I will give it to the
    elders to eat; they will divide the plant among them.
Its name is The-Old-Man-Will-Be-Made-Young.
I too will eat it, and I will return to what I was in my youth."

At twenty leagues they broke their fast.   283
At thirty leagues they prepared for the night's rest.

Gilgamesh saw a pool of cool water.
He went down into it and bathed in the water.
A snake smelled the fragrance of the plant.
It came up through the water and carried the plant away.
As it turned it threw off its skin.

That day Gilgamesh sat down, weeping.   290
Over his face the tears flowed.
He took the hand of Urshanabi the Boatman.
"For whom, Urshanabi, do my arms toil?
For whom has the blood of my heart dried up?
I have not won any good for myself;
it's the lion-of-the-ground that has won good fortune.
Now the floodtide will push it twenty leagues away.
When I opened the channel and entered the conduit,
what I found was a sign set out for me. Let us withdraw
and leave the boat on the shore."

                              At twenty leagues they broke
                                   their fast.   300
At thirty leagues they prepared for the night's rest. They
     arrived at Uruk of the Sheepfold.

Gilgamesh said to him, to Urshanabi, the Boatman,   303
"Go up, Urshanabi, onto the walls of Uruk.
Inspect the base, view the brickwork.
Is not the very core made of oven-fired brick?
Did not the seven sages lay down its foundation?

In [Uruk], house of Ishtar, one part is city, one part orchards,
     and one part claypits.
Three parts including the claypits make up Uruk."   307

NOTES TO TABLET XI, COLUMN vi

On the numbering of lines in Tablet XI, see notes to XI.i. In the final column of the tablet, the narrative takes a tragic turn. The irony is heightened by the fact of the wife's generosity.

258–260. In one sense, Utnapishtim has given Gilgamesh much—even the "robe of life," but the wife chides Utnapishtim on his hospitality.

261–262. In a poem that is not marked by much that resembles modern realism, the little act of lifting the pole is an interesting, probably ironic touch.

263–270. The first part of Utnapishtim's speech is briefly in the repetitive style. Utnapishtim's gift is, appropriately, a secret, *amat niṣirti*. The plant in line 268 is simply *šammu*, a general word for plant, and the plant is likened to the boxthorn. The magical or sacred plant, judging from the context, is one that will restore life (line 270).

271–276. Gilgamesh makes a last perilous journey. This one takes him through a tube he must open, *raṭu*. The plant lives in the *apsû*, or abyss, the dwelling-place of Utnapishtim's god, Ea. (Enki/Ea is traditionally associated with plants, which have their roots in the waters underground.) The technique Gilgamesh uses in his dive is used today by the pearl-divers of Bahrain.

277–282. A most important speech. Gilgamesh has made yet another "opening," and this is the plant of "opening," *šammu nibitti*. Through it one can obtain "his life," *nabbisu* (that is, *napištu*), "in his heart," *ina libbišu*. Notice that Gilgamesh does not immediately eat the plant. Rather, he will carry it back to Uruk, and like the good king, distribute it to the elders, who will find their youth restored. (The distribution of the plant suggests a kind of communion.) He gives the plant its name, *šíbu iṣṣaḫir amēlu*, a return to a man in his prime (not simply immortality). Only then does Gilgamesh think that he, too, will partake of the plant—a priority of the other before the self that recalls Gilgamesh's naming of Enkidu before himself.

283–289. A cruel turn, the reverse of Gilgamesh's purification, when he was given the robe of life: a serpent, *ṣēru*, seizes the plant—and is revived, casting off its old skin.

290–299. Once again, Gilgamesh must weep. Only the "lion of the earth," the serpent, *nēšu ša qaqqari*, has gained by his toils. For Gilgamesh there is only bitter knowledge. In the conduit he discovered a sign, *itti*—a variant is "his place"—and in this sober, brief remark the terrible truths are accepted.

300–301. Note the atypical breaking of the line, beginning a subdivision of the narrative in midline.

303–307. The return to Uruk. While there is no indication of joy or delight, there is also no indication of flat despair in the speech by which Gilgamesh ends his journey. The walls of Uruk are the only lasting remains. We take this as a denial of personal immortality but a recognition of something that will carry on the hero's reputation. Typical of the late version, the perspective is one of the fullness of city life, not one that dwells on the adventures of the fighting man. Uruk at the end is seen once again as the house of Ishtar, a final recognition of the feminine. We take the division of the city into one which emphasizes that the uncultivated claypits, source of clay tablets, but also a symbol of the dead, is the fitting comment on life that is, in the words of Martin Heidegger, being-toward-death. The final lines of the tablet repeat almost exactly the opening of the poem, I.i.16–21. As suggested there, the likelihood is that the poet, speaking in his own voice only in the prologue, anticipated these lines in composing the prologue, and established a connection between the secret-bringer Gilgamesh and the role of the poet.

A colophon at the end of Tablet XI gives the catchline for XII.i, indicating that the work is not complete in only eleven tablets.

TABLET XII
Column i

"Would that I'd kept the drum in the house of the Carpenter!   1
If only I'd left it with the Carpenter's wife, who was like a mother
    to me!"   2

"Lord, why is your heart not good?   3
I will bring up now the drum from the underworld, land of the
    dead;   4
I will bring up the beater from the mouth of darkness."

Says Gilgamesh to Enkidu,
"If you will go down to where the earth groans,
take in the secret thing my words uncover.
Here is my advice. Take it."

Gilgamesh says to him, to Enkidu:
"Any man who goes down today into the underworld,
let him draw my advice into his heart!   13
  Do not put on a clean garment:
  It will mark you as a foreigner.
  Do not smooth your skin with sweet-smelling oil from the
    bowl:
  They will swarm and settle all around you.
  Do not throw the throwing-stick in the underworld:
  Those the throwing-stick hits will turn, unharmed, and menace
    you.
  Do not carry a staff of power in your hands:
  The shades will besmut you with a dark curse.
  Do not put sandals on your feet.
  Make no bellow in the place of the cry-out-of-the-earth.
  Kiss not your beloved wife,
  nor strike the wife you hated;

kiss not your beloved child,
nor strike the child you hated.

The song of the dead will snap around you: 28
She who sleeps, she who sleeps, the Mother of Birth and Death, who
*   sleeps,*   29
Her clean shoulders no garment covers,
Her breast like a stone bowl does not give suck.''

NOTES TO TABLET XII, COLUMN i

Tablet XII is the most difficult part of *Gilgamesh* for the modern reader, with his expectation of a straight, linear ordering of the events of a story, to accept. The colophon at the end of Tablet XI.vi makes it clear that the twelfth tablet is indeed part of the late version. Tigay (49) argues that it was not part of the Old Babylonian *The Epic of Gilgamesh*. It is, then, along with the prologue (I.i.1–26) and the Flood story (XI.i–iv), one of the major additions of the late version to the Gilgamesh series (Tigay, 103).

The obvious problem is that in Tablet XII Enkidu is alive again and his death is narrated in a very different way than in Tablet VII. There are other unusual features of the text. It is conventional to number the lines of Tablet XII consecutively (as in Tablets VI and XI), without regard to column numbers. We follow R. Campbell Thompson's A-text (K.2774) in restoring the columns, but retain the consecutive numbering for convenience in following scholarly discussions of the text. While it is the usual six-column arrangement, however, the text of Tablet XII is quite brief, with columns of about thirty lines instead of fifty lines, the usual length of the late version column.

Tablet XII is also unusual in its fidelity to a Sumerian source called "Gilgamesh, Enkidu and the Nether World." (See Samuel Noah Kramer, *History Begins at Sumer* [Philadelphia: University of Pennsylvania Press, 1981], pp. 194–198; A. Shaffer, "The Sumerian Sources of Tablet XII of The Epic of Gilgameš" [Ph.D. dissertation, University of Pennsylvania, 1963]; and Tigay, esp. 105–109.) Tablet XII is a close translation into Akkadian of the Sumerian original. While there are some changes that are characteristic of the late version's handling of traditional materials, the most obvious feature is the care to preserve the Sumerian style and most of the Sumerian material intact. Another unusual feature is that Akkadian translations (as opposed to creative adaptations) of Sumerian works are usually produced as bilingual texts, with the Akkadian providing an interlinear translation of the Sumerian; the Sumerian is not produced here (Tigay, 49).

While Tablet XII is faithful to the Sumerian, it does not reproduce the whole of "Gilgamesh, Enkidu and the Nether World." The Sumerian poem opens with a mythological prologue and then tells the story of the heroes as they help the goddess Inanna (the Ishtar of *Gilgamesh*) rid a *huluppu*-tree (perhaps a willow) of some demonic figures who had come to dwell there. The tree is then cut, and Inanna gives the base of the tree to the heroes to fashion a *pukku*, the nature of which is still debated, and the crown of the tree, from which is fashioned a *mikku*, something used with the *pukku*. The poem is quite difficult at this point, but it appears that at the outcry of the women of Uruk, the *pukku* and *mikku* fall into the netherworld (Kramer, pp. 195–196). Tablet XII takes up the story at this point and translates it until the end, modifying only the last lines of the original (and expanding a few lines).

Tigay (189–191) has noticed that the outcry against Gilgamesh for using the *pukku* and *mikku* in a way that oppresses the people is quite similar to the complaints against Gilgamesh in I.ii.7–29. He also notes (105) that the depiction of the netherworld in Tablet XII is something of a doublet of Enkidu's vision of the world of the dead in VII.iv. It would appear, then, that Tablet XII is not just a sudden afterthought of Sîn-leqi-unninnî. We take it that the poet used the Sumerian material in reordering his version, and that what would have concluded the first part of *Gilgamesh*, Enkidu's death (for some outrage, for which he is made to die in an unusual way) and vision of the world of the dead, has been decentered. It returns as something of an epilogue, which picks up a number of motifs of *Gilgamesh* I–XI and puts them in a new light. Tigay (107) points to the possibility that Sîn-leqi-unninnî, an incantation/exorcist priest (*mashmashshu*), may have found Tablet XII particularly appropriate because of his professional interest in the world of the spirits. It has been noted all along that the late version prefers to give *Gilgamesh* the look of a Sumerian composition by using certain stylistic effects borrowed from Sumerian literature. Tablet XII goes this one step further, perhaps because of a sense of its sacred nature, and here the poet is reticent to tamper much with the Sumerian material at all.

Although Tigay (105–106) dismisses the idea, we feel that one aim of Tablet XII is to show Gilgamesh the full nature of death now that he is resigned to it. Note especially the way Gilgamesh is presented in column i: one who possesses the secret of the way in and out of the world of the dead. Now he is the one dispensing advice, rather than receiving it, as he had from Shamash, Ea, and Utnapishtim earlier.

This is a somewhat modified version of "Gilgamesh XII," which appeared in *MSS*, 2 (1983), 165–172. John Gardner's "Notes on Gilgamesh, Tablet XII" appeared in the same issue, pp. 159–164. Gardner's conclusion is worth repeating here: "The tablet is now half in ruin; much of what it says had fallen into the cracks of time. All we know for sure is that it's good to have sons, probably bad to fall from the mast of a ship into nothingness, good to die quickly and painlessly, good to die in battle, bad to die in the wilderness, unnoticed, and unspeakably bad to die unloved. Mainly what we know is that to die at all is a terrible thing, but to die without having truly lived—without having loved and left loved ones—is to be garbage surviving through eternity on garbage."

1. The poem opens suddenly, with Gilgamesh speaking to Enkidu. The "drum" is the *pukku*, about which there is much controversy. Another suggestion is that *pukku* and *mikku* are parts of a game the heroes played with. *Gilgamesh* picks up the story just in the midst of the hero's lament that the drum had fallen into the netherworld. We take it as a shamanic drum. The Sumerian passage from which this is taken is this:

> "O my *pukku*, O my *mikku*,
> My *pukku* with lustiness irresistible,
> My *mikku* with dance-rhythm unrivaled,
> My *pukku* which was with me formerly in the house of the
>   carpenter—
> The wife of the carpenter was with me then like the mother who
>   gave birth to me,
> The daughter of the carpenter was with me then like my younger
>   sister—
> My *pukku*, who will bring it up from the nether world,
> My *mikku*, who will bring it up from the 'face' of the nether
>   world?"

(Translation: Kramer, p. 196).

If the drum is an exorcist's drum (or is taken as such), many of the details of Tablet XII come at least partly clear. On the importance of the exorcist's drum (a copper kettledrum), see A. Leo Oppenheim, *Ancient Mesopotamia* (Chicago: University of Chicago Press, 1964), pp. 178–180.

2. Note that the late version picks up the Sumerian reference to the wife of the carpenter, but not the daughter of the carpenter. Balancing the male and female is characteristic of the late version, e.g., the Scorpion-man and his woman, Utnapishtim and his wife.

3. Note that the Akkadian retains the honorific, "my lord," in Enkidu's speech—though elsewhere in Tablet XII Enkidu is the "friend" and

"brother" of Gilgamesh, not his "servant," as he is in the Sumerian version.

4–5. "Land of the dead" and "the mouth of darkness" are added for clarity in identification; the Akkadian lines preserve the Sumerian habit of exact repetition, except for the *pukku* and *mikku* at the beginning of the lines.

13. The same term is used in lines 9 and 10, *aširtu*, "advice" or "instruction."

13–27. Gilgamesh offers advice for a shamanic journey. Note the reversal of ordinary life on earth, including nudity. The "shades" in line 21 are the *eṭemmu*, ghosts, spirits of the dead. The "cry-out-of-the-earth" (23) is for *rigma ana erṣetim*, which may be "noise in the netherworld." Gilgamesh's advice is indented to show the elegant pattern in the verse paragraphs.

28–31. The "song of the dead" is the lamentation of the netherworld, *tazimti erṣetim*, something of an echo of line 23. We take the three lines that follow as the words of the *tazimtu*. The first of the lines has the rhythmical movement of an incantation: *šá ṣallat šá ṣallat ummu ilu NIN.A.ZU šá ṣallat*. The Sumerian equivalent of the second and third lines adds material about the mother, having something to do with a *tigu*-instrument and plucking her hair out like "leeks" (Shaffer, pp. 76–77). Shaffer also points out two other parallel texts, the most accessible of which is Enki's advice for entering the netherworld in "The Descent of Inanna to the Nether World," lines 227–232 (Samuel Noah Kramer, "Cuneiform Studies and the History of Literature: the Sumerian Sacred Marriage Texts," *Publications of the American Philosophical Society*, 107 [1963], 485–525, and his "Sumerian Literature and the British Museum: the Promise of the Future," *PAPS* 124 [1980], 299–310). There it is clear that the goddess is Ereshkigal, depicted as a "birth-giving mother," lying ill in the netherworld "because of her children." Here the goddess is identified as the "mother of Ninazu"; Ninazu is a chthonic god of death. Sometimes his "mother" is merely the Mother Goddess, Mami; sometimes he is identified as the husband of Ereshkigal. In any event, we have tried to capture this quality of the birth-giving mother by calling the goddess "the Mother of Birth and Death."

Column ii

Enkidu was deaf to the words of revelation.   32
He put on a clean robe:
It marked him as a foreigner.
He smoothed his skin with sweet-smelling oil from the bowl;
at its scent they swarmed and settled around him.
In the underworld he threw his throwing-stick,
and those struck by the throwing-stick turned on him.
He carried a staff of power in his hands,
put sandals on his feet.
He set up a cry in the netherworld.
He kissed the wife he loved,
he beat the wife he hated;
he kissed the child he loved,
he beat the child he hated.

The lamentation of the netherworld seized him:
She who sleeps, she who sleeps, the Mother of Birth and Death,
  who sleeps,
Her clean shoulders no garment covers,
Her breast like a stone bowl does not give suck.

She did not let Enkidu rise again from the underworld.   50
Namtar the Fate-Cutter did not seize him; the sickness-demon
  did not seize him; the underworld seized him.   51
The deputy of Nergal the Unsparing did not seize him; the cry
  of the earth came up around him.   52
He did not fall on the field of battle. The earth seized him.   53

Then Lord Gilgamesh, son of Ninsun, wept for his servant,
  Enkidu.
                                                                                            54

To the House of the Dead, to Enlil the war god, he went, one
  man alone.

259

"Father Enlil, on the day the drum was beaten for me in the
    underworld,
and the beater was struck where the earth cries out,
Enkidu, who went down to bring them up, was trapped by the
    underworld."

NOTES TO TABLET XII, COLUMN ii

For the numbering of lines in Tablet XII, see notes to XII.i.

32–49. Following the Sumerian, the late version repeats the sequence and the language to show Enkidu's ironic refusal to take Gilgamesh's advice.

50–53. The lines expand the Sumerian original, characteristic of the late version (even in Tablet XII, where the poet is translating a Sumerian poem). "She" in line 50 may be the mother, Ereshkigal, seen as a personification of the underworld.

51. Namtar is the god of fate, death, and pestilence; he is a minister of Ereshkigal. "The Fate-Cutter" is our attempt to make the identification easy; it translates the Sumerian name. The "sickness-demon" is the *asakku*, mentioned earlier in VII.iii.32. In this and the next two lines, the usual causes of death are mentioned to show that Enkidu's death is unique. In every line it is the underworld itself, *erṣetu*, that "seizes" Enkidu.

52. Nergal, king in the netherworld and husband of Ereshkigal, is not the subject, but the *rabiṣu*-demon, called in the text "the unsparing."

53. On the (good) fate of the one who dies in battle, see XII.vi.149–150. Recall Enkidu's lament that he is not to die like one in battle, VII.vi.16.

54. Note again "lord" Gilgamesh and his "servant" Enkidu.

55. Enlil, the war god, has his dwelling in the temple, Ekur, "House of the Mountain" or "House of the Dead." Note the emphasis on Gilgamesh's going alone.

56–57. Note the play on the drum struck "for me" and the beater beaten "for me" in the final lines of the column.

Column iii

"Namtar did not seize him; the Plague-seas-demon did
    not seize him. The underworld seized him.   59
The deputy of Nergal the Unsparing did not seize him; the cry
    of the earth caught hold of him.
On the battlefield of man he did not fall. The earth seized him."

Father Enlil would not answer his word with a word.
                                      Gilgamesh
    went to the Moon God, one man alone.   62
"Father Sîn, on the day the drum was beaten for me in the
    underworld,
and the beater was struck where the earth cries out,
Enkidu, who went down to bring them up, was trapped by the
    underworld.
Namtar did not seize him; the Plague-seas-demon did not seize
    him. The underworld seized him.
The deputy of Nergal the Unsparing did not seize him; the cry
    of the earth caught hold of him.
On the battlefield of man he did not fall. Earth seized him."

Father Sîn would not answer his word with a word.
                                     He went to
    Ea, God of the Deepest Well—one man alone.   69
"Father Ea, on the day the drum was beaten for me in the
    underworld
and the beater was struck where the earth cries out,
Enkidu, who went down to bring them up, was trapped by the
    underworld.
Namtar did not seize him; the Plague-seas-demon did not seize
    him. The underworld seized him.
The deputy of Nergal the Unsparing did not seize him; the cry
    of the earth came up around him.
On the battlefield of man he did not fall. Earth seized him."

Father Ea, when he heard this—he whose words make what
 never was before—
to the Warrior, the hero Nergal, he said: 77
"Listen, Nergal, warrior, hero!
Open up now a hole to the underworld
that the ghost of Enkidu may issue from the darkness
and tell all the ways of the underworld to his brother."

Nergal, bold hero, listened to Ea's words.
He immediately opened up a hole now to the underworld.
The ghost of Enkidu issued from the darkness like a dream.   84
They tried to embrace, to kiss one another.
They traded words, groaning at one another.   86

NOTES TO TABLET XII, COLUMN iii

For the numbering of lines in Tablet XII, see notes to XII.i.

59–75. The journey of Gilgamesh to three gods, begun in column ii, is brought to a successful conclusion—but only after Gilgamesh has twice been rebuffed. Two gods, Enlil and the moon god, Sîn, cannot or will not help Gilgamesh. No explanation for their failure is given.

62. "Moon God": the text gives the name of the god, as in line 63. The epithet is added to ease identification. The episode with Sîn is exactly the same as with Enlil. He cannot or will not help in this matter. In the Sumerian original, only Enlil and Enki (often rivals in Sumerian stories) appear. Adding the moon god to the story may have been done only in the late version of *Gilgamesh*, but see Tigay (107).

69. Where the other gods fail, the one who succeeds is Ea, whose epithet we have added. The appeal is exactly the same. A second epithet is added in line 76.

77–81. Ea's fourth and final speech in *Gilgamesh* is much like the Sumerian original, but is slightly longer. The Akkadian is interesting in that it tries to keep not only to bilingual synonyms, but also to the word order of Sumerian, a language not at all related to Akkadian. A major change is having the underworld god, Nergal, act for him, where the Sumerian has Utu (the Shamash of our version). He orders Nergal to open a "hole," *takkabu*, through which the spirit, *utukku*, of Enkidu will pass. Line 81 adds a point not found in the Sumerian, that the purpose is to tell the ways of the underworld to his "brother," *ahu*.

84. When the ghost of Enkidu passes through the hole, it issues like a *zaqiqu*, like a "phantom" or a dream (the god of dreams carrying this name).

86. Since Enkidu is a spirit, we take the "groaning" of the last line, *anahu*, as full of lamentation.

Column iv

"Tell me, beloved, tell me, friend, 87
tell me the ways of the underworld that you've seen."

"I will not tell you, friend. I will not tell you.
If I must tell you the ways of the underworld that I've seen,
sit down and weep."

"I will sit down, I will weep."

"My body, that gave your heart joy to touch,
vermin eat it up like old clothes.
My body, that gave your heart joy to touch,
is filled with dirt."

"Agh!" he cried out, and threw himself to the earth, saying—
threw himself into the dirt, saying—
"Have you seen the man who has no son?"
                              "I have seen him. 99
He . . ."

"The one with one son: have you seen him?"
                              "I have seen him.
He lies under the wall, weeping bitterly."

"The one with two sons: have you seen him?"
                              "I have.
He lives in a brick house and eats bread."

"The one with three sons: have you seen him?"
                              "I have.
He drinks water out of waterskins filled from deep wells."

———

"The one with four sons: have you seen him?"
                    "I have.
His heart rejoices."

"The one with five sons: have you seen him?"
                    "I have.
Like a good writer, scribe to a king, his hand is revealed.
He brings justice to the palace."

"The one with six sons: have you seen him?"
                    "I have.
Like the man who guides the plow, he feels pride."

"The one with seven sons: have you seen him?"
                    "I have.
Like a man close to the gods, he . . ."   116

. . .

NOTES TO TABLET XII, COLUMN iv

For the numbering of Tablet XII, see notes to XII.i.

87–98. The horrors of the world of the dead are too dreadful to tell. Like the medieval *memento mori*, the passage dwells on the creatural disgust with the decay of the body.

99–117. The catalogue of the fates of man concludes column iv—and columns v and vi continue the catalogue until the end of *Gilgamesh*. The catalogue begins with the one who has left no son and brightens as the greater the number of sons is told. The traditional concern for sons is certainly evident here—but also, as the end of the poem shows, it is a matter of having someone to care for the dead, at least the memory of the dead. The fate of the man with no offspring is not known; the text is broken. In all likelihood, it is the worst of fates, comparable to that of the spirit at the end of the poem that has no one to tend to its needs. The fates of those who have five, six, and seven sons are considerably better. (There is no mention in *Gilgamesh* of the number of sons, if any, that Gilgamesh himself has.) The man with seven sons is "close to the gods." The text is broken at the end, with one line missing entirely (117). Possibly the seven is the completion of the series, and the last line adds another simile. (Column v begins with two lines of similes—possibly continuing the blessed state of the man with seven sons.)

Column v

NOTES TO TABLET XII, COLUMN v

For the numbering of Tablet XII, see notes to XII.i. Very little remains of column v or its Sumerian original. Clearly the catalogue of fates continues from column iv. The first two lines may still refer to the man who has seven sons, but that is not certain. About twenty-five or twenty-six lines are missing after that. When the text is clear again, it appears to deal with unusual types of death, and the fate of the man who fell from a mast does not appear to have been a good one. Note that in none of the cases is there a judgment about sinful lives, although there may have been a concept of the blessings of life pertaining to one's keeping "his god," thought to dwell in him, in the proper way.

Column vi

"The one who died a sudden death: have you seen him?"
                            "I have.
He sleeps at night on a couch and drinks pure water."

"The one who was slain in battle: have you seen him?"
                            "I have.
His father raises his head and his wife tends the corpse."

"The one whose body was thrown into the wasteland: have you
    seen him?"
                            "I have.
His spirit does not rest in the underworld."

"The one whose spirit has no one left alive to love him: have you
    seen him?"
                            "I have.
The left-overs of the pot, the scraps of bread thrown into the gutter
[what no dead dog will eat]
he eats."   154

NOTES TO TABLET XII, COLUMN vi

For the numbering of Tablet XII, see notes to XII.i. With only eight lines, column vi is by far the shortest in *Gilgamesh*, far shorter than the thirty lines that are average for Tablet XII. (Short sixth columns, however, are not uncommon.)

The end of *Gilgamesh* is brutally abrupt. Even the Sumerian lines have been reordered in the translation. Certainly the last few cases are mixed. The one who dies a sudden death and the one slain in battle are thought to have positive fates. The last two, the one tossed into the wilderness and the other, with no one to care for him, are certainly the worst of the lot. Tigay notes (106) that it is just such cases of uncared-for spirits that Gilgamesh, once deified as a judge of the netherworld, is entreated to help. The line in brackets has been added to the text by the translators, but the intensity of the left-overs, the offal tossed to the unloved spirit is clear in the text. The end of the poem would seem to be appropriate to the role of Gilgamesh and to the role of the exorcist like Sîn-leqi-unninnī. In a negative way, it reinforces, however, the theme of love that pervades the work.

A colophon at the end of column vi indicates that the *Gilgamesh* series is complete at this point.

Appendix

TRANSLATING
GILGAMESH

The more remote the text, the more decisions about translating it multiply. Two well-preserved passages from *Gilgamesh* illustrate procedures taken to arrive at a reasonable translation of poetry from at least as early as the Middle Babylonian Period (1600–1000 B.C.) of Akkadian literature. Both are speeches, one by the god Shamash to Enkidu (VII.iii.33–48), the second by the god Ea to Utnapishtim (XI.i.36–47). Speeches in Sumerian and Akkadian literature are usually quite formal and well-organized, as these are. Because they are designed well, the speeches shed light on the way the poet composes poetic units longer than the line or line-pair. The second, especially, raises questions about the use of figurative language in Akkadian poetry, something we have come to expect in poetry, perhaps, but a feature of ancient works difficult to translate.

GILGAMESH VII.iii.33–48

Enkidu, nearing death, has cursed the woman who has brought him from the wild to fully human life—and with it suffering and the anticipation of death. Shamash responds:

Shamash heard, opened his mouth,   33
and from afar, . . . from the heavens called to him:
"Why, Enkidu, do you curse the love-priestess, the woman
who would feed you with the food of the gods,   36
and would have you drink wine that is the drink of kings,
and would clothe you in a great garment,
and would give you beautiful Gilgamesh as a companion?

Listen: hasn't Gilgamesh, your beloved friend,   40
made you lie down in a great bed?
Hasn't he made you lie down in a bed of honor,
and placed you on the peaceful seat at his left hand?
The world's kings have kissed your feet.

He will make the people of Uruk weep for you, cause them to
    grieve you,
[will make the women], the whole city, fill up with sorrow for
    your sake.
And afterward he will carry the signs of grief on his own body,
putting on the skin of dogs and ranging the wilderness."

CENTIMETERS	1	2	3	4	5	6	7	8	9	10
INCHES		1		2		3			4	

The small text, upper left, provided R. Campbell Thompson with VII.iii.33–40, as can be seen from his handcopy of the tablet on page 279. The right-hand portion of VII.iii.33–48 is from another tablet (see photo opposite). The text on the right is actually a joining of three fragments. It provided Thompson with the larger part of XI.i.36–47 (see photo on page 293). Photograph reproduced by Courtesy of the Trustees of the British Museum.

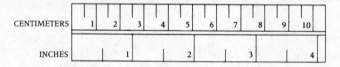

CENTIMETERS	1	2	3	4	5	6	7	8	9	10
INCHES		1		2		3		4		

The broken clay tablet, lower left, provided Thompson with VII.iii.33–48. (Note the small tablet, upper left, whose face is so obliterated that no signs can be read.) Photograph reproduced by Courtesy of the Trustees of the British Museum.

The Akkadian text of Gilgamesh VII.iii.33–48 in transliteration

33 ^{ilu}šamaš iš-ma-a-[ma ip-t]ì pi-i-šu
34 ul-tu ul-la-nu-um-ma . . . [ul-tu] šamê(e) il-ta-na-sa-aš-šu
35 am-me-ni ^{ilu}en-ki-dù ḫa-rim-[t]i ^ršam-ḫat ta-na-an-za-ar
36 ša u-ša-ki-lu-ka akla si-mat ilu-u-ti
37 ku-ru-un-na iš-qu-ka si-mat šarru-u-ti
38 u-lab-bi-šu-ka lu-ub-ši ra-ba-a
39 u dam-qu ^{ilu}gilgāmeš tap-pa-a u-šar-šu-ka ka-a-ša
40 [e]-nin-na-a-ma ^{ilu}gilgāmeš ib-ri ta-li-me-ka
41 [uš-na]-a-al-ka-a-ma ina ma-a-a-ali rabî(i)
42 [i-na] ma-a-a-al tak-ni-i uš-na-al-ka-ma
43 [u-ši]š-šib-ka šub-ta-ni-iḫ-ta šu-bat šu-me-li
44 [ma-al]-ka ša qaq-qa-ri u-na-aš-ša-qu šepâ^{II}-ka
45 [u-šab]-kak-ka niše^{meš} ša uruk^{ki} u-šad-ma-ma-ak-ka
46 [šam-ḫa-a-ti] niše^{meš} u-ma-al-lak-ka dul-la
47 [u šu]-u ar-ki-ka u-ša-aš-ša-a-ma-la-a pa-gar-[šu]
48 [il-tab-bi]-iš maš-ki kal-bi-im-ma i-rap-pu-ud ṣ[êri]

(Transliteration: after R. Campbell Thompson, *The Epic of Gilgamesh: Text, Transliteration, and Notes* [Oxford: Clarendon Press, 1930], p. 45.)

Thompson's handcopy of Tablet VII. The lines mark the two texts that provide VII.iii.33–48. Used with permission of Oxford University Press.

The passage does not present translators today with the maddening problems that come when large gaps in the text appear or when the vocabulary is odd or used in an unusual way. Even in the earliest translation of the lines, made by George Smith just after he discovered the tablets, the main points are clear:

> And Shamas opened his mouth
> and spake and from heaven said to him:
> . . . and the female Samhat (delightful) thou shalt choose
> they shall array thee in trappings of divinity
> they shall give thee the insignia of royalty
> they shall make thee become great
> and Izdubar thou shalt call and incline him towards thee
> he Izdubar shall make friendship unto thee
> he shall cause thee to recline on a grand couch
> on a beautiful couch he shall seat thee
> he will cause thee to sit on a comfortable seat a seat on the left
> the kings of the earth shall kiss thy feet
> he shall enrich thee and the men of Uruk shall make silent
>   before thee
> and he after thee shall take all . . .
> he shall clothe thy body in raiment and . . .[1]

It is worth comparing the two versions to show the kinds of materials translators used then and now. Smith already knew the passage had something to do with "divinity" and "royalty," something "great" given to Enkidu, the friendship of Gilgamesh, a bed of honor, and the "kings of the earth" kissing the feet of Enkidu. Otherwise, the passage seems a bit vague, and Smith misses a line near the end, where the passage sort of dwindles away. What he did was remarkable in the 1870s. And, though Smith did not leave his own transliteration of the passage behind, it can be shown that he read the cuneiform signs properly. How did he manage to get so close and yet translate the passage in such a different way?

Look at the handcopy of the passage made by R. Campbell Thompson (1930) for what is still the standard text of *Gilgamesh*.[2] Plate 28 is Campbell Thompson's handcopy of the end of Tablet VII, column iii. He has marked in the line numbers. (Ignore the small fragment at the bottom, marked K.10536.) The signs used by the ancient scribes are called "cuneiform" or "wedge-shaped" signs. They were impressed most often in the still-wet surface of a tablet made of clay with a reed stylus. By turning the stylus, the scribe produced small wedges horizontally (►) or vertically (▼), large wedges of the same type (►—) and (▼), and small and large wedges at an angle (▲) and (◣), called "Winkelhaken." Cuneiform signs are made up of combinations of the marks. Sometimes spaces in a line of text (read left to right, top to bottom) indicate separate words, but as often as not, words are not clearly separated from one another.[3] When signs are jammed together on a line, as they are in lines 34 and 39, finding the separate words can be tricky. Add to that the peculiarities of a scribe's handwriting, and it is difficult to tell where one sign begins and another ends. The clarity in which they appear in Campbell Thompson is already the result of many decisions made about just what signs have been impressed in the clay. To produce a new edition of *Gilgamesh* —as opposed to a new translation based on existing edited texts—would require a painstaking reconsideration of every sign on every line of all the fragments and duplicates that have been discovered. Note the last two signs in line 31, for example. Signs along every break can present impossible problems, and the wear and tear on the clay can lead to the rubbing away or breaking off of a small clue that might help reconstruct an entire line.[4]

Scribal handwriting is not the only problem facing the modern reader, or epigrapher. The signs, which were originally pictographic but had become highly stylized in the Third Millennium,[5] changed gradually over the three thousand years they were used. To take a simple example, the first two signs in line 33 form the name of the god Shamash. The signs appear as they do in the Neo-Assyrian (1000–400 B.C.) Period, the period in which the *Gilgamesh* was recopied for the Library of Ashurbanipal. The first sign, called *dingir* (after the Sumerian word for "god"), is a silent determinant, indicating that the sign or signs following it form the name of a god: ►▼— . The second sign by itself means "sun" and "sun god," Shamash: ▒▼ . In an Old Babylonian text of Gilgamesh (2000–1600 B.C.), the two signs would appear differently, the *dingir* as: ►▒ , and "sun" as: ▒▼ . Of course, the very changes that complicate the writing system give important clues to the date of a text that is unearthed.

Once the signs are recognized, they must be read, that is, interpreted. A fully pictographic text could, presumably, be read by anyone in any language, but such texts are very rare. (Consider just how universal the modern equivalents, international road signs, really are. Although the technology of automobiles and highways is very widespread, even today there are many people who would fail to grasp the meaning of the signs.) The Neo-Assyrian text of *Gilgamesh* has no true pictographs. The signs are of three types: logographs, syllable-signs, and determinatives. The "sun" sign is a logograph. Reading it would depend upon the language of the text, here *shamash* in Akkadian as opposed to, say, *utu* in

Sumerian—or any of the several other languages written in cuneiform (Hittite, Hurrian, Ugaritic). But the meaning would be clear even if we did not know the name in that language. The "god" sign, *dingir*, is both logographic (if pronounced, it would be *ilu* in Akkadian) and a determinative, as pointed out above, an unpronounced indicator of a god name. Most of the signs in the text are syllable-signs.

Look at line 39, "and would give you beautiful Gilgamesh as a companion." The line consists of seventeen cuneiform signs, read *u dam-qu* *^{ilu}Gilgamesh tap-pa-a u-šar-šu-ka ka-a-ša*. In this "transliteration" into Akkadian syllables, the words have been separated, although it is not obvious from the text where the breaks occur. The line includes the name Gilgamesh, written with four signs: ⊨⊨⊨⊨. (Note that the *dingir* determinative, written in superscript *d* or *ilu*, does *not* mean that the whole name is a god name. As often happens with Sumerian and Akkadian names, the name is theophoric, that is, it contains the name of the god and something about the god, usually flattering to the bearer of the name, possibly for good luck. When George Smith read Enkidu as "Heabani," he was reading the signs in Akkadian, whereas we now prefer to read the signs in Sumerian, since Gilgamesh and Enkidu were originally Sumerian figures. In the name Gilgamesh, the *dingir* governs only the next sign in the complex, i.e., *GIŠ*. In the Old Babylonian Gilgamesh texts, his name is regularly shortened to just *^{ilu}GIŠ*. Even so, it does not mean that Gilgamesh is a god because he has a theophoric name.) The reading of the hero's name is still a matter of debate after a hundred years of scholarly study. Smith called him Izdubar; now some claim he should be called Bilgamesh. What is significant is that the complex *^{d}GIŠ-GÍN-MAŠ* can potentially be read in quite a number of different ways. "Gilgamesh" has been the conventional reading since late in the nineteenth century (A.D.), and so has been followed here.

The debate over the reading of the name Gilgamesh tells us another important fact about the cuneiform writing system. Even when the individual sign is isolated and the language of the text is known, there are still many possibilities for reading the sign. In our one line of seventeen signs, for example, the first sign, *u*, has only one pronunciation as a syllable, but we know of at least five Akkadian words the sign could stand for *(bēlu, buru, gigurû, pilšu, ubānu)*, if it did not stand for the *u* meaning "and." The second sign, read *dam*, could also be read *tam*, or it could point to the Akkadian word *aššatu*, "wife." The third sign, read *qu*, could also be *kum* or *qum*, or it could stand for an Akkadian word meaning "to crush," and so forth. One sign, read here *pa* (in the word *tap-pa-a*, "companion"), has no fewer than nine possibilities as a syllable-marker *(pa, ḫad, ḫat, ḫaṭ, ḫáš, ḫáṣ, sàk, sìg, zák,* and *zaq)* and at least nine different possibilities as a complete word, from "scepter" to "bird." This is not to consider that the signs enter into combinations with one another in long strings that vastly multiply the power of the system.[6]

With such a bewildering array of sign values, some of which were active in one period, some in another, there is little wonder that it took years of study in the *é-dub-ba* (scribal school) for a scribe to achieve competency. Even kings took pride in knowing the mysteries of the system. Borger lists just about 600 signs in his sign list. With various logographic possibilities, many syllabic readings, and a host of combinatorial chances, one can see why only a tiny minority of the population would be literate. A simple alphabet, with twenty to forty characters, seems almost a miraculous invention after such complexity. And such did happen. The alphabet we use is a greatly simplified (and much transformed) system derived from cuneiform.[7]

The great advantage of the syllabic system is that it allows us to reconstruct the pronunciation of Akkadian with a greater fidelity than, say, biblical Hebrew, although the Hebrew texts are centuries later than the Akkadian texts. Biblical Hebrew was originally written in only consonants; only much later, after the language had changed, as languages will, was an attempt made to add vowels to the Hebrew text. The situation with cuneiform is much different. Perhaps because the cuneiform system was used in a bilingual situation at a very early date—as early as 2650 B.C. there were scribes writing Sumerian texts who had Semitic names as well as scribes who had Sumerian names[8]—the pronunciation of the signs was important. Even in the northern Syrian city of Ebla in the Third Millennium, bilingual lexical texts were concerned not only with the equivalence of words in two languages (in that case, Sumerian and Semitic Eblaite), but with the vocalization of the texts as well.[9] The literary dialect of Akkadian, called Standard Babylonian, had the following phonemes: stops /b, p, d, t, ṭ, g, k, q/, sonants /m, n, r, l/, and vowels /a, e, i, u/. There were also five spirants /z, s, ṣ, š, ḫ/. Some of the phonemes are not found in English but are common in Semitic languages. The "hard t" /ṭ/ is one; the velar palatal /q/ is another (not the /kw/ we represent by *qu* in English). The pharyngealized sibilant /ṣ/ is another "hard" phoneme. The voiceless /š/ is another sibilant, this one familiar to us as *sh,* as in Shamash. Finally, /ḫ/is not our *h* but a tongue-based laryngeal.[10] Thanks to numerous bilingual Sumerian-Akkadian lexical texts and bilingual compositions, the ancient scribes have given us many clues to the vocalization of their texts—although there have been no native speakers of Akkadian for over two thousand years.

Akkadian is a language in the Semitic family of languages. Because it is related to living languages like Arabic and Hebrew that have been much studied, Akkadian grammar was reconstructed rather early. (By contrast, the Sumerian language, in spite of the great help from the ancient grammarians themselves, still contains mysteries that elude scholars today; it is unrelated to any known language.) Thus both phonological and grammatical features of Akkadian are known to us.[11] Dictionaries of Akkadian were begun in the mid-nineteenth century, but only recently have the vast lexical resources of the many thousands of clay tablets become available to the non-specialist, with the completion of Wolfram von Soden's *Akkadisches Handwörterbuch*. The twenty-one-volume *Chicago Assyrian Dictionary* is not far behind. Based on experience gained in compiling *The Oxford English Dictionary* and the Berlin Egyptian Dictionary, the CAD has now published fourteen of the twenty-one volumes.[12]

In the line from *Gilgamesh* VII.iii mentioned above, we have an example of the assistance modern dictionaries give the translator. Line 39 reads *u damqu* [ilu]*Gilgāmeš tappâ ušaršuka kâša*, which we have seen as the end of a sequence of gifts the prostitute has given Enkidu: "and would give you beautiful Gilgamesh as a companion." We learn in CAD 3(D).68–74 that much is known of the word written in two signs on the tablet, *dam-qu*. The word can be written syllabically, as it is here, or it can appear as a single sign, called *SIG₅*.[13] There are lexical texts from antiquity which give *damqu* as the equivalent of the Sumerian word *sig;* and bilingual texts show how Sumerian texts were translated by Akkadian scribes. The CAD is particularly generous in providing clauses and sentences from a variety of sources to show how the word is used in context. The word *damqu* can mean "good fortune" and "kindness," but these are rather unusual. Far more often the term is used as one of the relatively few adjectives in Akkadian. The CAD detects nine distinct meanings of *damqu* as an adjective and points out the distribution of each in different periods of the language. The word means "good" ("fine," "pleasant"); "beautiful" or "handsome"; "of good family"; "expert"; "of good quality"; "gracious"; "propitious"; "effective" and "canonical." The nuances are especially helpful to the translator. We follow the CAD, which cites the line, in thinking the sense here is "handsome" or "beautiful."

The peculiarities of clay tablets and the cuneiform sign system, the different values of the signs, and the range of meanings make translating Akkadian a slow and painstaking process—one that demands a word-for-word and syllable-for-syllable transliteration before any larger complexes can be addressed. Fortunately, the popularity of *Gilgamesh* among cuneiformists has meant an ample commentary on the philological features of the text. The typical Akkadian poetic line, as in our example above, helps to fix the word within the context of a clause. The poetic line, whatever metrical features it may have, usually consists of one or two clauses. Sometimes two lines are closely related couplets, the clauses of one line answering to clauses in the other. Enjambed or run-on lines occur, but infrequently. In *Gilgamesh,* enjambment appears to be the mark of a special stylistic turn. The poetic line and the heavily formulaic character of Akkadian are the reasons why a complete clause can often be reconstructed from a few signs in a highly fragmented line of text.

Reconstruction can be dangerous, though. Return to the two translations of VII.iii.33−48 above. The first four lines illustrate the problem.

now: "Shamash heard, opened his mouth,"
Smith: "Shamas opened his mouth"

now: "and from afar, . . . from the heavens called to him:"
Smith: "and spake and from heaven said to him:"

now: "Why, Enkidu, do you curse the love-priestess, the woman"
Smith: ". . . and the female Samhat (delightful) thou shalt choose"

now: "who would feed you with the food of the gods,"
Smith: "they shall array thee in trappings of divinity"

Why was Smith in 1876 so close and yet so far from the mark? In this case, the answer is visible from Campbell Thompson's handcopy (Plate 28) of the text. The four lines are those just below the line drawn across the text above line 33. The first three lines have a large gap right in the center of the text, and the fourth line has one sign in the middle that is broken at the top. Notice, though, that Campbell Thompson has put together two fragments, one in the upper-left corner (lines 27−40), the other right and center (lines 31−51). Notice how the broken side on the left of the larger text can be traced by the many dots in Campbell Thompson's text through broken signs. Just in the middle, a dotted line circles four signs in line 38, one sign in 39, and one sign in line 40. These are signs found on both texts. Campbell Thompson notes the variants, since the two texts sometimes disagree. The smaller text in the upper-left has the British Museum number K11659; the larger text, right and center, has another British Museum number, K3389.

The solution to the puzzle is soon clear. Smith, who discovered the K-numbered texts at Nineveh, did not join the two fragments. (Considering the many thousands of small fragments, often with only a few cuneiform signs on them, it is surprising how many Smith was able to recognize and place in his, the first, attempt at the *Gilgamesh*.) He had, in other words, only K3389 and not K11659. For the four lines in question, he tried to reconstruct the whole line from only a few signs on the right. From the first line, he could read *pi-i-šu*, "his mouth," and from that small clue he could guess the shape of the opening of a speech, a formulaic expression. From the second line, he could read that the person was called "from the heavens," and so was able to surmise that the speaker was the sun god, Shamash. The "female Samhat (delightful)" is our "love-priestess." Smith thought that the woman had a proper name, Samhat, that meant "delightful." The "female" is a silent determinative indicating that the word following, *šamḫatu*, is in a class of females; normally, it is not vocalized or translated. Smith had the verb form in the line, but guessed "choose" instead of "curse" because he did not have the larger context of Enkidu's cursing the prostitute. Indeed, he chose to place this fragment, not in Tablet VII (notoriously difficult to piece together), but in Tablet II! With what he had of the text, he concluded, quite reasonably, that the fragment was a *prediction* of what would happen to Enkidu—not a curse after the fact, when Enkidu was near death.

This is not to fault Smith. What he was attempting, with far fewer resources than we now have, is not essentially different from what is attempted today. The last of the four lines reinforces the strengths and weaknesses of the process. Again, Smith had only the end of the line to work with. He knew that the line was paired with the next line. One had something to do with the gods, the second with kings. Just what it was could not be read from the fragmented lines. So he surmised "trappings of divinity" and followed it with "insignia of royalty." With greater hindsight, we can see that he was wrong. The second fragment helps recover the true pairings, "food of the gods" and "the drink of kings." Smith did not have the verb in the line. He thought that, besides Samhat, there was yet another woman involved, and that led him to "they" as the subject; since he had thought the line involved "trappings of divinity," "they shall array thee" seemed reasonable for the first part of the line. One would like to wait until a "complete" text of *Gilgamesh* is available before translating it. One hundred years of work have not produced that complete text. In the meantime, risks have to be taken—and mistakes will be made that are likely to fill later generations with as much amusement as Smith's pioneering work occasions in us—or more, as with Leonidas Le Cenci Hamilton's 1884 *Ishtar and Izdubar*.

Recall that *Gilgamesh* VII.iii.33–48 is one of the *best*-preserved sections of the poem, that there is little controversy today about the reconstruction of the text. Even with two good fragments, the lower-left (lines 40–48) is still missing and must be reconstructed. And the gap in line 34 remains. No one has a reasonable surmise about the signs in the break. Consider what would have been the case if the few signs in lines 49–51 had not survived. We would not know what Enkidu did when he heard Shamash's advice. The episode ends with Enkidu's angry heart growing still. Enkidu, ever the very figure of rebellion, comes close here to the resignation of the lordly Gilgamesh. But for a handful of signs at the end of a column, the whole resolution would have been lost.

Translating *Gilgamesh*, then, involves careful weighing of many features peculiar to cuneiform texts, thousands of small decisions that reflect the state of the art at the moment the text is engaged. There are larger questions of translation, though, that can be illustrated in this passage.

The first thing to notice about Shamash's speech to Enkidu is that it is well designed. After the introductory formula (33–34), the speech itself falls into three clear sections (36–39, 40–44, 45–48) of roughly equal length. The second section has one more line than the other two, but it also contains the only example of enjambment in the speech (40–41) and so the sections have rather equal development. The first section tells Enkidu of the gifts the prostitute has given him. The second and third sections turn to gifts Gilgamesh has given him and will give him in future. Gilgamesh is also the last and highest of the gifts the prostitute has given Enkidu (line 39), and the two sections are thus elegantly tied together (39 and 40). There is, of course, no attempt to capture the hesitation, wavering, fragmentary quality of ordinary discourse, the way a modern novelist might want to capture it. Instead, the speech illustrates Akkadian poetic technique beyond the single line and the line-pair.

The introductory formula itself (33–34) is worth noting. One reason why there is hesitation about reconstructing the signs in the break (line 34) is that the introduction is an unusual variation on what is usually very standardized language. As Tigay (p. 233) has pointed out, there are two distinct introductory formulas for speeches in *Gilgamesh*. "A said to him, to B" (A *ana šâšu/šâšima izzakkar[a] ana* B), and (A *pâšu īpušamma iqabbi izzakkara ana* B), "A opened his mouth to speak, saying to B." The first is typical of Old Babylonian Akkadian in *The Epic of Gilgamesh;* the second is a formula found only in late texts. The first line of our speech, *ilušamaš iš-ma-a-[ma ip-t]ì pi-i-šu,* "Shamash heard, opened his mouth," is, as we have seen, close enough to the late formula that George Smith felt he could reconstruct the line only from the last three signs. But it is not really the same, and the second line is far different—"and from afar, . . . from the heavens called to him." The free and unusual reworking of a traditional formula is a characteristic of Sîn-leqi-unninnī's technique.

If we consider further that there is no parallel to the episode—Enkidu's curses, Shamash's advice, the change in Enkidu, Enkidu's blessings—in the Old Babylonian *The Epic of Gilgamesh*, it would appear that this passage is one of the best to show the poet's individual technique. Even the *carpe diem* motif present in the passage, a motif so characteristic of the Old Babylonian version, is modified in line with the increasing seriousness of Sîn-leqi-unninnī's work.

Schematically, the passage looks like this:

33–34. Introductory speech formula.
    35. Opening of the question that ties 36–39 together,
        Why do you curse the prostitute who . . . ?
36–39. Gifts of the prostitute: food of the gods
                       the drink of kings
                       a great garment
                       Gilgamesh as a companion.
40–44. What Gilgamesh has given you: to lie in a great bed
                               to lie in a bed of honor
                               to place you at his left hand
                               kings have kissed your feet.
45–48. What Gilgamesh will do for you:
        A. He will have the city mourn your death.
        B. He will mourn your death.

Even in outline, the careful building of sections is clear. The gifts are the whole life of mankind in civilized life, from those things needed to survive (prepared food and drink), to what marks Enkidu as human and not merely animal ("great garment"), to Gilgamesh himself and the trappings of power and prestige. Even the city's mourning is part of the process. Enkidu will be remembered, his death marked by the city and, returning to the personal, by Gilgamesh. In the last two lines, ironically, the expression of Gilgamesh's grief blends into the loss of self and Gilgamesh's attempt to become what Enkidu was before he was civilized, "ranging the wilderness" *(irappud ṣ[êri])*.

What Sîn-leqi-unninnī has managed is perhaps so obvious that its importance is missed. At a moment of great change for Enkidu, just before his death when he is asked to understand what has happened to him and to accept the meaning of his life, the poet recapitulates the whole movement we have called the Apollonian movement in *Gilgamesh*. As is typical of this poet, he summarizes the action of the poem without explicitly mentioning battle; the heroic fighting of Gilgamesh and Enkidu, like the *carpe diem* motif, is made implicit and at the same time transformed in the process, subordinated to a vision of existence that includes death and understanding. The lines are beautifully lucid and make good use of hierarchical design. The speech is, of course, an *argument*. And it is an argument that the poet skillfully designed to be convincing. It convinces Enkidu, who turns his curse of the prostitute into a blessing.

That the passage develops an argument should be enough to dispel the notion that ancient myth is incompatible with reasoning, or that one is likely to find only "pre-logical" or "primitive" thought before the Greeks. Story, myth, still predominates. (Think of the different interpretations offered for Gilgamesh's return to Uruk at the end of Tablet XI. There narrative carries the entire theme of Gilgamesh's "recognition" and "resignation," without any need for the sort of explicit comment found here.)

The passage is a divine revelation. The poet emphasizes the transcendence of Shamash. Where he had inspired the men through dreams, he now speaks directly, without ambiguity—but "from afar, . . . from the heavens." Yet there is nothing magical about the speech. It has nothing to do with a Shamash cult. It does not serve to establish the fates. Ironically, the force behind Enkidu's curse and blessing, like Jacob's curses and blessings of his sons (Genesis 49), comes from the magical power of the word. Enkidu cannot simply change the fate of the prostitute (the entire history of prostitutes, note, not just that of the particular one who seduced him); he can only add blessings. He cannot simply cancel the curse, once uttered. Both sides stand as if Enkidu's words alone were sufficient to secure them. But Shamash's words have no such force. They are words of persuasion, not of force. And if they mollify the angry heart of Enkidu, it is because the words have convinced him.

If the outline of the passage and the themes contained in it can be captured without great difficulty by the translator, there remain a number of smaller, subtler matters that are difficult to convey in translation. In general, we do not like formal repetition in our literature today. Typically, we strive to obscure the basic orderliness of our compositions. This makes it difficult to appreciate, for example, Sumerian poetry, which seems to find as much delight in the discovery of order as we take in the discovery of chaos. Large patches of Sumerian poetry are repeated word for word, line for line. Akkadian heroic poetry, which depends for so much on Sumerian poetry, is different. Subtle variation is often preferred to straight repetition. Still, Akkadian poetry is much closer to Sumerian poetry than to modern British and American poetry.

The handling of the verbs in this passage is an example. There are a number of places where word order and the placing of words in the poetic line serve aesthetic rather than semantic purposes. The transition between sections one and two is very strongly marked. Line 39 ends the list of the prostitute's gifts by naming Gilgamesh the *tappû*, or companion, and concludes the sequence of lines 35–39 (one full sentence) with a full stop. The next sequence opens with the strong, *[e]-nin-na-a-ma*, "Now then!" or "Listen!" But instead of giving us the usual line-clause, the poet repeats the name Gilgamesh and emphasizes the companionship by not one but two appositives, *ib-ri ta-li-me-ka*, "the equal, the one with whom you are intimate," or as we have rendered it, "your beloved friend." Here the variety more than, perhaps, the precision of the terms keeps the lines separate and at the same time ties them together. The verbs and objects in the passage show a similarly elegant variation.

In the first section, the verb forms are subjunctive, after the *ša* ("who") that begins the sequence in line 36. The subjunctive forms are not simple past-tense forms; they do not merely indicate that the prostitute has fed Enkidu, given him drink, a garment, and Gilgamesh. Rather, the forms tend to define the role of the prostitute (without, at the same time, casting the fate—where the poet would have used precative forms or imperatives). We have translated the sequence with the modal "would." Why curse the woman "who would feed you . . . ,/ and would have you drink . . . ,/ and would clothe you . . . ,/ and would give you beautiful Gilgamesh as a companion?" At the same time we have tried to capture something of the repetition-with-variation in the word order. In line 36, for example, the Akkadian has a sequence V + Obj. + Appositive; the next line has Obj. + V + Appositive, where both appositives are in the construct form. The next two lines again vary V + Obj./ Obj. + V—but also add adjectives, one following the noun, which is the ordinary word order (*lu-ub-ši ra-ba-a*), the second fronting the noun (*dam-qu* ^ilu^*Gilgāmeš*), "garment great" and "beautiful Gilgamesh."

Similar play can be shown in sections two and three, where causative past and future forms are employed by the poet. The point, though, is that the Akkadian manages to be correct, elegant, and beautifully clear in the passage. It is an address appropriate to Shamash, god of light. There is a kind of wisdom uttered that is the equivalent in story to the myth of the sun god battling the monster of darkness. There is skill here, but it is subordinated to a cool, dispassionate, and unambiguous rhetoric of persuasion. The trick is to translate the discourse without losing the light touch and falling into the aged heaviness of King James Version prose style.

GILGAMESH XI.i.36–47

Gilgamesh travels to see the sage Utnapishtim in order to find life—and is given a story, the Flood. The poet seems to have anticipated the story, for Tablet I opens with Gilgamesh's most important act, his carrying back "word of the time before the Flood." In a very detailed comparison of the late version of *Gilgamesh* XI with the Old Babylonian *The Epic of Gilgamesh* on the one hand, and the versions of the Flood story known from what is called *Atra-ḥasīs* on the other, Tigay (214–240) concludes that the hero's journey to Utnapishtim was part of the Old Babylonian Gilgamesh story—but that the Flood story was not. Thus, he divides *Gilgamesh* XI into the Flood story and the non-Flood episodes. The Flood story is very close to versions of *Atra-ḥasīs*, some of which also date to the Old Babylonian Period. The poet of the late *Gilgamesh*, then, added the interest in the Flood, making it the chief discovery of the heroic quest, and used traditional materials to compose the Flood narrative.

Tigay also noticed an odd stylistic variation in *Gilgamesh* XI. The non-Flood episodes show a great deal of stylistic similarity to the late version of *Gilgamesh* generally; but the Flood does not seem to have been revised to fit the late style. A number of details are not fully assimilated into a harmonious narrative. One traditional feature Sîn-leqi-unninnī retains in the telling of the Flood story is the speech of the tricky god, Ea (called by his Sumerian name, Enki, in Old Babylonian *Atra-ḥasīs* texts). Ea speaks three times in the Flood story (XI.i.19–31, 36–47, and iv.177–188) and once in Tablet XII. One of the speeches has gained great prominence in cuneiform literature: it contains the most famous use of metaphor in any Akkadian text. Because the translation of metaphor presents a number of special problems, the speech is worth looking at in some detail.

Ea informs Utnapishtim (through a wall) of the Flood ordered by the god Enlil and tells Utnapishtim what to do to escape the Flood. Utnapishtim has a problem. How can he get the boat constructed without telling the citizens of the Flood? In a masterpiece of indirection, Ea tells Utnapishtim what to say to the people. He need not lie to the citizens. Rather he need only exploit the resources of language itself to trick the people into helping in the project.

> "Ea shaped his mouth, saying,
> saying to me, his servant,
> 'You, you may say this to them:
> Enlil hates me—me!
> I cannot live in your city

> or turn my face toward the land which is Enlil's.
> I will go down to the Abyss, to live with Ea, my lord.
> He will make richness rain down on you—
> the choicest birds, the rarest fish.
> The land will have its fill of harvest riches.
> At dawn bread
> he will pour down on you—showers of wheat.' "

The final five lines are richly metaphorical. The beginning of the speech, too, is filled with wordplay. Indeed, the piece is the most conspicuous sustaining of figurative language through a complete poem in *Gilgamesh*. The figures are sustained in order to avoid the lie.

The speech is not given directly, as was Shamash's in VII.iii.33–48, but within the context of Utnapishtim's first-person account of an event that took place in the past. As Utnapishtim recounts it, Ea addresses him, but avoids using the human's name—perhaps because it preserves the ruse of the reed-wall. Ea can still claim in the assembly of the gods (XI.iv.186–187) that he did not "unhide the secret of the great gods" because he did not address the sage by name. In any event, the avoidance of Utnapishtim's name brings into prominence the pronouns that refer to him. Independent personal pronouns are not needed, ordinarily, in Akkadian, because the pronominal function is included in the verb form or appears as a suffix. One consequence of the use of pronouns in the passage, which are emphatic when they are used, is a play on the name of the god, $^{ilu}é$-a, and the first-person pronouns ia-a-tu (37), ia-a-$ši$ (39), and the suffix -ia-a-ma (41). Utnapishtim is to tell the elders: Enlil hates ia-a-$ši$, hates -an-ni-ma. It is a simple statement, true on one level, but it contains a kind of play that will increasingly dominate the passage. It prepares the hearer (Gilgamesh/the reader) for the language to become more intensely figurative.

The reader needs to know that the Flood will come soon to appreciate otherwise straightforward statements. Utnapishtim will indeed not be able to gaze upon the "earth" of Enlil. The three gods, Anu, Enlil, and Ea, were thought to divide the universe: Anu (heavens), Enlil (earth), and Ea (the below, the *apsû*). Utnapishtim, unable to turn his face to the land, will "go down" to the Abyss, the dwelling-place of Ea. This is true only in the sense that the earth is covered—and the *apsû* is let loose in flood upon the earth. The boat does not otherwise "go down" to the *apsû*.

The "he" of "he will make richness rain down on you" (43) is perhaps ambiguously Ea or Enlil, but the point is a minor one compared with the scandal of misdirection by which the waters below *(apsû)* and

The lines mark the text that provided R. Campbell Thompson with XI.i.36–39. (The larger part of XI.i.36–47 can be seen in photo on page 276.) Photograph reproduced by Courtesy of the Trustees of the British Museum.

The Akkadian text of Gilgamesh XI.i.36–47 in transliteration

36 ^{ilu}é-a pa-a-šu i-pu-uš-ma i-qab-bi
37 i-zak-ka-ra ana ardi-šu ia-a-tu
38 lu-u at-ta ki-a-am ta-qab-ba-aš-šu-nu-ti
39 [e(?)]-di-ma ia-a-ši ^{ilu}en-lil i-zi-ir-an-ni-ma
40 ul uš-šab ina â[li-ku]-nu-ma
41 ina qaq-qar ^{ilu}en-lil ul a-šak-ka-n[a] pani-ia-a-ma
42 [ur-r]ad-ma apsî it-ti ^{ilu}é-a [be]-li-a aš-ba-ku
43 [eli k]a-a-šu-nu u-ša-az-nak-ku-nu-ši nu-uḫ-šam-ma
44 [ḫi-iṣ-bi] iṣṣuri (?) pu-zu-ur nûni^{meš}-ma
45 [išarrakkunūš]i meš-ra-a e-bu-ra-am-ma
46 [ina šēr(i)] ku-uk-ki
47 [ina lilâtu u]-ša-az-na-na-ku-nu-ši ša-mu-tu ki-ba-a-ti

(Transliteration: after R. Campbell Thompson, *The Epic of Gilgamesh: Text, Transliteration, and Notes* [Oxford: Clarendon Press, 1930], pp. 60–61.)

Thompson's handcopy of Tablet XI. The lines mark the two texts that provide XI.i.36–47. Used with permission of Oxford University Press.

the waters above *(zanānu)* produce the great Flood. Vegetation as well as marine life is sustained by the waters below. The verb *zanānu* means both "to rain" and "pour out" and "to provide food," "to provide an institution with means of support." [14] The lines play upon Ea's traditional role, bringing waters from below and above to produce the fertile land. Compare a Sumerian Enki hymn:

> At my word the stalls are built, the sheepfolds ringed about:
> when it nears the above, a rain of plenty rains from above;
> when it nears the below, there is a carp-flood of flooding water;
> when it nears the green flood meadow,
> at my command piles of grain are piled up inside and out. [15]

Where the Sumerian is straightforward, though, *Gilgamesh* XI is devious. The result of the god's actions will be "the choicest birds" and a *puzru*, the "rarest" of fish. The waters will produce "riches" *(mašru)* and a "harvest" *(ebūru)*. The elders can hardly be expected to guess what sort of baleful harvest it will be.

In fact, the people of the city are delighted. Drink is poured as if it were the water of a river (XI.ii.73). The city makes a festival like the New Year's Festival (XI.ii.74) when the boat is built. And no wonder. Through Utnapishtim Ea offers "bread" at dawn (46) and "showers of wheat" in the night (47): a pun on both *kukku*, a kind of bread or cake, and *kukkû*, "darkness" (used as a name for the netherworld); and on *kibtu*, "wheat" but also "misfortune"—both senses are exploited here. What the elders expect is bread and wheat; what they will get is darkness and misfortune.

The passage presents the usual problems of reading the cuneiform signs and putting together a text line that is broken in places. Campbell Thompson, as seen in Plate 45, used two different texts to construct lines 36–47. His D-text (S.2131) is actually a join of five small fragments; and his E-text (K.8517), of two. Even so, the lower left hand is broken away. Since the readings of the last few lines are particularly important, reconstruction of the passage is crucial. In this case, the task is eased because the last two lines are repeated in XI.ii.87, 90. That is something of a surprise, but the repetition of the key lines, "At dawn bread/ he will pour down showers of wheat" (without the suffix, "on you," note) reinforces the importance of the lines. The repetition in XI.ii.87 has been a bit of a puzzle. Many think Shamash (who is himself a surprise in the context of the Flood story) speaks the line. [16] This is not necessarily the case. In both 87 and 90, the repetition of the lines follow a reference to the "time" *(adannu)* set for the Flood to begin. The two lines, we think, have become the *name* of the Flood.

There is also a partial parallel to the lines in *Atra-ḫasīs*. The text is found in III.i.15–35 of that work,[17] a speech of Enki/Ea that conflates the first two speeches of Ea in *Gilgamesh*. As in *Gilgamesh* XI.i.19–31, Ea tells the sage (through a reed-wall) to build a boat. The details of the *Gilgamesh* follow *Atra-ḫasīs* very closely, although the two accounts are not entirely the same. The sequence is the same. The *Atra-ḫasīs* account does not, however, include Utnapishtim's question about what he should say to the elders of the city. Instead of ending the speech the way it is ended in *Gilgamesh*, it concludes abruptly with two lines that recall the end of *this* speech: "I will rain down upon you/ an abundance of birds, a basket of fishes!" (34–35). There is no ambiguity in Ea's speech in *Atra-ḫasīs* about whose responsibility it will be to bring the waters, as there is in *Gilgamesh*. The lines are metaphoric, but they are not devious. So far only *Gilgamesh* has preserved this extended, tricky speech of Ea.

Most commentators consider the Flood story in *Gilgamesh* a digression.[18] If the Flood story was not part of the Old Babylonian *The Epic of Gilgamesh*, why is it given such prominence by Sîn-leqi-unninnī? If he was the first to insert the tale—and to announce it in the very beginning of Tablet I—one might guess that there is more to the story for Gilgamesh than is usually considered. This is especially intriguing if the poet took over the old materials without changing them into the style of the rest of Gilgamesh's visit to Utnapishtim. We think that the answer lies with Ea —that the clue is not so much in the story of the saving of life itself but in the saving of life through what Ea and his servant, Utnapishtim, represent: cunning. This is most obvious in Ea's third speech, where Gilgamesh is told to listen closely to Ea's words—a sure way of tipping off the audience. But the same kind of cunning dominates all three speeches— though this one is even more conspicuous than the others, as cunning has entered fully into its form and texture.

Ea's speech illustrates a problem in translating texts that draw on traditional materials. In some ways *Gilgamesh* is quite free and innovative, making new connections between old Gilgamesh stories, adding a Flood story, or, as we have seen in the previous passage (VII.iii.33–48), carefully bringing a series of tales about Enkidu to closure by an exchange in which Enkidu's life is recounted, clarified for him, and recognized by Enkidu just before his death. Like Chaucer and Shakespeare in the English tradition, Sîn-leqi-unninnī did not hesitate to use old materials in new ways. Still, comparisons of *Gilgamesh* with older versions of Gilgamesh stories and with other versions of the Flood, such as we have here, indicate great respect for the literary tradition. Unless there is a clear need to change things, the poet is content to follow the sequence, details, and even the wording of texts in the stream of tradition. The last lines of our passage, the most famous example of figurative language in the tradition, may themselves have been traditional, a saying about the Flood that had become virtually the name of the event, like the date-formulas used in ancient texts to indicate a year in a king's reign. Translating figurative language is always tricky. The problem is in knowing how many contexts are involved.

Once isolated for purposes of analysis, a speech like Ea's may turn out to be organically unified or merely a string of originally unrelated sayings. Translating this passage demands that we work backward from the two lines that close the speech. Because the openings of speeches in Sumerian and Akkadian literature are usually marked explicitly by introductory formulas, the speech is usually a convenient unit for the study of compositional techniques. (The same could not be said about, say, modern fiction, where an attempt is made to capture something like naturalistic dialogue, with all its give-and-take, guided by the modern assumptions of highly individualistic characters.) This speech does appear to play with language in a certain way from the start. The reader is set up to expect increasingly clever ambiguity. The old notion, going back to Aristotle, that figures like metaphor are exchanges of names for objects, that a one-to-one correspondence holds between the "real" name of an object and the name chosen to replace it—that notion has given way to the idea that metaphor appears only in the context of, at minimum, a clause.[19] The play of metaphor in this speech extends to the last two lines and, beyond that, we suggest, to the speech as a whole.

We take the speech of Ea, then, as something more than a string of loosely related sayings. (The parallel in *Atra-ḫasīs* III.i.15–35, on the other hand, has the look of just such a string of sayings.) The context extends to the speech as a whole. But must we go further? The relevant contexts are within *Gilgamesh* and also beyond *Gilgamesh*. Ea's speech is one of three in the Flood episode. The speech occurs within a long address by Utnapishtim to Gilgamesh. Utnapishtim's "secret of the gods," the Flood story, is itself part of the narrative of Gilgamesh's visit to Utnapishtim, which consists of several episodes in *Gilgamesh* X and XI. *Gilgamesh* opens with what looks like an anticipation of the Flood story, crediting Gilgamesh's knowledge as his most important heroic achievement. And as the *Gilgamesh* advances, it becomes clear that the journey to Utnapishtim is Gilgamesh's goal after the death of Enkidu. This is all to say that it *appears* the speech is part of a larger, well-ordered composition. But, as has been seen, even the series of episodes that make up

Gilgamesh's encounter with Utnapishtim show such stylistic variation that one must be very cautious with a top-down translation of even the Flood story itself.

Add to this the intertextual connections between other versions of the Gilgamesh stories, which may or may not have been available to the poet; between the Flood in *Gilgamesh* and in Sumerian and Akkadian accounts of the Flood, especially *Atra-ḫasīs;* and between Ea's speeches in *Gilgamesh* XI and a tradition of composing Ea's speeches. About this last, already more than ninety speeches of Enki/Ea have been collected in the Sumerian, Akkadian, and Hittite languages. Because Ea is the talking god, there seems to be a much greater interest in representing Ea's speech than the speech of other gods—including Shamash. The "wisdom" tradition does not show such an interest in the speeches of the gods.[20] Many of Ea's speeches are part of magical rites and had magical power. Even when, as is the case here, Ea speaks because someone (usually a god; only very rarely a human) has a problem of such complexity that only the god of cunning can solve it, he *only* speaks. Sumerian literature represented Enki/Ea in a variety of activities, usually involving sexual activity and the creation of strange beings. In Akkadian literature he is mainly a problem solver. When Ninurta exclaims to the Assembly of the Gods (XI.iv.174–176) that only Ea could have tricked Enlil and saved mankind from the Flood, he is just reflecting a long tradition in the Enki/Ea literature. The tradition at least leads us to anticipate that a speech by Ea is likely to display a cunning in the play of words appropriate to Ea's "character."

We feel that this cunning *is* the point of including the journey of Gilgamesh to Utnapishtim in *Gilgamesh* and, in particular, the point of the Flood story. It is not the confident "wisdom" of Shamash, but its complement, its underside, as it were. Utnapishtim, servant of Ea, represents the devious, ironic, often brutal truth of existence that Ea presents in his role in cuneiform literature. If Shamash convinces Enkidu on his death-bed that life in its fullness is valuable in itself, Ea and the "overly wise" Utnapishtim make the point again and again: life preserved is not life as perfect happiness or life eternal. To seek life is necessary; to seek truth, bitter but the highest good of mankind. In its very indirection, the Flood story is like the dark center of a labyrinth. Or gazing at the *nagbu*. Gilgamesh resists the existential horror as long as he can. His recognition and return to Uruk are marked, not by joy, but by the resignation in winning a tragic knowledge, a kind of dark *gnosis*.

We have, then, considered the different contexts of Ea's speech and, in spite of the difficulties, decided for translation purposes that the speech and its context in *Gilgamesh* disclose a unified narrative and a well-worked theme. Structurally, Ea's role in what we have called the Dionysian phase of *Gilgamesh* is similar to Shamash's in the Apollonian phase. It is not the drunkenness of Dionysus (which has its counterpart in the *sparagmos* of Gilgamesh), but the tragic knowledge, the mad "secret" that comes like inspiration, that has, finally, urged this notion of a Dionysian phase.

Finally, it is worth noting that Gilgamesh's long journey, which takes him in agony to Utnapishtim, is a journey into the archaic. Where Shamash is the god of light and the clarity of reason, which gives us a stable world of past, present, and future, Ea is the old father, with a very different grasp of existence. Gilgamesh does not only leave the here-and-now world of Uruk to travel through a strange space. He also travels in time. Utnapishtim has escaped human time—the only human to have done so. But he represents the past, history divided by the Flood. He lived before Gilgamesh, and his Flood story is a tale of the past. This archaic character is especially evident in the Ea literature, where his young son is, typically, the one calling upon the old father to set things straight. The gods exist in a kind of non-time, the time of origins;[21] the Flood exists in imagination, and so can be told; Gilgamesh slips out of history for the time of his journey across the waters of death. Again, like the labyrinth or the abyss, the spiral takes Gilgamesh into intimacy with a terrible truth.

Ea's speech is speech about language. Only the cunning one, the poet, can lead into the archaic and lead us back to Uruk.

NOTES TO THE APPENDIX

1. George Smith, *The Chaldean Account of Genesis* (New York: Scribner, Armstrong and Co., 1876), pp. 197–198. A. H. Sayce made no changes in this passage when he revised Smith's *Account* in 1880. Paul Haupt, who edited the text for first time in *Das Babylonische Nimrodepos* (Leipzig: J. E. Hinreichs'sche, 1884), presents only the right fragment (=K 3389), not the left (K 11659), p. 15, #4.

2. R. Campbell Thompson, *The Epic of Gilgamesh: Text, Transliteration, and Notes* (Oxford: Clarendon Press, 1930).

3. The overwhelming majority of the hundreds of thousands of texts already discovered are clay tablets, sometimes sun-baked, sometimes baked in ovens. Others are cut into stone or metal. Some are painted on glazed terra-cotta. A few wooden tablets covered with beeswax have been found; but whereas baked clay tablets are virtually indestructible, the wooden tablets have not survived except in very peculiar circumstances. On the tablets and the "stream of tradition" that preserved texts, see A. Leo Oppenheim, *Ancient Mesopotamia* (Chicago: University of Chicago Press, 1964), pp. 8–30.

4. Here the tendency of cuneiform documents to be written in standard forms and formulas helps greatly to reconstruct a line from just a few signs. As an example of the simple wear and tear on tablets, some twenty lines in George Smith's translation appear to show that he had more of the text in the 1870s than was available to Paul Haupt in the early 1880s; signs worn from the surface can be reconstructed from Smith's translation of the lines. (Smith left no handcopy or transliteration of his *Gilgamesh*.)

5. Sign-lists include Rykle Borger, *Akkadische Zeichenliste* (Neukirchen-Vluyn; Verlag Butzon and Bercher Kevelaer, 1971), and René Labat, *Manuel d'épigraphie akkadienne* (Paris: Imprimerie Nationale, 1963). The earliest version of these two signs would give a clue to the meaning (in any language): the eight-point star ✳ and the sun rising ◠ (Labat, pp. 48, 174). For the origin and development of cuneiform writing from pictography to stylized signs, see Samuel Noah Kra-

mer, *History Begins at Sumer* (Philadelphia: University of Pennsylvania Press, 1981), pp. xxiii, 381–382. For an overview of writing systems, see I. J. Gelb, *A Study of Writing* (Chicago: University of Chicago Press, 1963).

6. See Borger, p. 47 (#295, *pa*). For combinations, consider the *pa* and the *dingir* signs together: read *pa-an*, it is the Akkadian *parṣu* ("divine attribute"); read *an-pa*, it could be either the god Nabû or the Akkadian complex *elât šamê*, the zenith. There are other god names beginning with *pa* but consisting of more than one element, e.g., *ᵈḤendur-sag-ǵa*.

7. Walter J. Ong points out the technological differences between alphabets and scripts like cuneiform in his chapter "Writing Restructures Consciousness," in *Orality and Literacy* (New York: Methuen, 1982), pp. 78–116.

8. Robert Biggs, *Inscriptions from Tell Abu Ṣalabikh* (Chicago: University of Chicago Press, 1974), p. 12.

9. See René Labat, "L'écriture cunéiforme et la civilisation mésopotamienne," in *L'écriture et la psychologie des peuples*, with Marcel Cohen et al. (Paris: Librairie Armand Colin, 1963), pp. 73–86, with discussion, pp. 87–92. On the bilingual lexical texts discovered at Ebla, see Giovanni Pettinato, *Old Canaanite Cuneiform Texts of the Third Millennium*, tr. Matthew L. Jaffe (Malibu: Undena, 1979), pp. 10–11; also his "The Royal Archive of Tell-Mardikh-Ebla," *Biblical Archaeologist*, 39 (1976), 50. Kramer, "The First Case of Apple-Polishing," in *History Begins*, p. 11, tells of a Sumerian student who took the tablet he had prepared in the scribal school home and recited it before his father—likely a common event for a student in the schools.

10. Erica Reiner, *A Linguistic Analysis of Akkadian* (The Hague: Mouton, 1966), pp. 34–35.

11. A useful grammar is Arthur Ungnad and Lubor Matouš, *Grammatik des Akkadischen* (Munich: Verlag C. H. Beck, 1969).

12. For a history of Akkadian lexicography and the plan of the *Chicago Assyrian Dictionary*, see I. J. Gelb, "Introduction" to volume I(A), Part 1 (1964), pp. vii–xxiii.

13. The subscript 5 after the *SIG* (named from its Sumerian value) indicates it is the fifth sign discovered that can be read *sig*. By convention,

the first sign discovered carries no indication (*sig*); the second is marked by an acute accent (*síg*); the third by a grave accent (*sìg*). After that, the subscript 4, 5, . . . x is attached. The accents, then, do *not* indicate vowel quality. On the other hand, vowel length is marked, as in *ᶦˡᵘgilgāmeš* and *tappâ*.

14. CAD 21.41–43.

15. The transliteration and a translation of the poem from which this is taken can be found in Carlos A. Benito, *"Enki and Ninmah" and "Enki and the World Order"* (Ph.D. dissertation, University of Pennsylvania, 1969), 11. 89–93.

16. E.g., E. A. Speiser, tr., *The Epic of Gilgamesh*, in *Ancient Near Eastern Texts Relating to the Old Testament*, ed. James B. Pritchard (Princeton: Princeton University Press, 1969), p. 93; Tigay, 235.

17. W. G. Lambert and A. R. Millard, *Atra-ḫasīs* (Oxford: Clarendon Press, 1969), p. 88.

18. Tigay, 239–240, offers this as an explanation: "Perhaps the contribution of the full account [of the Flood] to *Gilgamesh* is not to be found in its meaning, but in its artistic function as a digression within the epic. With Gilgamesh having finally reached Utnapishtim, the epic's audience is anxious to know whether he will at long last learn the secret of immortality, a secret the audience, too, would no doubt like to learn. Depending on individual members of the audience, the digression may have the effect of building suspense or relaxing it. Perhaps at the beginning of the flood narrative the suspense would be heightened, but as the narrative continues, its own intrinsic interest would begin to distract attention from Gilgamesh's quest and ultimately relax the suspense over that quest. Such relaxation might help prepare the audience's mood for Utnapishtim's disappointing answer and the subdued conclusion of the epic. Like all such suggestions, this one is obviously speculative."

19. Paul Ricoeur, *The Rule of Metaphor*, tr. Robert Czerny (Toronto: University of Toronto Press, 1977), develops the point and traces the history of explanations of metaphor from Aristotle to the present. Metaphor is the subject of much investigation today, e.g., issues of *New Literary History*, 6 (1974) and *Poetics*, 4 (1975) devoted entirely to metaphor.

20. Shamash's advice is compatible, we feel, with what Giorgio Buccellati, "Wisdom and Not: the Case of Mesopotamia," *Journal of the American Oriental Society*, 101 (1981), 35–48, considers the "wisdom" tradition, Ea's with what he calls the "other" tradition.

21. This is Mircea Eliade's "mythical time" of his *The Myth of the Eternal Return* (Princeton: Princeton University Press, 1954), p. 35; elsewhere he refers to it as *illud tempus*, sacred time; see *The Sacred and the Profane*, tr. Willard R. Trask (New York: Harcourt, Brace, 1959), pp. 80–85.

ABOUT THE TRANSLATORS

John Gardner was accorded wide praise for his works of imagination, of criticism, and of scholarship. He was born in 1933 in Batavia, New York. Among the universities at which he taught are Oberlin, Northwestern, San Francisco State, Bennington, and the State University of New York, Binghamton. He died in 1982.

John Maier is Associate Professor of English at the State University of New York College at Brockport. He has also taught at Duquesne University and at Clarion State College. He is a contributor of book reviews and articles to various scholarly journals and the co-editor of a book entitled *The Bible in Its Literary Milieu*. He lives in Brockport, New York.

Richard Henshaw studied Assyriology and the Old Testament at Hebrew Union College, the University of Chicago, and Cambridge University. He is currently teaching at Colgate Rochester Divinity School in Rochester, New York.